Readings in Daoist Mysticism

Livia Kohn

Three Pines Press
Magdalena, NM 87825
www.threepinespress.com

9 8 7 6 5 4 3 2 1

Printed in the United States of America
⊗ This edition is printed on acid-free paper that meets the American National Standard Institute Z39.48 Standard.
Distributed in the United States by Three Pines Press.

Library of Congress Cataloging-in-Publication Data

Kohn, Livia, 1956-
Readings in Daoist mysticism / Livia Kohn. — 1st ed.
p. cm.
Contains some translations from the Chinese.
Includes bibliographical references.
ISBN 978-1-931483-13-1 (alk. paper)
1. Mysticism—Taoism. I. Title.
BL1923.K68 2009
299.5'14422—dc22

2009034659

Contents

Preface

This book was inspired by an edited project on the subject of "Teaching Mysticism," organized by Bill Parsons at Rice University. In the process of writing my contribution on "Teaching Chinese Mysticism," I realized two things:

One was that there was no good resource for students to read short and pertinent selections of original sources in translation. The other was that, since the publication of *Early Chinese Mysticism* in 1992, I had written a number of conference papers and articles on different aspects of the tradition that were either unpublished or scattered in different publications. They could well bear updating, re-editing, and putting together into a comprehensive collection.

I am much indebted to Bill Parsons for his inspiration. I very much hope that the volume will help professors and students alike in creating a deeper appreciation of the Chinese mystical tradition and placing it more actively into a comparative context.

Part One

Studies

Chapter One

Mystics in Training: Living the Daoist Body[1]

> Lord Lao said: A long human life lasts for a hundred years, but with proper moderation and preservation, one can extend that to a thousand. It is like the wax of a candle: use it sparingly and it will last long.
>
> The multitude are full of great words—I speak only little. They have many vexations—I hardly remember anything. They are aggressive and violent—I never get angry.
>
> I don't let my mind get entangled in human affairs; I don't pursue the work of service or employment. Serene and at peace, I rest in nonaction, my spirit and *qi* spontaneously satisfied. This truly is the medicine of no-death. (*Yangxing yanming lu* 1.7b)

The Daoist body has been studied widely and from many perspectives ever since Kristofer Schipper's seminal article of the same title (1978). Scholars have examined it as a microcosm of the greater universe and a replica of social and administrative systems (Kohn 1991b), inquired into its cosmic inner landscape and presentation in charts and diagrams (Despeux 1994; Komjathy 2008), described the gods that inhabit it in various forms and shapes (Homann 1971; Robinet 1993; Saso 1995; Kroll 1996; Bumbacher 2001), and placed it into the active co of Daoist organization and ritual (Schipper 1994; Andersen 1994; Saso 1997). In a less cosmological or social dimension, they have also paid increasingly close attention to its transformation through Daoist self-cultivation, most importantly with the help of diets and fasting (Levi 1983; Arthur 2006), sexual hygiene and internal alchemy (Wile 1992; Winn 2006), breath control and the absorption of *qi* (Engelhardt 1989; Despeux 2006; Jackowicz 2006), physical stretches and other exercises (Kohn 2008a), as well as various modern Daoist-inspired

---

1 This paper was presented at the Conference on Daoist Studies, held in October 2008 at the University of British Columbia in Vancouver, Canada.

practices such as qigong and taiji quan (Kohn 2005; Bidlack 2006; Komjathy 2006).

All these various studies have in common that they focus largely on the Daoist body as a unique, cosmic, and powerful entity that relates the person directly to Dao. It stands aside from other body visions and modes of relating to physical reality, be they Western, indigenous, or even classically Chinese. The impression is thus created that the body in Daoism is only relevant for highly specialized practitioners and is first and foremost a way of transforming the self toward oneness with Dao. While this is certainly the case, it only reflects one part of the larger picture, which also includes the Daoist body as a living, breathing, and interactive entity within the larger context of Chinese (and increasingly modern Western) society.

In other words, there is a dimension to the Daoist body that underlies the more advanced visions and practices associated with it: the body that Daoists live in their day-to-day life—Daoists here being not only the reclusive specialists of the monasteries and the would-be immortals of the deep wilderness but also lay followers and general practitioners. This body, too, has to be treated as a holy vessel and with great care, and texts provide ample advice on how to relate to it psychologically, how to use it ethically among other beings, and how to treat it with care, dignity, and moderation in various lifestyle modes. These texts, it turns out, although contained in the Daoist canon, are not of the highly esoteric and mysterious quality often associated with medieval Daoist documents. Rather, they also appear in medical classics and actively participate in the tradition of Chinese longevity or nourishing life (*yangsheng* 養生), which began as the preventative branch of Chinese medicine in the Han dynasty and only gradually merged with hermit practices to form part of the Daoist tradition.

A major compendium of relevant passages is the *Yangxing yanming lu* 養性延命錄 (On Nourishing Inner Nature and Extending Life, DZ 838; *Yunji qiqian* 32.1a-24b), a summary of nourishing life practices in six sections that is linked with various masters in the bibliographies but is most likely a work of Sun Simiao 孫思邈 (581-682) or his disciples.[2] Many passages in the text also appear in Sun's *Qianjin fang* 千金方 (Priceless Prescriptions) and other medical works of the

---

[2] A complete Japanese translation with ample annotation appears in Mugitani 1987. Sections 2 and 3 on diet and taboos are translated in Switkin 1987. Sections 4 and 5 on *qi*-absorption and daoyin are rendered in Jackowicz 2003. For a brief discussion, see Schipper and Verellen 2004, 345-47.

early Tang. Its overall outlook and dominant tendencies, moreover, match Sun's other writings on life extension, such as the *Baosheng ming* 保生銘 (On Preserving Life, DZ 835), a concise treatise extolling moderation, a regular lifestyle, and virtuous attitudes; the *Fushou lun* 福壽論 (On Happiness and Long Life, DZ 1426), a presentation of the workings of fate and various ways to enhance it; [3] the *Sheyang lun* 攝養論 (On Preserving and Nourishing [Life], DZ 841), an account of dietary and other health methods for each of the twelve months of the year; and the *Zhenzhong ji* 枕中記 (Pillowbook Record, DZ 837, *Yunji qiqian* 33.1a-12a; see Engelhardt 1989), a collection of longevity techniques in five sections that also emphasizes ethical and lifestyle aspects.

In addition, the *Yangxing yanming lu* contains numerous passages that also appear in the chapter on longevity in the Japanese medical collection *Ishinpō* 醫心方 (Essential Medical Methods; trl. Hsia et al. 1986) of the year 984, thus replicating a classic pattern of medieval materials, notably surviving from fourth-century south China. Among them the most important is the *Yangsheng yaoji* 養生要集 (Long Life Compendium) by the aristocrat and official Zhang Zhan 張湛, better known as the first and most important commentator to the *Liezi* 列子 (Book of Master Lie; trl. Graham 1960), which supports a similar view of the body.[4]

Beyond this, there are also several treatises in the Daoist canon, such as two lifestyle advisories based on Ge Hong's 葛洪 (283-343) *Baopuzi* 抱朴子 (Book of the Master Who Embraces Simplicity, DZ 1185; trl. Ware 1966). They are the *Pengzu shesheng yangxing lun* 彭祖攝生養性論 (Preserving Life and Nourishing Inner Nature As Practiced by Pengzu, DZ 840; abbr. *Pengzu lun*) and the *Baopuzi yangsheng lun* 抱朴子養生論 (Nourishing Life According to the Master Who Embraces Simplicity, DZ 842; abbr. *Yangsheng lun*). Although in title and edition linked with esoteric Daoist and hermit traditions and probably compiled on the basis of eremitic documents (see Schipper and Verellen 2004, 362, 357), they closely match Zhang Zhan's attitude and

---

[3] This is probably the same as the *Fulu lun* 福錄論 (On Happiness and Prosperity), ascribed to Sun in the early bibliographies (Sivin 1968, 132). On these two texts, see Schipper and Verellen 2004, 535, 743.

[4] The *Yangsheng yaoji* survives only in fragments, many found in the *Ishinpō*. The fragments are collected, translated, and analyzed in Stein 1999. For more on the text, see also Sakade 1986.

recommendations. Like other longevity texts, they do not speak of mountain isolation, alchemical elixirs, ecstatic visions, or radical transformation, but rather emphasize the need for moderation, ethical behavior, and personal care in daily life, thus helping to create a comprehensive vision of how best to live the Daoist body. Another, slightly more technical text that yet includes much of the same information is the *Shenxian shiqi jin'gui miaolu* 神仙食氣金櫃妙錄 (Wondrous Record of the Golden Casket on the Spirit Immortals' Practice of Eating *Qi*, DZ 836, 16a; abbr. *Jin'gui lu*), which may go back to the fourth century.[5]

Fundamental Attitudes

The most important attitude to develop in living the Daoist body is a sense of destiny and one's place in the large scheme of things. Thus Sun Simiao notes in his *Fushou lun* that health and long life are functions of good fortune. As such they relate directly to one's karma and inherited patterns and also depend on the good and bad deeds one performs in life (1b). The key to goodness, aside from accumulating "hidden virtues" by doing good deeds that may not even be recognized, is to appreciate one's standing within the greater scheme of things or to remain within one's allotment (fen 分)—an important concept in the *Zhuangzi* interpretation of Guo Xiang (d. 312) who defines it as the "share" one has in Dao which manifests in one's inner nature (*xing* 性) and combines it with "principle" (*li* 理), the determining factor of one's social setting and outward circumstances, described in terms of destiny (*ming* 命).[6] For Sun Simiao, the "share" or "lot" means one's entire position in the greater universe, including things such as rank and status, carriages and horses, wives and concubines, servants and slaves, houses and residences, silks and brocades, clothes and garments, food and drink, as well as profit in business (2a-3b).

[5] The *Jin'gui lu* is ascribed to Master Jingli 京里 or Jinghei 京黑 who supposedly lived in the fourth century. The text may be a Tang compilation but in contents predates the Sui. See Loon 1984, 130; Schipper and Verellen 2004, 355. A modern Chinese presentation is found in Ma 1999.

[6] On Guo Xiang and his understanding of share and destiny, see Robinet 1983; Knaul 1985a; 1985b; Kohn 1992a.

Continuing his essay, Sun emphasizes that it is most important to gain a basic understanding of how Dao works in the world, so that one can discern when to move forward and when to retreat, when to accumulate more and when to leave well alone. He then distinguishes nine different kinds of people:

> Sages who embody Dao in nonaction;
> worthies who know some misfortunes but do not cheat to avoid them;
> accomplished ones who obey destiny and do go beyond their level;
> faithful people who guard their faith and rest in calm tranquility;
> benevolent folk who are modest and diligent, caring and circumspect;
> knights dedicated in service who always maintain respect;
> ordinary people who observe the principles but are careless in implementation;
> ignorant ones who are obstinate and egotistic and pay no attention to Dao;
> small men who actively go against Dao, busy without thinking in larger terms (1a).

Sun then notes that one should examine oneself to see which category fits, then cultivate the attitude of the next higher level, so that one ends up with clear perception and a dedication to service, benevolence, and destiny. Whatever good fortune, moreover, one may find, one should keep a sense of detachment: "Reside in wealth and not love it, reside in nobility and not cherish it" (4b).

As regards the body, Sun Simiao in his *Zhenzhong ji* further specifies that one should nurture one's spirit by maintaining an attitude of awe and care. Awe and care, as the *Jin'gui lu* already says, "are the gateway of life and death, the key to rites and good teaching, the cause of existing and perishing, the root of good and bad fortune, as well as the prime source of all auspicious and inauspicious conditions" (14b). If lost, moreover, "the mind will be confused and not cultivated, the body will be hectic and not at peace, the spirit will be scattered, the *qi* will go beyond all bounds, and will and intention will be deluded" (14b). This condition, which we would describe as stress today, is accordingly the ultimate antithesis to long life and the preservation of health. Sun continues along these lines and defines the first principle of "prudence" in terms of awe and care, which he defines further as the basis of all moral actions and virtuous thoughts. This quality creates great benefit. As the *Zhenzhong ji* has:

> One who is able to understand these things is safe from harm by dragons when traveling on water, and cannot be hurt by tigers or rhinoceroses when traveling on land. Weapons cannot wound him, nor can contagious diseases infect him. Slander cannot destroy his good name, nor the poisonous stings of insects do him harm. (Sivin 1968, 118; Engelhardt 1989, 281)[7]

To maintain prudence, moreover, the other great principle Sun expounds is moderation: one should avoid overindulgence in food and drink as well as other sensual and sexual pleasures, observing instead guidelines for healthy living. The principle of moderation goes back far in the literature and is the key topic of most longevity texts, from Ge Hong's work all through the middle ages.[8] A major way in which the texts express it is in the format of twelve things to do only in "little" increments. They are:

Think little, reflect little, laugh little, speak little, enjoy little, anger little, delight little, mourn little, like little, dislike little, engage little, deal little.

> If you think much, the spirit will disperse.
> If you reflect much, the heart will be labored.
> If you laugh much, the organs and viscera will soar up.
> If you speak much, the Ocean of Qi will be empty and vacant.
> If you enjoy much, the gall bladder and bladder will take in outside wind.
> If you get angry much, the fascia will push the blood around.
> If you delight much, the spirit and heart will be deviant and unsettled.
> If you mourn much, the hair and whiskers will dry and wither.
> If you like much, the will and qi will be one-sided and overloaded.
> If you dislike much, the essence and power will race off and soar away.
> If you engage yourself much, the muscles and meridians will be tense and nervous.
> If you deal much, wisdom and worry will all be confused.

---

[7] See also *Yangxing yanming lu* 1.2b.

[8] It plays also a key role in Xi Kang's 稀康 *Yangsheng lun* 養生論 (On Nourishing Life). See Henricks 1983.

> All these attack people's lives worse than axes and spears; they diminish people's destiny worse that wolves and wolverines.[9]

In other words, harmony with Dao manifests itself in mental stability and physical wellness, and any form of agitation or sickness indicates a decline in one's alignment with the forces of nature. The various mental activities and strong emotions will harm key psychological forces and thus bring about a diminishing of *qi*, which takes one further away from Dao and reduces life. As the *Yangsheng yaoji* says: "Dao is *qi*. By preserving *qi* you can attain Dao, and through attaining Dao you can live long. Spirit is essence. By preserving essence you can reach spirit brightness, and once you have spirit brightness, you can live long" (23.17ab; Stein 1999, 172).[10]

Citing the ancient immortal Pengzu, the *Yangsheng yaoji* further details its instructions on moderation by pointing out that heavy clothing and thick comforters, spicy foods and heavy meats, sexual attraction and beautiful women, melodious voices and enticing sounds, wild hunting and exciting outings, as well as all strife for success and ambition will inevitably lead to a weakening of the body and thus a reduction in life expectancy (Stein 1999,178; also in *Yangxing yanming lu* 1.10b-11a). Along the same lines, the *Yangsheng lun* has a set of six exhortations to release mental strain and sensory involvement. It says:

> 1. Let go of fame and profit.
> 2. Limit sights and sounds.
> 3. Moderate material goods and wealth.
> 4. Lessen smells and tastes.
> 5. Eliminate lies and falsehood.
> 6. Avoid jealousy and envy. (1b)

In other words, to successfully live the Daoist body, one must place oneself firmly in the larger context of universal transformation and individual destiny, understand self and body as manifestations of Dao

---

[9] The version translated here appears in *Yangsheng yaoji* as cited in *Ishinpō* 29 (Stein 1999, 170-71). It is also found in *Yangsheng lun* 1b-2a and *Jin'gui lu* 16a. In the enviroment of Sun Simiao, it is cited as from the *Xiaoyou jing* in *Yangxing yanming lu* 1.5b.

[10] The *Yangxing yanming lu* similarly notes: "Life is the foundation of spirit; the body is its tool. If you use spirit a lot, it will be exhausted; if you exert the body a lot, it will perish" (pref.1a).

and *qi*, and maintain an attitude of fundamental goodness and moderation in all things—both physical and psychological. As the *Zhuangzi* says: "Focus on the essence of life and do not trouble yourself with what life cannot do" (ch. 19; Watson 1968, 197).

Ethical Behavior

The clearest discussion of ethical guidelines in relation to bodily well-being appears in Sun Simiao's *Zhenzhong ji*, in the second section after "Prudence" under the heading "Prohibitions." Here Sun encourages closer alignment with Dao by observing moral precepts, temporal taboos, and dietetic regulations. Presenting a set of ten precepts, he says that one should stringently avoid:

1. licentiousness
2. stealing and doing evil
3. intoxication
4. uncleanliness
5. eating the meat of the zodiac animal corresponding to the year of one's father's birth
6. eating the meat of the zodiac animal corresponding to the year of one's own birth
7. eating any meat at all
8. eating raw food or the five strong vegetables[11]
9. killing a sentient being, including even insects and worms
10. urinating while facing north (Yunji qiqian 33.6a; Engelhardt 1989, 284)

These ten precepts include first of all the classic five precepts against killing, stealing, lying, sexual misconduct, and intoxication, central in both Daoist and Buddhist ethics as well as in moral systems all over

---

[11] The five strong vegetables (*wuxin* 五辛) are onions, leeks, scallions, chives, and garlic, all plants in the genus *Allium* (Anderson and Anderson 1977, 328). Yang-enhancing and warming foods, they serve as important herbal remedies in the Chinese pharmacopoeia (see Stuart 1976) and were originally part of the diet of Daoist hermits and immortals, who used them to replace grains and ordinary nourishment. They were prohibited in Daoist communities because their consumption was seen as leading to diminished purity of the organs and could result in socially obnoxious phenomena, such as bad breath and flatulence, which in turn might have a negative impact on discipline and community cohesion (Kohn 2003, 127).

the world, thus often called the great universal rules (see, e.g., Gert 1970). In Daoism, they feature most prominently in the *Laojun jiejing* 老君戒經 (Precepts of Lord Lao, DZ 784) of the late fifth century. Here each precept has a distinct impact on a certain aspect of the body, as punishment for every breach is meted out through its corresponding organ as defined in the system of the five phases:

> The precept to abstain from killing belongs to the east. It embodies the *qi* of Germinating Life and honors natural growth. People who harm and kill living beings will receive corresponding harm in their livers.
>
> The precept to abstain from stealing belongs to the north. It embodies the essence of Great Yin and presides over the resting and storing of nature. People who steal will receive corresponding calamities in their kidneys.
>
> The precept to abstain from sexual misconduct belongs to the west. It embodies the material power of Lesser Yin and preserves the purity and strength of men and women. People who delight in licentiousness will receive corresponding foulness in their lungs.
>
> The precept to abstain from intoxication belongs to the south and the phase fire. It embodies the *qi* of Great Yang and supports all beings in their full growth. People who indulge in drink will receive corresponding poison in their hearts.
>
> The precept to abstain from lying belongs to the center and the phase earth; its virtue is honesty. People who lie will receive corresponding shame in their spleens. (14a-15a; Kohn 1994; 2004, 32, 150)

The way this works, as outlined in the *Zhengyi wujie pin* 正一五戒品 (Five Precepts of Orthodox Unity; in *Wushang biyao* [DZ 1138], 45.16b), is through the senses and psychological agents associated with the five organs:

liver	eyes	spirit souls
kidneys	ears	essence
lungs	nose	material souls
heart	mouth	spirit
spleen	body	intention

As people indulge in activities involving the five senses, they engage and labor the five psychological agents. For example, "the eyes desire to see the five colors; overwhelmed by color, the spirit souls are labored" (16b). As a result, the five organs do not function properly and induce the person to engage in further sensory excesses which lead to violations of the precepts. Vice versa, as people violate the precepts, the five psychological agents are more exhausted and cannot maintain a proper spirit presence in the organs which duly fall ill, leading to the karmic consequences of sickness, misfortune, and eventually death.

The *Yangxing yanming lu* expresses a similar concept when it says:

> The reason why diseases arise is because of the five exertions. Once these are present, they will affect the two organs of the heart and kidneys which will in turn be subject to wayward *qi*. Then organs and viscera will equally become diseased. [3b] The five exertions are [creating exertion through] (1) the will, (2) thinking, (3) the mind, (4) worry, and (5) fatigue. They create six forms of extreme pressure [stress] in the body, in (1) *qi*, (2) blood, (3) tendons, (4) bones, (5) essence, and (6) marrow. These six in turn cause the seven injuries which transform into the seven pains. The seven pains create disease. (2.3b)

Remedies not only involve sensory moderation along the lines of "awe and care," but also include the five Confucian virtues that, too, are linked with the body through the five phases: benevolence to counteract aggression and the urge to kill (liver), wisdom to help with the push to steal and take what is not freely given (kidneys), righteousness and social responsibility to ward off the tendency toward sexual misconduct (lungs), propriety to release the desire for intoxication and other forms of uncontrolled behavior (heart), and honesty to prevent lying and cheating in every form (spleen).[12] Ideally all virtues should be practiced equally to prevent the negative impact of ethical violations on health and long life, but it is perfectly acceptable to work mainly on a central one—often described as honesty (spleen)—and thereby set a positive cycle of cosmic awareness into motion.

In addition, Sun Simiao also includes specific dietary regulations and concrete taboos in his set of ten precepts, such as against eating animals with specific cosmic connections and offending Dao by urinating while facing north. His list is typical for the intricate mixture in Dao-

---

[12] The *Zhengyi wujie pin* provides a slightly different version, agreeing on the connection liver—killing—benevolence and spleen—lying—honest, but then connecting lungs—stealing—righteousness, heart—sexual misconduct—propriety, and kidneys—intoxication—wisdom.

ist thinking of behavioral guidelines of different levels (personal, social, cosmic) and types (regulations, prohibitions, taboos) to enhance a cosmic awareness of human behavior.

An earlier example of similar taboos appears in the *Lingshu ziwen xianji* 靈書紫文仙忌 *(Immortals' Taboos According to the Purple Texts Inscribed by the Spirits*, DZ 179),[13] which similarly prohibits the consumption of the five strong vegetables, then lists several kinds of that meat practitioners should avoid:

> Do not eat the flesh of animals associated with the day of your parents' birth.
> Do not eat the flesh of animals associated with the day of your birth.
> Do not eat the flesh of the six domestic animals.
> Do not eat the meat of armored [shelled] animals like turtles or dragons on the days of Six Armored Gods [liujia 六甲].
> Do not eat pheasant on *bingwu* 丙午 days.
> Do not eat the meat of black animals on *bingzi* 丙子 days.
> Do not eat fish on the ninth day of the second month. (2ab; Bokenkamp 1997, 365)

Rules like these further appear in Sun Simiao's *Sheyang lun*, where he also lists food taboos concerned with specific days of the month. For example, he says that days including the cyclical signs *jia* and *yin* are dangerous because they mark the time when the demons fight each other and people are given to tension and nervousness.

Not just food, but also personal relations are subject to ethical guidelines. Thus Sun continues his discussion in the *Zhenzhong ji* noting that practitioners should keep themselves and their surroundings scrupulously clean and always maintain emotional harmony. They should move frequently to prevent getting involved with ordinary people and to avoid any deep relationships with the opposite sex. Female adepts should not get pregnant; male practitioners should not approach pregnant or menstruating women. Both should strive for greater self-reliance and venerate the gods and goddesses but not

---

[13] The text is connected to the *Lingshu ziwen*, which appeared as part of the Highest Clarity (Shangqing) revelations in the mid-fourth century and probably dates from the fifth century. See Robinet 1984, 2:412-15; Kleeman 1991, 176; Yoshioka 1961a, 66-67. Similar taboos are also found in the *Shangqing xiuxing jingjue* 上清修行經訣 (Scriptural Instructions on Highest Clarity Cultivation (DZ 427), 22b-25a; and in *Yunji qiqian* 40.11b-12a. Tao Hongjing's *Zhen'gao* 真誥 (Declarations of the Perfected, DZ 1016), too, variously mentions taboos of a similar nature.

> The method of nourishing life involves not spitting far and not walking hastily. Let the ears not listen to excess; let the eyes not look around extensively. Do not sit until tired; do not sleep beyond your needs. Wait until it is cold before you put on more clothes; wait until it is hot before you take them off. Do not get too hungry, because hunger harms the qi, and when you eat beware of overindulging. Do not get too thirsty before you drink and do not drink too deeply at a time. If you overeat, your bowels will be blocked and obstructed to the point of illness; if you drink too deeply, phlegm will accumulate into lumps. (2a; also in *Yangsheng lun* 2a; *Baopuzi* 13; Ware 1966, 223)

Along very similar lines Master Blue Ox, identified as Feng Heng 封衡, *zi* Junda 君達, a *fangshi* in the environment of Emperor Wu of the Han, says:

> People should not desire to feel exhilaration, since exhilarated people do not live long. No matter what, they should make sure not to overdo physical activity and force: never let yourself be talked into lifting anything heavy, digging into the earth, or doing anything else that is hard and creates fatigue without proper rest. This will only lead to muscles and bones tiring and being exhausted. Overall, it is easier to engage in some physical exertion than learning to avoid exhilaration. If you are constantly active with something from morning to night and do not plan proper rest periods, you'll get nervous and tense. Just make sure you are aware of your extreme point and take a good rest, then begin your activity anew. (*Yangxing yanming lu* 1.10a)

To ensure a healthy pattern of life, all texts strongly recommended regular scheduling, encouraging people to undertake certain activities at the same hours of the day. For example, it is best to get up early in accordance with the general rule, expressed in practically all Daoist and longevity texts since antiquity, that the universe like the human body is a living and breathing entity (Maspero 1981, 500). Creating the patterns of the circadian rhythm which govern human wake and sleep cycles, the cosmos has an inhalation or living breath (*shengqi* 生氣), which is dominant from midnight to noon, and an exhalation or dead breath (*siqi* 死氣), which controls the period between noon and midnight. For example, the *Baopuzi* says: "The circulating of *qi* should be undertaken at an hour when the *qi* is alive and not when it is dead" (Ware 1966, 139). Similarly the *Jin'gui lu* notes that one should "always practice after midnight [and before noon] in the period of living *qi*. . . . In this *qi*-practice, the time after noon and before midnight is called the period of dead *qi*. Do not practice then" (8a). Most exercises are accordingly scheduled to occur in the wee hours after midnight and around dawn, enhancing the quality of *qi* in the body through the rising energies of nature—a tendency that has continued to the present day, with qigong and taiji quan practitioners coming to the parks in the early morning.

Bathing and sleeping are two other areas that are discussed variously in the texts. For one, they should be part of a regular schedule and not be interrupted or undertaken at odd hours. As the *Yangxing yanming lu* notes about ordinary people: "The whole pattern of their lives, their rhythm of waking and sleeping is completely without moderation or regularity. Thus they can't even make it to fifty without going into decline" (1.7b).

In addition to early and at the same hour, it is recommended to go to sleep only after a proper period has been allowed for food digestion—ideally aided by a walk for several *li* after the evening meal. "Going to sleep immediately after eating a good meal leads to disease and causes back pain" (1.13a). It is also important not to engage in intense conversations, singing, or chanting right before bedtime (1.15b) and preferable not to sleep "with your mouth open because over a longer time this will cause great thirst and loss of blood coloring" (1.16a). As to the bed, it should—in good fengshui fashion—not be placed "right under windows and beams, which might cause the six spirits to become uneasy" (1.16b). The direction of the head, moreover, changes with the seasons: "For sleep in spring and in summer, have your head toward the east; in fall and in winter, toward the west" (1.16b).

As for bathing, the general rule is: "Bathing without regularity is inauspicious; so is bathing in mixed company. Bathing and soon getting drunk and filling oneself up, then going for a long walk will lead to great fatigue and the inability to engage in the bedchamber arts" (1.15a). The other great concern is the exposure of the wet body and hair to the elements, especially wind, known to cause diseases of the worst sort. After a bath or after getting sweaty during exercise or work, one should therefore dry off immediately and never expose the unprotected head to the wind (1.15b, 17a).

Perspiration, in general, is a cause for great care, as is the maintenance of other body fluids—semen, saliva, tears, mucus, and urine—

all understood as major sources of *qi*-loss (*Yangxing yanming lu* 2.5a). The text says:

> When perspiring do not tiptoe or hang your legs; if you do this for a long time you will get rheumatism; your feet feel very heavy, and your hip starts to ache. When the feet are perspiring, do not put them into cold water, because this might cause rheumatism in the bones as well as arterial blockages.
>
> Also, do not hold off on urinating for a long period, lest your knees become cold and numb and you invite rheumatism into your joints. If you start to sweat from eating hot food, do not expose yourself to the wind; this might create blockages and headaches, which in turn may lead to blurred vision and great sleepiness. (1.15b)

Overall, living the Daoist body thus involves the proper understanding of human life and destiny, the appreciation of ethical rules and guidelines, and a major effort at taking proper care of one's *qi* in daily living. Exercises and breath control help, but there is no need to leave society behind and become a mountain hermit. The main effort lies in being in the world while remaining conscious of larger, cosmic connections, following prudent ethical guidelines, and moderating one's lifestyle into a regular and careful pattern. As Master Blue Ox summarizes it:[15]

> The body always move.
> Your food always reduce.
> In moving, never reach extremes.
> In reducing, never get to naught.
> Eliminate fat and heavy things,
> Control all salt and sour tastes.
> Diminish thoughts and worries,
> Lessen joy and anger.
> Get out of being fast and rushing,
> And watch out for sexual exhaustion.
> Do this always—
> And you'll see results! (1.10b)

---

[15] This also appears in a later version of Feng Heng's biography. See Campany 2002, 399.

Chapter Two

The Mystical Process: Healing and Immortality[1]

Daoist mysticism centers on the attainment of immortality or transcendence, which occurs on three levels also applicable to contemporary qigong practice:[2] harmony with nature, perfection of nature, and transcendence of nature. First, it is an ideal of immortals not to meddle with the course of nature, to go along with the changes and patterns that nature prescribes.[3] Then again, immortality is understood as the perfection of nature, finding the perfect order inherent in the Dao. On a third level immortality is the transcendence of nature, the realization of the supernatural, a state which implies the conscious separation from normal society and ordinary human habits.

To attain these three levels, which can also be described as successive stages of Daoist attainment, practitioners first identify their particular station in the grander scheme of things, note their specific physical makeup and geographical situation, and adjust to the natural rhythms of yin and yang as they manifest in their surroundings. They take care to eliminate any potential diseases or disorders, ascertain that their vital energy is strong and flowing smoothly, and move in fruitful accordance with the patterns of life. Second, they use more subtle forms of nourishment to refine their bodies, often substituting regular foods with crude or refined drugs, and align themselves in even more detail with the patterns of the cosmos, absorbing the *qi* of the sun and the moon at the proper times and following not only the obvious but also the inherent tendencies of the various forces of the

---

[1] This paper first appeared as "Levels of *Qi*gong Practice as Seen from a Traditional Daoist Worldview" in *The Empty Vessel* 7.4 (2001), 23-31.

[2] On the history and relevance of modern qigong, see Bäumer 2004; Chen 2003; Cohen 1997; Heise 1999; Jahnke 2002; Liang and Wu 19977; Palmer 2007.

[3] This is reflected in modern qigong in the emphases placed by Jiao Guorui on the "Natürlichkeit als übergeordnetes Prinzip." See Lienau 1999.

universe. Doing so, they match themselves to the powers underlying nature and thus reach a state of higher and subtler naturalness.

Third, Daoist seekers take food unfit for normal people and refuse normal ways of nourishment, completely replacing grains with drugs, minerals, and *qi*. They also enter into a direct relationship with non-human cosmic agencies, such as the gods who govern and control nature, but are not themselves part of it. Practitioners' bodies become residences and pathways of the divine, their spirits become parts of the larger universe, and their true abode is no longer the earth but the sky with its planets and celestial palaces. Death at this point is avoided: even though there may be the appearance of death, the vital structures of the corpse still continue to function, and the immortal does not languish in the underworld but ascends to meet his celestial partners on high.[4]

Taking these three levels or models together, a certain degree of contradiction appears. That is to say, if the decay of the human body is unavoidable and if one is not to meddle with the course of nature, how can one ever strive for immortality? If the first two levels are the key focus, if one is bound by the laws of nature and all one can attain is a slowing-down of the natural decay, there is no room for transcendence or immortality. Turning this around, it means that immortals, in order to achieve the very goal of their lives, must meddle with nature, overcome nature as a continuous, inescapable process.

At this point of contradiction the medical and immortality practitioner part ways, and different levels and directions of health and religious practices emerge. The physician and the longevity master accept decay as inevitable and do all they can to slow it down and make it smoother and easier. They devise exercises and take or prescribe medicines to make people stronger and healthier, but there they stop—right where the religious practitioner starts. His incentive is less to live as healthily and for as long as possible, to enjoy this life as much as he can. Rather, he wishes to attain a more perfect, a more enduring life, one that is found in the higher subtlety of the natural world, but ultimately rests beyond it.

All three levels of healing, extension of life, and transcendence of nature, are essential in both traditional Daoism and the modern prac-

---

[4] I first formulated this understanding of immortality in a review of Ute Engelhardt's book (1987). See Kohn 1988. For more on Daoist fasting practices, see Eskildsen 1998.

tice of qigong. How do they work together? How are they realized within the human being? What do people have to do to work on one or the other of them?

Qi and the Souls

A key to understanding these issues is found in ancient theories of the human body and soul (s). The classical belief was that human beings consisted of *qi* 氣 or vital energy. *Qi* is the material aspect of Dao, which accumulates to create life. The softest and weakest force in the world, this vital energy yet constitutes all; it makes beings what they are, causes the sky to be high and clear and the earth to be low and turbid.

The *Xisheng jing* 西昇經 (Scripture of Western Ascension, DZ 726), a fifth-century Daoist mystical text associated with the Northern Celetstial Masters that follows the tradition of the *Daode jing*, describes the process of creation as depending entirely on this cosmic energy or *qi*. It says:

> *Qi* is the ground of all life: it comes together, coagulates, and gradually becomes solid.
>
> Thus there are different tastes and various shapes, such as sweet, bitter, spicy, salty, and sour.
>
> When *qi* moves, there are the many and the few; the strong and the weak are not the same.
>
> They arise together, yet differ in name and appearance. Each follows its own intention in being born.
>
> Thus they have different inner natures and natural movements, develop different bodies and selves.
>
> They are raised through Dao of yin and yang; thus following separate ways they are yet akin. (5.4-5.9; Kohn 1991a)

As all things are created and animated by *qi*, so are people. Within the human person, moreover, this *qi* was understood to come in two basic forms: a yang part that was provided by Heaven and appeared as the *hun* 魂 soul, and a yin part that was given by Earth and manifested as the *po* 魄 soul.[5] The gestation of the human embryo was defined as the coming-together of these two types of *qi*, the death of the

---

[5] An illustrated description of this soul is found in Schlicht 1999, 57.

751). Whatever one does, if done by the *zi*, is done of itself, by the self as a spontaneous, independent organism, not by an organized object-centered self. In this sense, the *zi* can give rise to an inner feeling of shame, it can have a spontaneous inclination towards good or back fortune, it can develop spontaneous knowledge, or attain true spontaneity within.[15]

These two types of self as defined in traditional Daoism can be related to the modern understanding of the self as proposed by Arthur Deikman. He suggests that people have both an "object self" and an "observing self" (1982). According to him, the object self unfolds together with human consciousness, when infants begin by understanding the world through the medium of their bodies and the first abstract, yet humanly fundamental concept emerges that object = body = self (Deikman 1982, 68). One's very own body, the agent that processes the sense data and translates them into needs and desires, is seen as an object in itself, as one more object from which to receive stimuli and toward which to direct wishes.

Consciousness of the object self can be divided according to three distinct functions: thinking, feeling, and acting. The thinking self contains one's conception of who and what one is. It is a "me" defined by society and culture, bound by relativity and the dependence of opposites, based on measurements and comparisons, on the establishment of categories and classifications. The feeling self contains the emotions: anger, fear, worry, sadness, joy. All these are reactions of feeling toward a given object or objective. They are intimately linked with desire and classify the world according to whether it is at any given moment desirable or undesirable and reacts with feelings and emotions accordingly. The acting or functional self contains all that we do. It is an awareness of oneself as an acting individual. I know that I do; I realize the capacity I have to act in the world. I feel my body as an instrument of outer activity; I direct my feet and hands, my facial muscles, as well as my vocal chords in a particular direction, producing a particular effect. The acting self manipulates the world around it. It pulls objects and objectives toward it or pushes them away (Deikman 1982, 92-94).

The development of such an object self is a necessary stage of human development, an evolutionary phase that is essential for survival of both individual and culture. On the other hand, as children develop,

---

[15] See *Lunyu* 12.23, *Mengzi* 2A.4, *Zhuangzi*, chs. 4, 15.

so evolution proceeds further, and eventually the object self can and must be overcome for the greater attainment of the higher stages of life. These, according to Deikman, are approached when another mode of consciousness is first learned—the "receptive mode," a way of perception which diminishes the boundaries between self and world and gives people a sense of merging with the environment (1982, 71).

This mode is realized in the observing self. Originally at the center of one's being, this self is the deep inner root of one's existence, an ultimate and transcendent sense of being alive within. It is there, yet cannot be consciously known, felt, or manipulated: it cannot be objectified in any way. Rather than thinking, feeling, and doing things actively and with regard to an object, the observing self allows things to happen spontaneously. Instead of as objects, people then see themselves and the world as flowing streams of energy, intensely alive and perfectly individual, yet ultimately interconnected in a cosmic whole. The observing self has no limits; it is transcendent and yet most deeply immanent in all.[16]

Although perception in the receptive mode of consciousness is unifying and free from classification, thinking still takes place. Only, instead of clear-cut value judgments and the evaluation of things as objects, there is now a sense of fluidity of values, an openness to other points of views. Similarly, there is still feeling, but there are no emotions that are intrinsically related to the desires of the ego. Rather, emotions are now replaced by compassion, charity, kindliness, and perhaps sadness about the shortcomings of life (Maslow 1964, 82). Also, people in this state still can and do act in the world. But their actions are not based on single-minded categorizations nor on ego-centered emotions. Instead, they give service to others and hope to aid them in their health and longevity. In Daoist terms, therefore, people who have realized their observing self flow along with Dao and live in harmony with themselves and others, never wasting but only nurturing and even increasing their inner *qi*. This self, moreover, becomes the main stepping stone for the attainment of immortality, the

---

[16] The observing self, as Deikman describes it, is in many ways similar to Abraham Maslow's concept of Being-cognition. Being-cognition is the opposite of Deficiency-cognition. Where the latter is constantly aware of something missing, something needed, the former is content and calm, receptive as it were, and merely observing. See Maslow 1964, 83. For a more extensive discussion in the context of comparative meditation, see Kohn 2008b.

opposing forces possible" (von Brunn 1999, 85) and increases the mental awareness of oneself as part of a larger flow of energy which rises and ebbs, comes and goes, moves and halts. As one reaches a state of mental quietude and greater stability in one's heath, the practice leads on towards a more encompassing understanding of self and world, which also includes a sense of wonder, of gratitude towards the natural world and the greater universe (see Middendorf 1999, 90). The tense, ego-bound self loosens and a sense of open *qi*-flow takes its place. Healing moves on to longevity, and as cosmic awareness increases, even to immortality.

Chapter Three

The Ethical Universe:[1] Precepts and Mystical Practice

Mystical attainment in Daoism being the close identification with Dao and its ongoing spread of cosmic goodness, ethics and moral rules form a key to fundamental practice. Part of ancient Daoist thought,[2] ethics have found also extensive expression in the Daoist religion, including not only numerous lists of rules and precepts but also theoretical concepts of guilt, sin, and expiation.[3]

Although most mystical traditions emphasize ethics, Daoism is unique in that its rules are neither solid entities to be observed at all cost nor formalities taken as an entry to a higher plane. Rather, the precepts in Daoism form a conduit for the power and energy of the cosmos as it works in and through practitioners, both individually and communally. The rules lay the foundation of an attitude that realizes universal interconnectedness in everything one is and does. Daoism with its strong emphasis on the flow of *qi* in the larger cosmos strives to create a form of human behavior that activates the direct consonance of the life-giving power of the universe with personal and communal reality.

True to its mission of transforming individuals into aspects of pure Dao, Daoism does not isolate human conduct in the human sphere, separating it from nature, but finds it located fully in the larger con-

---

1 An earlier version of this article appeared under the title, "The Wisdom of Moral Conduct: Why Daoists Practice the Precepts," in *Wisdom in China and the West: Essays in Honor of Julia Ching*, edited by Vincent Shen and Willard Oxtoby (Washington, D.C.: The Council for Research in Values and Philosophy, 2005), 259-86.

2 There are some discussions of the ethics in early Daoist texts. See for example, Graham 1983; Girardot 1985; Peerenboom 1991; Ames 1992; Kjellberg and Ivanhoe 1996; Kirkland 2001; and Vankeerberghen 2001.

3 Discussions of Daoist ethics appear in Kleeman 1991; Kohn 2004a. Daoist rules in relation to overall Chinese values, such as filial piety, are discussed in Liu 1990, 133-46. For an analysis of guilt and sin in Chinese popular religion, see Eberhard 1967.

text of the cosmic flow. Individual rules, as a result, are not as important as the sense of the codex as a whole. Compliance can be handled flexibly and carries merit primarily if undertaken as an expression of cosmic spirituality. As such, the precepts are neither foundational nor separate, but constitute a key aspect of practice that affects the nourishing powers of Heaven and Earth and ultimately leads to the mystical transformation of the individual into a cosmic being.

Daoist precepts, as the rules that regulate Daoist community life, first arose with the earliest Daoist communities of Great Peace and the Celestial Masters in the second century C.E. They have proliferated ever since and come to form an important foundation of practice in all different schools, both in the middle ages and today. As a result, a total of over seventy precepts texts remain in the Daoist canon and its supplements. Using predominantly sources from the middle ages, i.e., third to eighth centuries, this presentation will address the question of the precepts' justification. Why did Daoists believe the precepts were essential to religious practice? What benefits did they expect from their observation? How did they argue to skeptics and outsiders that following the precepts was the best way of living in the world and attaining the Dao?

Justification

Justification of moral actions has been a key issue in the discussion of morality among ethicists and still is essential today. Ideally, as Immanuel Kant demanded (1959), being morally good should be a goal in itself and bring its own reward; one should be good for its own sake, behaving morally should be the rational thing to do, and morality should not need an exterior motive. The argument here is that the moral rules are so self-explanatory, so logical, so universal, that any thinking and feeling individual would follow them no matter what (Green 1987, 96). Still, even Kant admitted to the need for supra-empirical beings "because of the severity of the rational dilemma raised by moral obedience" (Green 1978, 74), the fundamental conflict between natural instincts of self-preservation and submission to the rules or the service of others, between inclination and duty (Kant 1960). There has to be a level of benefit and wellbeing beyond preserving the self and one's material existence if moral action is to be logically defensible. This level can only be of a supernatural, divine, or cosmic nature (Green 1978, 76, 109); it could be the belief in justice, God, karma, or ancestral wrath.

Other justifications for moral behavior acknowledged by ethicists include utilitarianism (or prudence) and soteriology (divine command). The utilitarian or prudential position claims that people act morally because it is useful for them and for society. "It is, by and large, advantageous to be a morally upright person and disadvantageous to be an immoral one" (Green 1987, 95). The cost for breaking rules and precepts, both on the psychological and social (material) levels, is enormous. It is thus easier, and more useful, to comply. Much of the modern penal code and prison system relies on this concept, imposing harsh punishments for misdeeds in the hope that people will see their uselessness.[4] Vice versa, the ancient Buddhist propagation of the five precepts included a distinct set of benefits for laymen, such as wealth, good repute, self-confidence in public, an untroubled death, and rebirth in heaven (Gombridge 1971, 247; Obeyesekere 1968, 28; Keown 1992, 44-45).

Unlike this explanation for moral behavior, the soteriological viewpoint, also known as "divine command morality," emphasizes the belief in a superior deity or law. People act morally not because it is logical and good to do so, nor because it gives them distinct advantages, but because a divine agency, a root power of the universe, has so decreed. The rewards of morality, despite all apparent futility on this earth, are of a higher nature; the purpose of the rules is beyond the limited faculties of human reason and perception to comprehend. Problems with this particular approach arise when the deity demands actions that are not only incomprehensible but even cruel and repulsive. At this point the devotion to the divine has to be tempered with human reason, and conflict arises.[5]

Religiously based morality in general tends to be of the soteriological group. Within this framework, however, modifications apply. Buddhist ethics, for example, has been identified as an ethics of intention, as a form of moral determinism, and—especially in its *Māhāyana*

---

[4] For more on the utilitarian model, see Mabbott 1969, 15-30; Hare 1965, 112-36; Baier 1958; Richards 1971; Williams 1980. For readings from original texts, see Taylor 1972, 136-95. A summary of all the different Western positions on ethical motivation is found in Becker and Becker 1992.

[5] For a detailed discussion of these issues, see Idziak 1980. More information on the problems of religion and morality is also found in Outka and Reeder 1973.

form—as a system that promotes altruism over all other considerations.

Intention in Buddhism is considered the central factor for all actions, whether mental, vocal, or physical. "By the law of karma, every intention good or bad will eventually be awarded or punished" (Gombrich 1971, 246), often independent of the actual outcome of any given deed—or vice versa, the same outcome will be treated differently depending on the original intention of the perpetrator. The classical example of the latter is the case of the masturbating monk contrasted with one who has a seminal emission during a dream. The former is guilty and punishable according to the *Vinaya*, the latter is not.[6] The goal of the Buddhist path with all its disciplines and meditations accordingly is to create a "choosing will" (Horner 1936, 280) that is based on right knowledge and will always opt for actions in accordance with the best intention and the purest mind. "One wills to act because his actions are in conformity with his own inward state that has been cultured by awareness derived from right knowledge" (Holt 1981, 67). It is the purity of mind and moral quality of intention that brings about the desired soteriological results, i.e., improvement of karma and the eventual complete release from the chains of conditioned existence (see Varma 1963, 41).

In terms of moral determinism, Buddhist ethical thinking assumes that the life and good fortune of the individual are determined by his or her moral actions, that there is "a law of just recompense in the world" (Varma 1963, 26), which will make sure one reaps exactly as one sows. This viewpoint stands in contrast to materialistic accidentalism, according to which everything happens at random and is due entirely to chance; it is also significantly different from divine election or fatalism, which maintains that decisions about one's life and fate are made on a supernatural plane and have nothing to do with one's actions or intentions (Varma 1963, 26). Moral determinism takes into account three factors: the motivation or intention for one's action; the physical and instrumental steps taken to carry it out; and the consequences resulting from it (Varma 1963, 27; Obeyesekere 1968, 22-24). Aside from providing a reasonable answer to the fundamental questions of fate and good fortune, it also encourages social conservatism (since social status is due to previously gained merit) and individualism (since one is fully responsible oneself) (Varma 1963, 42-46).

[6] For a discussion, see Holt 1981, 53-55; Sadhatissa 1970, 74; Sasaki 1956; Pachow 1955.

A third characteristic of Buddhist ethics its is orientation toward altruism, defined as "a willingness to act in consideration of the interests of other persons, without the need of ulterior motives" (Nagel 1970, 79; Munroe 1996, 6). It can be motivated by various emotions such as benevolence, sympathy, love, or compassion; or it can be pure, an act done for its own sake and the welfare of others (Nagel 1970, 80). The key to altruism is perspective and cognition: it involves a different way of looking at the world, regarding oneself as merely a person among others, finding identity as part of a larger whole, imagining oneself in the situation of others, and seeing fellow human beings where ordinary people only see strangers. As a result of this perception, altruists typically state that their unselfish actions are entirely natural and that they do not have a choice over whether or not to help someone.[7] In Buddhism, especially vows and resolutions serve the purpose to create this kind of mindset, a bodhisattva way of looking at the world as a whole and seeing every creature as a suffering being striving to realize buddhanature.

Religious Daoist ethics as expressed in the precepts presents a mixture of the soteriological and utilitarian positions, with a strong Buddhist influence. Ultimately one acts morally because the gods and Heaven demand it, but doing so also brings distinct advantages in this life. Within this framework, Daoist ethics like Buddhist is a form of moral determinism, since everyone will receive their just rewards on the basis of exact record-keeping by the celestial administration and the workings of the law of karma. It is also an ethics of intention, but less so than in Buddhism, since the physical execution of an action and its social consequences are also taken into account. A strong emphasis on altruism, as opposed to merely not harming one's fellow beings, too, is obvious mainly under Buddhist influence and begins in particular with the Lingbao school.

Overall, the various texts on Daoist precepts justify moral actions on four distinct grounds:

— administrative, because the recording officers in heaven keep detailed records of every thought and deed and impose appropriate punishments;

— medical, because noncompliance will bring about disease;

---

[7] For a detailed discussion of the altruistic perspective, see Munroe 1996, 9-14, 197-216; Nagel 1970, 82-83, 100-2.

— ritual, because only physically and morally pure agents can conduct rites to their proper effect;

— karmic, because all intentions and actions will have a clear reverberation in one's future fortune and existence;

Taking all this together and examining the metaphors and images used for the precepts, it becomes clear, moreover, that moral behavior and observance of the rules are undertaken because they afford a maximum of control over the vicissitudes of life, providing a guarantee of good fortune and benefits no matter what the outside circumstances may be.

Administration and Medicine

The first and most commonly cited ground for moral action in Daoism is administrative. According to this, Daoists act morally because the agents of the celestial administration keep close track of all actions with infallible certainty and punish evil deeds by reductions in luck, subtractions from the individual's life, and banishment to the underworld prisons or hells. The notion of a hierarchically organized otherworld with supervising functions over the living goes back far in Chinese history and can be traced back to the Shang dynasty and its ancestral worship.[8] It continued to develop through the Zhou and Han dynasties and was inherited by Daoism, which expanded and formalized it further.

In the middle ages, the Daoist otherworld became an elaborate construction of bureaus and offices. As the *Siji mingke* 四極明科 (Illustrious Regulations of the Four Ultimates, DZ 184), a fifth-century Shangqing text, describes it, there are three central offices in heaven:

> 1. the office to the left presides over transgressions of a yang nature, such as killing, theft of celestial treasures, unwarranted spread of sacred texts, cursing and swearing;
>
> 2. the office to the right presides over transgressions of a yin nature, including harboring schemes in one's heart, disobedience, planning harm to others, and never remembering the Dao;

---

[8] For a discussion of the early system, see Chang 1980; Keightley 1978a; 1978b. On its later development, see Poo 1997; Shahar and Weller 1996.

3. the office in the center presides over more essential shortcomings, such as doubts and duplicity, lack of reverence and faith in heavenly perfection, desecration of heavenly treasures, thoughts of stealing Daoist scriptures, or of defiling perfected writings (1.4b).[9]

All these offices were, moreover, thought to control a big staff, including their own divine guards and bailiffs as well as the Five Emperors and other, more locally placed agents and officials (1.5a). The latter resided in the nine provinces of earth and were typically staffed by 120 officials, 1,200 bailiffs, and 50,000 troops. They ruled the souls of the sinful dead, and kept them revolving in the cycle of transmigration for countless kalpas, letting them go only after unthinkable pain and torture (1.5b-6a). The only way to prevent all this was to act morally and with proper virtue (1.7b-8a), while also practicing the various Shangqing meditations and recitations described in the text (chs. 2-5).

To maintain a sense of what the celestial administration was doing, Daoists from an early period onward attributed specific numerical values to particular deeds—both good and bad, but mostly bad.[10] The currency selected consisted of single days of life, called a "reckoning" (*suan* 算), or stretches of sixty or one hundred days, known as a "period" (*ji* 紀). The earliest attributions of this kind date from the fourth century and are prominently continued in the sixth-century Celestial Masters code *Xuandu lüwen* 玄都律文 (Rules of Mystery Metropolis, DZ 188; trl. Kohn 2004b) and the monastic manual *Fengdao kejie* 奉道科戒 (Rules and Precepts for Worshiping the Dao, DZ 1125; trl. Kohn 2004c) of the early Tang.

Another tendency was to list numbers of good and bad deeds and specify the rewards and punishments one could expect in terms of

---

[9] These three are a development of the earlier celestial administration of the Celestial Masters, which was divided into the Three Offices of Heaven, Earth, and Water (see Kobayashi 1992). In Lingbao Daoism, the division appears under the name of the Three Primes, are each in control of different types of misdeeds (see *Sanyuan pinjie* 三元品戒, DZ 456; Kohn 2004a, 187-94). The *Siji mingke* also summarizes the various earlier models (1.5a).

[10] The one exception is a Dunhuang manuscript fragment of the *Fengdao kejie*, entitled "Compassionate Assistance" (P. 3682; Ofuchi 1979, 220-21; Tonkōkōza 1983, 175-76. For example, to develop the good intention that all beings should be free from obstacles and obstructions when one sees a broken bridge or blocked road will create an additional 420 days of life.

health, good fortune, descendants, and fate after death. The earliest version of this also appears in the fourth century, in the *Chisongzi zhongjie jing* 赤松子中戒經 (The Essential Precept of Master Redpine, DZ 185), a dialogue between the two classical immortals Huangdi and Chisongzi on questions of fate, reward, punishments, and family liability.[11] It is taken up in Du Guangting's 杜光庭 *Yongcheng jixian lu* 墉城集仙錄 (Record of the Assembled Immortals in the Heavenly Walled City, DZ 783) of the year 905, and eventually grows into the practice of keeping ledgers of merit and demerit, so popular in the Ming and Qing dynasties (see Brokaw 1990).

The calculation of deeds, the clear knowledge of what to expect for what activities, and the awareness of being constantly watched by the celestial officers provided a strong incentive to behave morally in medieval Daoism. There was no escape, there was no relief. The cosmos was working continuously and made no exceptions; every individual was forever tied into its web.

A second motivation for Daoists to be moral was medical. According to this understanding, failure to behave properly caused internal stress, harming the spirit, the souls, the essence, and the *qi* in the body and thus creating first psychological tension, then physical ailments, and eventually death. While early death and sickness were commonly thought of as administered by the celestial officers, there are also texts that present a more direct link between moral behavior and one's medical condition. Especially the fourth-century *Lingshu ziwen xianji* 靈書紫文忌 (Immortals' Taboos According to the Purple Texts Inscribed by the Spirits; DZ 179, a document of Shangqing provenance, emphasizes this feature. As the second of its ten items of moral conduct, it has:

> Do not steal or bring about misfortune and evil. As and when you bring about misfortune and evil, your Yellow Court [spleen] is thrown into confusion, and the three

---

[11] Cited already in Ge Hong's 葛洪 *Baopuzi* 抱朴子 (Book of the Master Who Embraces Simplicity, DZ 1186; see Ware 1966), 6.5a, this text goes back to fourth-century south China; however, as indicated by the preface, its present edition dates only from the Song dynasty (see Ren and Zhong 1991, 135-36; Yoshioka 1960, 730-31; 1970, 220). The text is mentioned in various Song catalogs (Loon 1984, 110) and cited in works of that period, such as the well-known *Ganying pian* 感應篇 (On Impulse and Response, DZ 1167), and to the present day forms a part of popular retribution culture (dat. 1127-1150; Hervouet 1978, 370-71; Suzuki and Carus 1973; Bell 1992; Liu 1990, 142-43). For a discussion of its notions of fate and quantification, see Kohn 1998c.

> worms delight in the kill. Your spirit souls and body gods start quarreling with each other; your material souls and inner demons fight for residence. The radiance of your eyes is besieged and scattered, and your mouth emits a noxious vapor. This is the second item that defeats the signs of immortality. (see also Bokenkamp 1997, 363)

The link between moral failure and illness is thus established through the action of inner forces, envisioned as deities and demons, who fight with each other for dominance in a person's body. Any disturbance of their equilibrium creates disorder and encourages the bad elements to rise to the fore, thus making the person sick. In some precepts, as those against sexual misconduct and intoxication, the connection is more directly physical—valuable seminal essence is lost or the spirit is deluded. In most, supernatural intercession is essential, reflecting the dominant Daoist view of the body as a microcosm of the universe and thus inhabited by countless deities or body gods.[12]

This view of the precepts is, furthermore, a direct reflection of the understanding of sickness and healing among the early Celestial Masters. They explained sickness entirely in supernatural terms as the attack by one or several demons, who could only gain entry into a person's body if the latter was weakened by sin. As a result, all Celestial Masters' healing took place through ritual and magic; acupuncture, herbs, and other medical treatments were expressly prohibited. First the sick person was isolated in a so-called chamber of tranquility or oratory (*jingshi* 靜室; see Yoshikawa 1987), an adaptation of a Han institution for punishing wayward officials involving solitary confinement. There he or she had to think of past sins, transgressions, and other moral misdeeds, if necessary tracing them all the way back to birth, thereby trying to find an explanation for the illness.

Once certain sins or misdeeds had been identified, a senior master would come to write them down—in triplicate and together with a formal petition for their eradication from the person's divine record. Next, the three copies would be transmitted ceremonially to the Three Bureaus of Heaven (by burning), Earth (by burying), and Water (by casting into a river). The divine officials would then set the record straight, expel the demons, and restore the person's good health. Additional measures of purification involved the ingestion of

---

[12] On the Daoist understanding of the body, see Schipper 1978; 1994; Kohn 1991b; Saso 1997.

"talisman water" (*fushui* 符水, the ashes of a talisman dissolved in water), healing exercises patterned on cosmic energy movements (*daoyin* 導引), and meditations (*jingsi* 精思).[13]

None of these measures worked, however, while sin was still present in the person and continued to open the gates to demonic influences. Moral behavior and a clear conscience were thus directly linked to physical health and mental wellbeing, a connection not limited to ancient China. Modern physicians, too, in explorations of psychosomatic medicine, have seen that "guilt-producing behavior, negative emotions, etc. tend to throw the body into a precarious position, to disturb necessary homeostasis, and to make the person more susceptible to the ravages of germs and bacteria, which up to this time have been kept under control by various natural barriers" (Belgum 1967, 50). Accident-prone people might, then, be seen as punishing themselves; and those already ill might have a harder time healing (or dying) while moral issues remain unresolved.[14]

The understanding of a close connection between morality and wellbeing—through natural links or mediated by demonic activities—together with the Daoists' wish for good health, strength, and a long life therefore provided a strong motivation to act morally and in accordance with the rules of the religion.

Ritual and Karma

Another justification for moral action lay in the fact that religious activity for Daoists was not possible and rituals could not be effective without the proper purification, both physical and moral. Even in ancient China purity was an essential prerequisite for the performance of rituals, typically undertaken as a set of purifications known as *zhai* 齋 that included baths, fasting, sexual abstention, and the avoidance

[13] On healing among early Daoists, see Kleeman 1998, 70-71; Kobayashi 1992, 22-25; Levy 1956, 217-18; Schipper 1984, 206; Tsuchiya 2002. The most thorough study of the relationship of religion and healing is found in Ohnuki-Tierney 1984.

[14] For more on the subject of guilt and healing, see Belgum 1967, 211-12; Siivals 1962; Simmons 1956, 55. It is commonly acknowledged that one cannot die a peaceful death with sinful matters weighing on one's mind. See Kübler-Ross 1979.

of death, blood, and other forms of defilement. The Daoist alchemical tradition, too, had a high esteem for purifications. Before even the first ingredient could be placed into the alchemical cauldron, the stage had to be properly set in an uninhabited area far removed from the impurities of ordinary folk, in a grove planted with the right combination of trees for proper *qi*, near an eastward flowing stream, and generally in a natural and pure environment. Then several ritual purifications had to be undergone. As the *Baopuzi* describes them:

> Begin by purifying yourself and fasting for one hundred days. Wash your body and hair in water enriched with the five fragrances and make yourself utterly clean. Never approach any defiling or dirty object or let ordinary people come anywhere near you! Let no disbelievers know of your plans. If they denounce the divine medicine, successful preparation will be impossible. (4.5b)

In addition, the seeker had to set up protective talismans, offer a sacrifice to the gods, swear an oath of secrecy, and make a formal pledge (often involving substantial gifts) to the master alchemist. All these measures served to create the proper atmosphere and mindset for the great work—which, as noted earlier, could not be completed without the virtues and merits created by following the precepts.

Formal purifications were also demanded for all sacred practices of Daoism, both meditations and rituals. Before one could practice visualizations and meditations in the oratory, for example, one had to undergo preparatory periods of fasting, bathing, and abstentions, then don proper garb, burn incense, and perform a series of bows, prostrations, and incantations (see Yoshikawa 1987). Similarly, the practice of purgations, the formal ceremonies of the Lingbao school, also called *zhai* (see Yamada 2000; Benn 2000), involved ten preparatory measures of physical purification as well as the taking of ten precepts for moral and spiritual preparation.

An early document on these rites is the *Dengzhu yuanyi* 燈祝願儀 (Observances for Lamps, Spells, and Vows, DZ 524), a fifth-century text ascribed to Lu Xiujing (406-477). It begins by listing ten purification measures to be completed before any ceremony:

1. taking baths in fragrant waters;
2. separating from worldly duties and ordinary relationships;
3. fasting to cut off desires for fancy foods and cleanse the organs and digestive tract;

4. donning proper garb to symbolize the majesty and power of the gods while encouraging humility in the practitioner;
5. maintaining silence to avoid speaking wrong or harsh words and only issue sounds to intone scriptures;
6. cleansing all intentions from the heart by avoiding false imaginings and harmonizing the six senses;
7. burning incense and sending up a memorial to invited the participation of the gods;
8. repenting one's sins and begging for forgiveness
9. developing compassion and empathy for all beings;
10. bowing down in faith, opening one's self to Dao, and pledging to follow the divine law in all (1b-2a; see Kleeman 1991, 179-80; Yoshioka 1961).

Already moving towards the right attitude as part of their preparatory purification, practitioners also had to aspire to mental and moral purity by taking the ten basic Lingbao precepts, a set based on Buddhist rules and combining the ten good deeds of the bodhisattva with the ten major precepts of the apocryphal *Fanwang jing* 梵網景 (*Brahmajāla sūtra*; see DeGroot 1893). The Daoist set, then, begins with the prohibition of "evil and envy in the heart," then goes on to discourage killing, debauchery, passions, impure speech (lying), intoxication, competitiveness, scriptural criticism, and quarrels. It ends with the general admonition that practitioners should always be "of even and unified mind" in all their activities.

This highly influential set of precepts first appears in the *Shangpin dajie* 上品大戒 (Great Precepts of the Highest Rank, DZ 177) and is then replicated in various other Lingbao texts (see Bokenkamp 1983; 1989; Yamada 2000). The ritual application of the rules is evident also from later texts, where they appear as necessary prerequisites for the performance of the nocturnal annunciation, the Golden Register Purgation, and the Rite of Mud and Ashes.[15]

---

[15] Materials on the precepts in these contexts are mainly contained in the sixth-century encyclopedia *Wushang biyao* 無上秘要 (Secret Essentials of the Most High, DZ 1138; see Lagerwey 1981). It cites the *Dajie jing* 大戒經 (Scripture of the Great Precepts) (35.6b-7b), the *Jinlu jing* 金籙經 (Scripture of the Golden Register [Purgation]) (48.5a-6a), and again the *Dajie jing* (50.3b-4a).

The tendency to require the taking of precepts as a necessary purification measure before the performance of any ritual activity also continued in later Daoism and played a role in the establishment of the ordination system, according to which only masters who had taken the highest and most extensive precepts were empowered to perform the loftiest and most efficacious rites.[16] It was a powerful justification for the taking of the precepts, which both served as prerequisites for all ritual actions and formed a key element of ritual success.

Another, even more important justification of moral action in Daoism was the karma doctrine, commonly and extensively cited in materials on precepts. The reason for this predominance may well lie in the fact that a complex culture of precepts only developed after the introduction of Buddhism and therefore under the influence of the karma doctrine. It may also have to do with the orientation of many precepts towards the alteration of individual behavior, the central feature of karmic concerns.

The karma doctrine, as is commonly known, has been part of Indian religion since the *Upanishads*. It states that all actions have inevitable consequences and, after a period of maturation, revert to their perpetrator. As the individual's soul or *ātman* is the carrier of this load, it must continue to be embodied in a physical form to receive the rewards and punishments necessitated by its former actions. Thus the notion of rebirth, including that in nonhuman and hellish states, became a close correlate to the idea of personally created and suffered-through karma (Mahony 1987, 262). In Buddhism, which denied the existence of an eternal soul, karma was understood very much as a function of the intention, transmitted in "consecutive moments of a psychic continuum," unstable and impermanent like the light of a candle (Mizuno 1987, 267). It was, at least according to ancient Buddhist doctrine, entirely centered within the individual and could be neither worsened nor improved by the actions of others.

This notion was later challenged by the Mahāyāna, whose followers claimed that good karma in the form of merit accumulated over long periods of time could not only serve as a positive inspiration to others but also be transferred to improve their lot (Mitomo 1991, 19). This gave rise to devotional cults toward savior figures or bodhisattvas, to

---

16 An example of the use of the precepts in Song-Yuan Daoism is found in the *Duren dafa* 度人大法 (Great Rites of Universal Salvation, DZ 219; 71.25b-26b), a Yuan dynasty collection of ritual methods (see Boltz 1987, 28-29).

rituals that would transfer merits for the sake of one's ancestors, and to the swearing of so-called bodhisattva vows. The latter placed the practitioner immediately on a high level of karmic attainment and gave him a "karmically protective coding" (Mizuno 1987, 267), with the help of which he or she could fulfill the spiritual goal of universal salvation and compassion for all that lives. Placing a strong emphasis on the community of all beings, Mahāyāna practitioners believed that the karmic activities of each being had an influence on all and that the country and even the world would benefit from the religious activities of the people. The king, therefore, participated to about one sixth in the merit or demerit created by all his subjects (Mizuno 1987, 268), and society as a whole became a forum for karmic and religious unfolding.

The Chinese, confronted with the karma doctrine in the first century C.E., found the intensely personal responsibility it implied not only surprising but abhorrent (Tsukamoto and Hurvitz 1985, 42). However, they could accept the more socially centered vision of its Mahāyāna developments; as a result Daoist precepts very much followed Mahāyāna lines. The justification for moral action was similar too in that it emphasized the horrors of hell for those who did not follow the rules, and the delights of future benefits and residence in heaven for devout observers.

The key issue in the Daoist understanding of the karma doctrine, aside from the general notions of retribution (*baoying* 報應), karmic connections (*yuan* 緣), causes (*yin* 因), and fruits (*guo* 果)—all closely adapted from Buddhism (see Kohn 1998c; 1998d)—was the contrast between "sin" and "good "fortune" (*zuifu* 罪福). The term *zui* here indicates three different aspects of wrongdoing: the bad deed itself, the guilt that accompanied it (see Eberhard 1967), and the resulting suffering through disasters and diseases, bad rebirths and the tortures of hell. Bad deeds can be acts of evil (*wu* 惡, as opposed to *shan* 善), transgressions (*guo* 過) or faults (*yan* 衍). They lead to *zui* as bad karma because one has violated or gone against the precepts; this will eventually bring great suffering (*ku* 苦), defined as physical pains, psychological frustrations, and an overall sense of hopelessness (see Bemporad 1987).

Fu, on the other hand, refers to the positive conditions attained through the practice of the precepts, both in this world and the next, from good health through wealth and intact family relations to fortunate rebirths and residence in heaven. It leads further to the creation of so-called *futian* 福田 or "fields of blessedness;" understood like physical fields plowed and cultivated by farmers (see Cole 1998), they are essentially areas of goodness that eventually lead to conditions necessary for liberation and immortality. In the Buddhist context, these "fields" refer to the acquisition of virtues, such as charity, kindness, and goodness toward all beings; they do not protect against the vagaries of karma but endow the person with the power to remain mentally calm and inwardly happy (Nakamura 1975, 1187; Mochizuki 1936, 4396b-97c). In Daoism, as described in the *Yinyuan jing* 因緣經 (Scripture of Karmic Retribution, DZ 336) of the Sui dynasty, they are more concrete, denoting the activities and wishes to create good living conditions for all beings, from the emperor and the state on down to the poor and orphaned (1.1a-9b). In addition, they guarantee that one will encounter mainly positive and fortunate situations, not only have the mental stamina to deal with adversities.[17]

Daoists also identify the punishments for evil deeds very concretely, adapting Buddhist notions, such as the "three bad rebirths" (*santu* 三途), "five realms of suffering," "eight difficult conditions," and "ten situations of intense suffering." As described in the fifth-century *Jieye benxing jing* 戒業本行經 (Scripture of Controlling Karma and Original Conduct, DZ 345), the three bad rebirths are in the hells, as hungry ghosts, or among animals (15b), while the five realms of suffering are any of the planes rebirth at all, including also the human and divine levels. The eight difficult conditions include life on the borders or among the barbarians; as a slave or servant; in poverty, as an orphan, or as a lowly person; as a sick or person; as a mentally retarded, mad, or disabled person; in situations of trouble and distress; with no filial piety or compassion for life and death; and in a country that lacks Dao (14a). And the ten situations of intense suffering are specific punishments in the hells:

1. to have to step on the mountain of knives;
2. to have to climb the tree of swords;
3. to be thrown in the boiling cauldron;
4. to be tied to the hot iron pillar;

---

[17] The *Daojiao yishu* 道教義樞 (The Pivotal Meaning of the Daoist Teaching, DZ 1129) of the late seventh century devotes an entire section to *futian* (sect. 30). It describes them as areas and qualities of life where future good karma can first blossom, based on good moral behavior and purity of mind (9.1a-2a).

5. to have to lie on the bed of spikes;
6. to be tied to a fiery chariot and plunged into icy water;
7. to have one's head grasped and the tongue twisted;
8. to have to swallow fire and eat burning charcoal;
9. to be tied and locked up by the three officers, hit with metal cudgels and beaten with iron staffs;
10. to come to life only to be tied be fetters, deeply in trouble and distress, and eventually killed (12b).[18]

These ten are adaptations of the hells of Buddhism, especially the eight fiery ones.[19] With visions of such suffering in store for wrongdoing, and with no escape from the burden of individual responsibility, it is not surprising that Daoists tended to place the notion of karma and rebirth centrally in their discussions of why people should observe the precepts—had, in fact, no other reasonable choice than to observe them.

Conclusion

Whatever the motivation and justification for moral action in accordance with the precepts, ultimately the Daoist vision of morality comes down to two central concerns: control over fate and its vicissitudes; and the emergence of the fully conscious human being in transcendental freedom.

---

[18] A more complete list of Daoist hells is found in the sixth-century *Taiji zhenren shuo ershisi menjie jing* 太極真人說二十四門戒經 (Twenty-four Precepts for Followers, Spoken by the Perfected of Great Ultimate, DZ 183). Each of its twenty-four precepts is associated with punishment in a specific hell—of the boilding caudron, the mountain of knives, the tree of swords, the stove full of coal, the iron plow that cuts the tongue, the steel pestles that grind down the body, the poisonous snakes that eat away the heart, the molten copper, the hot copper pillar, the iron wheel, the heavy boulders, the bed with iron spikes, the forest of swords, the lake of ice, and so on.

[19] Further descriptcions of hell are also found in the *Santu wuku jing* 三途五苦經 (Scripture of the Three Bad Rebirths and Five Sufferings, DZ 455) and the *Jiuyou bazui jing* 九幽八罪經 (Scripture on Removing Sins from the Nine Realms of Darkness, S. 957). A modern description of the punishments of hell, still taught in tantric Nying-ma practice, is found in Hopkins 1982, 64-72. For traditional Buddhist sources, see Mochizuki 1936, 1132a.

The problem of control becomes clear when examining the question of "moral luck." Moral luck means that, however morally correct a person may act, there are always circumstances that he or she has no control over which may seriously influence the outcome of his or her actions. For example, as Thomas Nagel points out:

> There is a morally significant difference between reckless driving and manslaughter. But whether a reckless driver hits a pedestrian depends on the presence of the pedestrian at the point where he recklessly passes a red light. (1979, 25)

Or again, there may be a careful driver who runs over a child just because she happened to run out into the street at that particular moment (Nagel 1979, 28-29). In other words, the outcome of our actions is determined not entirely by our intentions but limited by opportunities and factors beyond our control, subject to a broad range of external influences that are coincidental and can only be described as lucky or unlucky. Ascribing guilt to people on the basis of such external circumstances "amounts to holding them responsible for the contributions of fate as well as for their own" (Nagel 1979, 31)—and that is precisely what medieval Daoists are doing.

In Daoism, following the precepts means control not only over one's own intentions and actions but over the situations one will encounter. A person in good karmic standing will always step into lucky circumstances, while one who fails to follow the precepts will be haunted by back luck—the direct result of bad karmic connections, ritual inefficiency, medical violations, and punishments imposed by the celestial authorities. Obeying the precepts is thus a safeguard against the vagaries of fate. It serves as the ultimate control over things commonly associated with luck or external factors: infections and diseases, accidents and mishaps, natural disasters, political upheavals, even cosmic catastrophes.

The metaphors and images used for the precepts bear this out. For example, the *Jinjie jing* 禁戒經 (Scripture of Prohibitions and Precepts), a manuscript recovered from Dunhuang (S. 784; Ōfuchi 1979, 205-8), describes the precepts as "the medicine of the divine law" with the power to "eradicate life and death and all serious illness," as "the raft of the divine law which can take us beyond life and death and the ocean of suffering," as "the sharp sword of the divine law—they can cut down all entanglements and attachments of life and death" (l. 53-54). They are the guarantee of liberation, helping people to accumulate merit with every thought just as "polishing a mirror makes it gradually brighter," inevitably taking them beyond the ocean of life and death, just as "a boat will cross the great sea" (*Qianzhen ke* 千真科[Precepts for a Thousand Perfected, DZ 1410], 10a).[20]

Besides serving as the ultimate control mechanism for the vicissitudes of fate, the precepts are also the key factor in the creation of the fully conscious and individual person, one who has ultimate personal and transcendental freedom—in the sense that, as John Silber says in his discussion of Kant's *Religion within the Limits of Reason Alone*,

> by telling us what we *ought* to do regardless of what our inclinations and desires may bid us do, the moral law forces us to be aware of ourselves as agents rather than as mere creatures of desire. (1960, lxxxvii)

In other words, the active adoption and observance of the precepts raises the person from an entity driven largely by desires to a conscious, considerate, and thoughtful human being, an individual in the fullest sense of the term—an independent agent with clear intention and complete responsibility. This entails for the first time a sense of freedom from drives and desires and an inherent liberty to fulfill the ideal of the universal human—the accomplished mystic.

Vice versa, the commitment of evil is an act of bondage and the result of a failure to evolve. As John Silber says,

> Not even a wicked man wills evil for the sake of evil. His evil consists in his willing to ignore the moral law and to oppose its demands when it interferes with his non-moral incentives. His evil consists in his abandonment of the conditions of free personal fulfillment in favor of the adoption of the conditions of his fulfillment as a natural creature of desire. This represents the ultimate point in the abnegation of personality. (1960, cxxiv)

Daoists closely echo this statement when they describe sinners as being no better than animals:

---

[20] These and other images for the precepts echo the metaphors used for *sīla* in Buddhism, including those of a basis, such as roots, the earth, or the foundations of a city; of protection, e.g., a guide in the wilderness, a safeguard, and a destroyer of poisons; of motion, such as the raft crossing the ocean or the feet; of purification, including water, fire, and wind; and of precious objects, including perfume, jewels, ornaments, treasures, and fabric. See Keown 1992, 48-54.

> Sinful people, obstructive and evil, are close to animals—they may have entered the human realm but failed to obtain a human heart. In vain they engage in human relationships. Utterly polluted, they may listen to the divine law of the sages, yet their entire inclination is like that of animals kept in a dark pen. Even if all living beings were liberated, they would still not be awakened. With intentions of their low nature, they would only desire to return to their original bodies. (*Xuanmen shishi weiyi* 玄門十事威儀 [Ten Items of Dignified Observances for the Gate to the Mystery, DZ 792], 16b)

Punished for their obstinacy in extensive periods of hellish tortures, such sinners yet are not free from suffering but will retain their animal nature and show it in an even more obvious way.

> When they finally attain rebirth, they will come back in the body of a domestic animal, a pauper or lowly person, a dumb, deaf, mute or crippled man, with warped hands and deformed feet and an overall ugly and repulsive appearance. (*Jinjie jing*, line 75)

People without the precepts are described as being blind, lacking the basic ability to see, or as continuously hungry: they remain forever starved for Dao (*Qianzhen ke* 10a). They are not fully human and by choosing to follow their lesser instincts rather than the call to moral purity actively forego all chances of perfection and the attainment of immortality. The precepts, therefore, form both the essential foundation and the overarching network of the Daoist mystical endeavor, the line that divides the merely outwardly human from the fully perfected and transcendentally free.

Chapter Four

Mystical Philosophy: Theories, Logic, and Exegesis[1]

The Daoist religion grew in the Chinese middle ages (ca. 200-900 C.E.) under the heavy influence of Buddhism, then new introduced and the first and foremost model for organized Chinese religion. Beyond that, religious Daoism had its original base in a combination of ancient Daoist philosophy, the thought of oneness with Dao and harmony with the universe as described in the works of Laozi and Zhuangzi, and a variety of ascetic practices that served to extend life and allow adepts to reach higher mental states and spiritual immortality.

This base was firmly in place in the second century C.E., when the first Celestial Master Zhang Daoling experienced an ecstatic vision of Lord Lao. He received the Covenant of Highest Unity and founded the first messianically-oriented Daoist community, limited then to the southwest of China. Further revelations, notably those of Highest Clarity (Shangqing 上清) in 364, Numinous Treasure (Lingbao 靈寶) in the 390s, and the new Celestial Masters under Kou Qianzhi 寇謙之 in 415, together with the ever increasing Buddhist impact strongly furthered the development of Daoism as a religion (see Robinet 1991; 1997; Kohn 2001).

These various revelations and traditions were integrated into a coherent whole toward the late fifth century and by the Tang dynasty (618-906 C.E.), the heyday of traditional Chinese culture, served as the dominant organized religion of the country. This time was the most philosophical period of Daoism, when the originally tangled growth of the religion ad been basically integrated under the um-

[1] An earlier version of this was published under the title, "Daoist Scholasticism: A Preliminary Inquiry," in *Scholasticism: Cross-Cultural and Comparative Perspectives*, edited by José Ignacio Cabezon (Albany: State University of New York Press, 1998), 115-40.

brella of Highest Clarity and organized in the system of the Three Caverns (*sandong* 三洞) and was ready for a more subtle and complex form of presentation and analysis (see Assandri 2009).

The Tang, who succeeded the short-lived Sui that favored Buddhism (see Wright 1978), elevated Daoism to high status due to the identity of the imperial surname Li with that of Lord Lao, the deified Laozi,[2] as well as because of its overall political usefulness. Daoism at the time was made more coherent, controlled both administratively through a well-defined hierarchy of priests and doctrinally by an elaborate theoretics system under the teaching of Highest Clarity and with a strong Buddhist dimension.[3]

Mystical thinking with its "formal nature, its systemacity, its preoccupation with scriptures and their exegesis in commentaries, its rationalism and its reliance on logic and dialectics in defense of its tenets, its penchant for lists, classification and categorization, [and] its tendency toward abstraction" (Cabezon 1994, 15) flourished well in such an organized and centrally structured environment—an environment that made it politically and organizationally necessary to create coherence and general accessibility to a wide variety of doctrines, scriptures, and rituals (Panikkar 1973, 112).

Daoist philosophical systematization, then, was a direct function of the political unification and elevation of Daoism to the status of the major religious teaching under the Tang. It built strongly on past modesl, the basic doctrines, rituals, and hierarchies having been in place since the mid-fifth century. Even then eminent Daoists as Lu Xiujing 陸修靜 (406-77), Wang Daoyi 王道一 (447-510), and Tao Hongjing 陶弘景 (456-536) tried to integrate the religion and make it coherent in an plausible system of both priestly organization and religious doctrine. What distinguishes these earlier efforts from Tang thought is the intellectual thrust of the former. Pre-Tang Daoists

---

[2] On the importance of Laozi in the founding of the Tang dynasty, see Hendrischke 1993, 113; Bokenkamp 1994; Kohn and Kirkland 2000. For more on his various roles in legend, cult, and myth, see Graham 1990; Seidel 1969; Kohn 1989a; 1998a.

[3] Highest Clarity at this time was formally named the dominant Daoist school. Its second patriarch, Wang Yuanzhi 王遠知, became the founding saint of the dynasty, an inspired Daoist who not only foretold the victory of the Tang but also gave practical help to their generals. For a general outline of Tang patriarchs and the status of the school under the dynasty, see Schafer 1980. For more details on Wang Yuanzhi, see Yoshikawa 1992.

strove to authenticate and canonize scriptures, to establish a basic ethical code and ordination hierarchy, to create a religious organization on par with the flourishing Buddhist church. They had a concrete goal in mind, a goal more often than not linked with immediate political influence on the ruler of the day.[4] Nevertheless, they succeeded in the creation of a basically organized Daoist religion.

Daoist thinkers of the Tang were not only secure in their imperial favor but already had a fundamentally integrated, if very complex, religious system at their disposal. This freed them to turn to speculation, to intricate theoretical questions, to the exegesis of scriptures, the codification and logical interpretation of rituals. As Barbara Hendrischke points out, one of the new development of Daoism under the Tang was the tendency to make Daoist rituals useful to the court and Daoist teachings intelligible to a wider audience (1993, 139). For this, critical self-reflection and analysis were needed, a leisurely speculation on doctrines and practices that led, in due course, to the flourishing of advanced Daoist philosophy, an innovative and unique development in the history of Daoism.

Systematics, Logic, and Exegesis

The most prominent Daoist philosophical activities in the seventh century, besides the creation of more sophisticated new "Mahāyāna"-style scriptures,[5] were the systematization of the teaching in relation to Buddhist doctrines, exercises in Buddho-Daoist logic, and the reinterpretation of earlier texts, notably of the *Daode jing*, but also of re-

---

[4] This also holds true for the various debates among Buddhists and Daoists at the time. Although sophisticated and formal, dialectical and logical, arguments in these debates served the concrete aim of discrediting an opponent and had little or nothing to do with a systematic understanding of the doctrines. On the contrary, in many cases, the apparently well-structured analysis of certain concepts and ideas hides an intentional distortion of the opponent's views. See Kohn 1995a; Assandri 2009.

[5] The most famous of these were the *Benji jing* 本際經 (Scripture of Original Time) and the *Haikong jing* 海空經 (Scripture of Master Haikong). Both placed in the mouth of the Heavenly Worthy, preaching from a lotus-throne in the heavenly realm, they not only integrate the teachings of the various Daoist schools but also heavily rely on Buddhist doctrine and logic. For a detailed discussion, see Assandri 2009.

ligious scriptures, such as the *Duren jing* 度人經 (Scripture of Universal Salvation, DZ 1).[6]

An example of a the systematic description of the teaching is found in the *Daojiao yishu* 道教義樞 (The Pivotal Meaning of the Daoist Teaching; DZ 1129) by Meng Anpai of the late seventh century. Responding to Buddhist criticism, the text outlines the major tenets of the Daoist teaching in thirty-seven sections (see Yoshioka 1959, 309-50; Assandri 2009). Each section, in turn, provides a detailed account of the various doctrines relevant to its topic, integrating in a most sophisticated manner various Daoist views with corresponding Buddhist concepts. Doing so, the variety of Daoist doctrines, as they developed in the many different schools and lineages, are systematized and integrated actively with the current, well-known and already integrated, Buddhist visions of the time. Daoism as a religious doctrine becomes more encompassing and more sophisticated in the process; thinkers create wholeness and fullness out of partiality and doctrinal discrepancies.

The human body, for example, discussed in Section 2, had played a central role in religious Daoism since its early emphasis on physical practices and longevity (see Kohn 1991a). The body accordingly appears in the *Daojiao yishu* immediately after the most basic concepts "Dao and Virtue." The discussion, however, does not stop with the practical relevance and immortal potential of the body but also integrates the Daoist concepts with the Buddhist "body of the law" (*dharmakāya*). In Buddhism, this refers to the spiritual or true body of the Buddha, the essence of Buddhahood, and the ultimate nature of the universe. The Daoist vision, then, merges the traditional Chinese view with the Buddhist concept and takes the body of the law as referring to the cosmic nature of the human body, which appears both as the original body of Dao and as the body in the world (Kohn 1992a, 149).

A similarly systematic and even contrived mixture of theories is found in Section 17 on "Observation" or insight meditation. Here two fundamental kinds of observation are described, based on the Daoist distinction between energy (*qi* 氣) and spirit (*shen* 神):

---

[6] For a discussion and partial translation of this important scripture, see Bokenkamp 1997. On its later history, see Strickmann 1978.

> The two kinds of observation are the observation of energy and the observation of spirit. The two terms "energy" and "spirit" refer to the inner constituents of body and mind.
>
> The body belongs to the realm of being; it is subject to the delusions of the World of Form. Thus the term "energy" is used to refer to concentration.
>
> The mind belongs to the realm of nonbeing; it is difficult to fathom. Thus the term "spirit" is used to refer to the insight of emptiness. (5.3b; Kohn 1993a, 224)

In a second step, however, this basically Chinese system is further and more subtly distinguished as it is linked with the Chinese Buddhist—specifically Tiantai—analysis of contemplation:

> One does not reach enlightenment and perfection of body and mind through the two major kinds of observation alone. Rather, there are five different sets of three levels of observation. One such set of three is:
>
> 1. Observation of apparent existence.
> 2. Observation of true existence.
> 3. Observation of partial emptiness.
>
> Another set of three levels of observation consists of:
>
> 1. Observation of being.
> 2. Observation of nonbeing.
> 3. Observation of the Middle Way.
>
> (5.4b, 5b; Kohn 1993a, 225)

This section on observation has not survived in its entirety, but the first two sets cited here are instructive. Buddhist notions of emptiness and concepts of illusory existence as well as Mādhyamika ideas of the Middle Way are thoroughly and logically integrated into the Daoist vision, listed as different models and variants of the Way.

The *Daojiao yishu* shows a high degree of systematization, a tendency to make lists for clearer distinction, a pervase application of logic, and push to be all-inclusive. The goal of the text, even if it was originally molded in a polemical environment, is less the practical establishment of a teaching or the refutation of an opponent's argument than the creation of a theoretically comprehensive system of doctrines and interpretation of practices that merges all major lines of thought current at the time. It creates a complex and systematic reformulation of the teaching as a whole.

Mādhyamika Logic

Daoist thinkers of the Tang also believed in the importance of logic. Their main model of thinking in this respect is called by the same name as the major school of *Daode jing* exegesis: Twofold Mystery (*chongxuan* 重玄). The expression goes back to the line "mysterious and again mysterious" in the first chapter of the *Daode jing*. In the Tang, the word "mysterious" appears as a verb in the sense of "to make mysterious," making the phrase "mysterious and again mysterious" parallel with "decrease and again decrease" (ch. 48; see Robinet 1977). The idea is not only that one discards all desires in two steps. It also implies the theoretical approach to Dao in a twofold movement of making mysterious and decreasing.

This theoretical structure goes back to the Buddhist theory of the two truths, which in turn is part of traditional Mādhyamika thinking. The two truths were first in China formulated by Jizang 吉藏 (549-623). According to him, truth was realized in three distinct stages: first, through a passage from worldly truth to the absolute truth of emptiness; second, from emptiness, now understood as another form of worldly truth, to a new level of absolute truth now understood as complete nonduality—neither being nor nonbeing; third, from duality and nonduality to neither duality nor nonduality.

The two levels of truth and their application to three stages of mystical progress leads logically to the analytical method of the "Four Propositions" (*tetra lemma*), part of traditional Mādhyamika:

> affirmation of being;
> affirmation of nonbeing;
> affirmation of both, being and nonbeing;
> negation of both, being and nonbeing.
> (Robinson 1967, 57; Robinet 1977, 117; Assandri 2009, 1)

In Daoist philosophy, this is reformulated in terms of origin and traces and is applied immediately to practice and the immortal state of mind. As Cheng Xuanying 成玄英 of the seventh century says in his commentary to the *Zhuangzi*:

> There are four levels of meaning:
>
> First, the wonderful origin is empty and concentrated, one is serene and without movement.
>
> Second, the secondary traces develop through impulse and response, one is active and not serene.

> Third, origin and traces coincide, one is active and serene at the same time.
>
> Fourth, origin and traces are both forgotten, one has discarded both movement and serenity.
>
> (DZ 745, 9.13b; Robinet 1977; Kohn 1991a, 190; Assandri 2009)

The Daoist thinking of the period, as mainly exemplified in the philosophy of Twofold Mystery, is therefore an adaptation of Buddhist Mādhyamika logic and two-truths theory. At the same time it is also an active effort to integrate Daoist conceptions of the universe, the self, and realization into one logically coherent whole. The reliance on logic and the tendency toward unification and theoretical coherence is clearly evident.

The main body of texts, to which this logic was applied, consisted of the ancient philosophical works: the *Daode jing* and the *Zhuangzi*. Especially the former underwent a great renaissance in the seventh century, when it was formally named the primary text of the religion (Kohn 1992a, 141). Commentaries to the text—by scholars, recluses, even emperors—abound, going into ever more subtle details of intricate speculation, until Du Guangting (850-933), in his comprehensive commentary work, the *Daode zhenjing guangsheng yi* 道德真經廣聖義 (Vast Sagely Meaning of the Perfect Scripture of Dao and the Virtue; DZ 725; hereafter abbreviated *Guangsheng yi*), summarizes them according to five distinct tendencies or schools:

1. the Liguo 理國 school, which placed most emphasis on the "regulation of the country;"
2. the Lishen 理身 school, which concentrated on self-cultivation and the "regulation of the body";
3. the Shili yinguo 事理因果 school, which dealt primarily with the "cause and effect in the interrelation of affairs and principle";
4. the Chongxuan 重玄 school, centering their interpretation around the "mysterious and again mysterious" of the text;
5. the Xuji wuwei lijia liguo 虛寂無爲理家理國 school, which strove to "rule clan and country through emptiness and non-action." (pref.1a; Kohn 1991a, 189)

In all these different ways, then, Daoist philosophers of the Tang integrated and organized their teaching into a comprehensive whole. They combined various views through the use of sophisticated theoretical structures and developed elaborate listings. They applied formal logic to establish an active link between the purely abstract formulations of the doctrine and the practice of the active seeker and commented on the major scriptures of the time to explore, in ever more intricate detail, the depths of the divine words.

Major Thinkers of the Tang

Tang thinkers were court Daoists. They were trained in a monastic setting and each had a home monastery, but their institutions as well as their activities were court-sponsored. They moved freely and actively in the intellectual circles of the capital. Their roles and thinking, though similar in their overall pattern, were not static but changed over time, just as their outlooks were influenced by the evolving cultural and political climate and differed according to individual character. To provide a first impression, I shall describe the lives and works of three main thinkers: Li Rong of the seventh, Sima Chengzhen of the eighth, and Du Guangting of the ninth centuries.

Li Rong

Li Rong of the seventh century was also called Renzhenzi (Master Who Follows Perfection). Few concrete details are known of his life, since he does not have an official or Daoist biography. According to gleanings from a variety of sources and anecdotes, he came originally from Sichuan, more particularly from a district northeast of Chengdu. Here he became a Daoist monk in his early years and received basic training on Mount Fule. By the middle of the seventh century, he was already in the capital and engaging actively in court debates with famous Buddhists.[7] He was also a poet of some renown and a respected member of the literati, a friend of the famous poets Lu Zhaolin and Luo Binwang. They both wrote poems about him, in which he is stylized as a close friend of the immortals on high, having easy access to the peaches of immortality and continuing his existence in the various spheres of cosmic life forever and ever.

In addition to being an active contestant in the debates and poet in literary circles, Li Rong was the author of two major Daoist commen-

---

[7] Since the debates are reported in Buddhist sources, Li Rong is often depicted as dumbfounded or driven to mindless rage (Kohn 1991a, 196-99).

taries, one on the *Daode jing*, the other on the *Xisheng jing* 西昇經 (Scripture of Western Ascension; DZ 726). The latter text dates from the fifth century and purports to contain the oral instructions Laozi gave to Yin Xi when he transmitted the *Daode jing*. It is a mystical text of some importance in medieval China (see Kohn 1991a).

In both commentaries, Li Rong subscribes fully to Twofold Mystery philosophy and Mādhyamika logic, insisting on the necessity of increased forgetfulness in attaining the Dao. In addition, he combines Buddhist and Daoist thought by equating enlightenment with the natural spontaneity of Dao and by developing a subtle distinction between knowledge, wisdom, and insight. A Confucian, state-supporting element enters his thought when he defines the sage as a realized person who has the pleasure and the duty of leading others to salvation and saving the human community. In addition, a formalized ritual aspect of Li Rong's teaching is found in the Dunhuang manuscript *Xiyu shenxin jing* 洗浴身心經 (Scripture of Cleansing and Purification of Body and Mind; S. 3380; Ōfuchi 1979, 132), attributed to him (Sunayama 1980, 36).

A short text of only four pages, the *Xiyu jing* is set in the Seven-Jewelled Gold-Towered Palace of Purple Tenuity in the Jade Capital of heaven known as Mystery Metropolis. The Heavenly Venerable of Primordial Beginning addresses an assembly of the sages, emperors, kings, nobles, and commoners of the ten directions, including also all kinds of spirits, dragons, demons, etc. The sermon consists of a series of instructions on how to purify oneself properly for interaction with the divine: upon entering the meditation room known as the chamber of silence, one should scatter flowers, burn incense, and thoroughly cleanse one's body and mind. Doing so, one matches the activity of the celestials above:

> Every year, as the last days approach, the immortals, realized ones, and sages of the upper eight ranks as well as all the men and women in the universe bathe and cleanse their physical bodies in an effort to exhort all living creatures to return to proper accordance with Dao and eventually go beyond the sufferings of life and death. (Ōfuchi 1979, 133)

Altogether, Li Rong was a devout and active Daoist, a prominent participant in the aristocratic life of the capital, a court debater, a poet, and a philosopher. He lived the life of an established court figure, not that of a reclusive mountain dweller. Although firmly embedded in his religious beliefs and practices, he participated actively in the intellectual and political life of his times and formulated his ideas and treatises with the goal of contributing not only to a better understanding of the Daoist teaching but to creating a more powerful integrative doctrine that would benefit the human community as a whole.

Sima Chengzhen

A century later, Sima Chengzhen (647-735) also was an important public figure. The twelfth patriarch of Highest Clarity (Shangqing) Daoism, he was in fact the leading Daoist figure of his time and has merited various biographies, both in dynastic histories and in Daoist hagiographies, beginning with a stele inscription composed seven years after his death (Engelhardt 1987, 26-33). Born in Henan, the son of an aristocratic family of long-standing official service, he underwent Daoist training on Mount Song under Pan Shizheng, the eleventh patriarch of Highest Clarity. Succeeding the latter after his "transformation" in 684, Sima traveled to various famous mountains of Daoist repute to settle eventually, upon imperial command, on Mount Wangwu in easy distance from the capital. Serving at court as ritual master and teacher of doctrine, he was well regarded by the emperor and had much contact with the leading literati of his time. Throughout his life, he was a court Daoist in good standing (Engelhardt 1987, 36-61; Kirkland 1986, 43-71).

Sima Chengzhen was a prolific writer but not all his works have survived. Among those extant are various devotional works that include listings and descriptions of famous mountains and Daoist sages as well as a well-known inscription on the sacred sword he had made as a present for the emperor (see Fukunaga 1973; Schafer 1979). His major works, however, are instructions: treatises that systematize the Daoist teaching in its theoretical and practical aspects and make it accessible to a wider audience. Repeatedly he emphasizes in his prefaces that he saw his main task as being one of formulating the salvational teachings of Dao for all those ready to listen and practice. One of his works, the *Zuowang lun* 坐忘論 (Discourse on Sitting in Oblivion; DZ 1036), describes the seven-step meditation transformation of the mind and body into immortal emptiness. It survives also in an early inscription of the year 829 and can be traced back to lectures Sima gave to his disciples, possibly literati of the capital who joined him for a time on his mountain (Kohn 1987a, 40).

Sima Chengzhen's systematization of the Daoist teaching is closely related to his pedagogical concerns. A speaker for the Dao, he made the doctrines practically accessible to an audience of literati. Many of his surviving works fit into this pattern. In his *Daoti lun* 道體論 (On the Embodiment of the Dao; DZ 1035), he patiently explains the nature of Dao and its role in the world to an ignorant student who continues to ask questions, both complicated and foolish. In his *Fuqi jingyi lun* 服氣精義論 (How to Absorb *Qi* and Penetrate [Ultimate] Meaning; see Engelhardt 1987), he outlines the various kinds of physical and respiratory practices necessary to bring the body into line with Dao and to ready it for the higher stages. His *Tianyinzi* 天隱子 (Writings of the Master of Heavenly Seclusion; DZ 1026; Kohn 1987b), moreover, provides a comprehensive description of the Daoist path as a whole, dividing it systematically into five stages.

Between the seventh and eighth centuries, therefore, the main emphasis of the Daoist mystical thinking underwent a change. Li Rong still worked in an atmosphere of debate and defense of the teaching, striving, like the *Daojiao yishu*, to give a comprehensive logical picture of the Daoist teaching that also did justice to its Buddhist elements and served to convince the rivals of its validity. Sima Chengzhen, on the contrary, addressed primarily disciples of Dao and intellectuals who came to learn about a deeper, more meaningful level of life. He had no need to justify, and instead worked toward systematization, giving lists and logical explanations, interpretations and rational outlines. His goal was to develop a simplified, more accessible and eminently practical form of the Daoist teaching, motivated, as he himself states, by his desire to help the suffering people of his time.

Du Guangting

Du Guangting (850-933) again worked in a completely different environment. Where Li Rong was part of the consolidation of Tang power and Sima Chengzhen lived during its heyday under Emperor Xuanzong, Du Guangting was active during its decline, working in Sichuan, on the periphery of the empire, and serving the local ruler after the downfall of the Tang. He has not merited a biography in official sources but is mentioned honorably in Daoist hagiography and has left behind a large number of works that allow a detailed reconstruction of his career (see Verellen 1989).

Born in the environs of the capital of Chang'an, Du failed the imperial examination and turned to Daoism, which he studied on Mount Tiantai under Ying Yijie (Verellen 1989, 13; Cahill 1986, 129). First called to court under Yizong in 875, Du became a palace resident and editor of imperial memoranda, serving as counselor and participating in controversies with the Buddhists. Eventually he was promoted to commissioner of Daoist ritual. After the capital was sacked by rebels in 881, he withdrew to Sichuan, where he edited and compiled Daoist texts and liturgies (Verellen 1989, 86; Cahill 1986, 129). Following the court, he returned to Chang'an in 885 and with it fled back to Xingyuan in Sichuan a year later. In 901 the Tang exile government was overthrown by a local king, and Du joined the new ruler as royal tutor. He continued to be promoted by the Sichuan king until he retired from official service to Mount Qingcheng, where he compiled, edited, and composed Daoist texts until his death in 933 (Cahill 1986, 130).

Du Guangting wrote a large number of works, which Verellen classifies according to eight different groups: mirabilia, saints' biographies, liturgies, inscriptions, editions and commentaries, memoranda and official writings, poetry, and miscellanea. His efforts are found mainly in the first three and the fifth categories. His collections of mirabilia, for example, give a detailed and systematic record of various wondrous events documenting the power of the Daoist gods and their teaching, especially as it was evident in the Tang dynasty and in Du's own lifetime (see Verellen 1989, 206; 1992).

Hagiographies and the biographies of saints and immortals form another venue for Du's systematization of the Daoist tradition (Verellen 1989, 208-11). Here, his most famous extant work is the *Yongcheng jixian lu* 墉城集仙錄 (Record of Assembled Immortals of the Walled City; DZ 783), a collection of the lives of divine ladies—goddesses, immortals, and active Daoist practitioners.[8] His numerous works on liturgy, moreover (Verellen 1989, 212-15) are the most extensive collection of practical and formal manuals on Daoist ritual remaining from medieval China. Here Du Guangting's vibrant awareness of the changing times and the threats of shifting patterns of power to the Daoist tradition finds its most powerful expression. He compiled and systematized the practices as they were still undertaken in his time, creating a comprehensive corpus of hitherto unknown proportions.

---

[8] For a study of the Queen Mother of the West in this text, see Cahill 1993. For a more general discussion of women's practices in medieval Daoism as documented by Du Guangting, see Cahill 1990; 2006.

In addition, Du edited and wrote commentaries to a number of Daoist scriptures, including the *Shenzhou jing* 神咒經 (Scripture of Spirit Spells; DZ 335), the *Duren jing* (*Quan Tangwen* 932), the *Suling jing* 素靈經 (Scripture of Immaculate Numen; DZ 389), and others (Verellen 1989, 217-19). His commentary and summary of commentaries to the *Daode jing* in his enormous *Guangsheng yi*, consisting of fifty scrolls, is a masterpiece of theoretical systematization and integrative interpretation. In addition, before treating the text proper, Du outlines the pursuits of the cosmic deity Laozi (chs. 2 and 3), thereby laying the foundations for the standard Laozi hagiographies of the Song (Boltz 1987, 131-36).

Du Guangting, the greatest and most prolific among Tang thinkers, was much motivated by the political unrest and ongoing decline of the dynasty he served. He was a court Daoist, working for most of his life at court under a formal appointment and compiling his many Daoist works in an official context. His primary concern was the rescue of Dao as he knew it and the documentation of the power of the gods and the teaching. His powerful systematizations, editions, and new interpretations make him truly eminent but they also stand in direct relationship to the upheaval of his time. He created order in the face of overarching disorder, theoretical systems to last where social patterns crumbled.

In all three phases of the Tang dynasty, Daoist philosophy thus played a significant role. Carried by Daoists active in literati society and at court, it was an expression of the dominant intellectual climate and thus a direct outcome of the political situation of the time. Li Rong and the philosophers of Twofold Mystery established an integrated Daoist teaching, set up the predominance of the *Daode jing*, and interpreted its thinking in terms of Mādhyamika logic just when the Tang rulers were actualizing their claim to power. Sima Chengzhen created systematic descriptions of the teaching and organized paths to Daoist realization when Emperor Xuanzong was using the veneration for Laozi to strengthen his hold over the empire and to establish strong unified structures (see Benn 1987). Similarly Du Guangting, in his own time, compiled Daoist miracle tales, hagiographies, liturgies, and commentaries in immediate reaction to the evident destruction and disorder that grew all around him.

Integrated Vision

The three thinkers, though different in time and style, share certain basic concerns, which they express in their own ways. In all cases the main focus of their work is on finding ways of expressing the reality of Dao on earth and in human life. They all concentrate on defining Dao in its various aspects and on giving an impression of the ways in which it can be realized by human faculties and through human actions.

Li Rong in this context defines Dao as nature (*ziran* 自然), spontaneity or so-being) and delineates three different levels of knowing or realizing it. Sima Chengzhen presents a lengthy speculative discussion on the "Embodiment of the Dao" that is couched as a dialogue between teacher and disciple. Du Guangting, in his turn, excels in explaining the role of Laozi, highest deity of Dao and also known as Lord Lao, and gives lists and analyses of the god's names in his efforts to better understand Dao and bring it closer to humanity.

Knowledge and the Dao

Li Rong follows the *Xisheng jing*, which says that "Dao is nature" (DZ 726, 1.3a). He then proceeds to define "nature."

> Nature has no specific character within itself. It is free from all causes and dependencies on the outside. Clear and empty, in mysterious serenity, one cannot fathom its origins. Thus it is called "nature."
>
> The within and without of nature cannot be distinguished on the basis of self and other. The form and material substance of nature cannot be defined on the basis of being and nonbeing. The energy and symbols of nature cannot be fixated on the basis of yin and yang. The root and branches of nature cannot be penetrated on the basis of cause and effect.
>
> This is the great Dao of emptiness and nonbeing. This is nature. (1.3a; Kohn 1991a, 203)

Dao as nature for Li Rong is therefore utterly beyond the limitations of human understanding and the definitions of human language. It is free from the bounds of ordinary life and represents the state of permanent serenity sought by the adept of the Dao.

Though beyond all, this spontaneous nature is realized within the perfected human mind. Called sagacious virtue, it is beyond ordinary knowledge and understanding. Always active, it is yet deeply at rest; always radiant, it is yet intensely dark.

> Sagely virtue is broad and encompassing, there is nothing it does not accord with. Its knowledge can illuminate all mental states, yet despite its brightness it is always dark. Its substance can give rise to all kinds of functions, yet despite its activity it is always at rest.
>
> Thus one who is wondrously joined with names and principle, skilled at entering aloneness, concentrated and imbued with nonaction, is called one with Dao and nonaction. For him, there is nothing that is not done. (1.1a; Kohn 1991a, 203)

Realization of Dao is the actualization of the basic state of natural so-being in human life and mind. The limitless and ever changing, always active yet serene way of the world becomes the inherent mental function of the realized Daoist. Still, even within the realm of perfection, there are differences in degree. Li Rong proceeds to distinguish different kinds and levels of knowledge. In his commentary to chapter 33 of the *Daode jing*, he says,

> Knowing it by hearing is called sageliness. Knowing it by seeing is called wisdom. What is hard to know on the outside are other people. What is hard to know on the inside is oneself.
>
> Reflecting on others and knowing their good and evil is called wisdom. Illuminating oneself and learning about one's good and bad points is called enlightenment.
>
> Knowing goodness is to come closer to being a superior person. It is like acquiring the fragrance of an orchid. Knowing evil is to distance oneself from being an inferior person. It is like removing the stench of a fish-shop. Knowing how to acquire and fulfill goodness, one will develop a sense of loyalty. Knowing how to reject and abandon evil, one will find feelings of repentance. This is enlightened knowledge. (Yan 1983, 831; Kohn 1991a, 203-4)

Here Li Rong describes two approaches to realization that go together with two levels of knowledge: analyzing the outside world and observing the life within. Either way, conceptions are found to be mere constructs without solid reality. Nothing is permanent, and while both approaches ultimately must go together, the inner realization that the self is not solid is more important and leads closer to realization of Dao. More elementary and underlying these two levels of knowing is the correct understanding of good and evil, the knowledge how to best accumulate good and remove evil in one's life.

Sageliness, according to Li Rong, is thus divided into three levels: the knowledge of good and evil and its correct application in life; the knowledge of the outside world and the understanding that all conceptualizations are constructs without solid reality; and the knowledge of oneself as a floating immortal entity, the fully realized embodiment of no-self.

Li Rong then distinguishes these three terminologically as knowledge, wisdom, and insight. "Insight reflects emptiness, wisdom illuminates being," he says in his *Xisheng jing* commentary (2.15b). His views are strongly Buddhist at first sight, depicting an increase in wisdom by throwing things open to light and "awakening" illuminated insight. Nevertheless a traditional Daoist element remains in Li Rong's description of the ultimate state as the darkness of unknowing. Oblivion is the final characteristic of perfect nature or so-being; it is reached at the deep, dark center of the Dao. Commenting on the *Xisheng jing* statement, "To know without knowledge, this is the pivot of Dao," he says:

He says,

> Following the teaching without words, relying on the principle of nonaction, one spontaneously awakens to Dao and wisdom becomes omniscient. Although then there is nothing that is not known, one is yet in a state of unknowing. Only upon forgetting all knowledge does one attain the pivot of the Dao. (3.15b; Kohn 1991a, 205)

Also, in discussing the definition of Dao as "invisible and inaudible" (*Daode jing* 14), he comments,

> One goes beyond beings and returns to where there are no beings. In a state without beings there are no forms to be seen or sounds to be heard. Thus one joins with the invisible and inaudible. With these, one reverts to complete serenity (Yan 1983: 777; Kohn 1991a, 205)

Knowledge for Li Rong thus means a number of different things. On the lowest level, it is the superficial division of affairs into good and evil and is easily applicable in the outside world. In a second step, it becomes enlightened wisdom and means the understanding that all conceptualizations of self and world are constructs without a reality of their own. On the third level it is insight, the realization that one is without a permanent identity, and thus the active embodiment of no-self. In addition, the highest knowledge of all is unknowing, sensory oblivion and utter merging with Dao (Kohn 1991a, 204).

Li Rong's interpretation of the Daoist scriptures integrates the logic of the Mādhyamika and the Buddhist understanding of the progress toward enlightenment into the traditional Daoist worldview. He systematizes and explains, delimitates stages and levels and makes clear distinctions in terminology and understanding. His analysis is succinct and logical, his integrative interpretation a good example of early Tang thinking.

Dao and Its Embodiment

More complex and intricate, looking at problems from many different sides and defining terms in phrases like "both" or "neither," Sima Chengzhen's *Daoti lun* is a lengthy and highly abstract dialogue on the original nature and active presence of the Dao. The text is divided into three parts, focusing in turn on the *Daode jing*, the nature of Dao, and the embodiment of the Dao.

The text begins with a basic distinction of Dao and Virtue, the underlying cosmic power of the universe and its active principle in the world.

> Dao is all-pervasive; it transforms all from the beginning. Virtue arises in its following; it completes all beings to their end. They thus appear in birth and the completion of life. In the world, they have two different names, yet fulfilling their activities, they return to the same ancestral ground. They are two and yet always one. (1a; Kohn 1993a, 19)

It then moves on to discuss the different qualities of the two, Dao as the creative potential and Virtue as the nurturing quality of life, which again are "two and yet always one." Following logically, the question arises whether Dao is "the same or different from beings"? The text answers,

> Dao is always there, yet eternally other. Beings need Dao to embody themselves. At the same time, Dao needs beings to embody itself. Beyond the inherent oneness of all, there are good and evil, right and wrong, life and death, opposition and conformity. (2a; Kohn 1993a, 20)

Dao and beings need each other and depend on each other just as Dao and Virtue are two aspects of the creative power of life. They are different yet the same, separate yet one, nameless yet named, at rest yet in constant movement.

Names and reality, in particular, raise the problem of epistemology and knowledge of the Dao. Both names and reality ultimately belong to the same underlying structure that essentially can never be grasped. But they are also an active part of the world. This means that as practitioners of Dao strip off names and classifications in their minds, the "Chaos Perfected" nature of Dao emerges (*Daoti lun* 4b).

"Chaos" here means "without distinctions," something, not a thing, that cannot be called by any name. "Perfected" means "total and centered in itself," some not-thing that has no referent outside of itself. Speaking of self or beings as "Chaos Perfected" thus creates a dichotomy that is not there originally. Any name, even that attached to the human body, arises from a conscious self and is mere projection. The concept is a formal expression of a perceived difference—it is unrelated to the being as being, as Chaos Perfected (5a).

Knowledge of Dao is thus a contradiction in terms, yet that is precisely what Daoism is all about, what the practitioner strives to realize. It can only be attained in utter so-being, a state that is both empty and serene and not empty and not serene at the same time. In that it equals Dao, which both embodies emptiness and rests originally in serenity and is also actualized in the living world and moves along with beings and things (5b).

In its second part, the discussion of the *Daoti lun* concentrates especially on the Dao. Although ineffable and empty, it is yet the beginning and mother of all things, manifest both in the nameless and the named (7b); both negative and affirmative, elusive and visibly embodied (8a). The discussion here leads to the question of why, "if there is no difference between all beings and Dao, one should cultivate it?" The answer given is that "cultivation makes up for the discrepancy, however minor, between the root and its embodiment, and leads back to original nonbeing" (8b).

The third part, then, focuses on the embodiment of Dao and its reality in the world and among living beings. Again, the basic nature of Dao is discussed, new and additional terms are defined and the problem is looked at from yet more and different angles. For example, we find,

> Question: But if beings are Dao that means that Dao also lives and dies. Or doesn't it?
>
> Answer: Living and dying or not living and dying are both attained naturally. That is to say, if Dao embodies itself in beings, then beings are the Dao.
>
> Since beings live and die, Dao also lives and dies. As the Treatise says, "It shares the same pattern with beings, active and resting, empty and full." So it ends and begins anew. The text also says, "When spirit radiance joins the hundred transformations, it goes along with the living and dying of beings. Square or round, nobody knows its root."
>
> Good and evil, life and death can be compared to the way fishes both live and die in water. Life and death happen to the fish, but the water does not change.
>
> Again we may say, once there are distinctions, there is life and death, but Dao contains all equally, and so it is free from life and death. In yet other words: Life and death happen to beings, but what destruction could ever touch the Dao? Thus Dao is free from living and dying. (10b)

Looking, therefore, at the problem from the perspective of beings' living and dying, Dao is inherent yet beyond, changes as beings change yet stays always and ultimately the same. In life beings are with Dao as they continue to change, yet they are also permanent in and through their transformation as Dao is one and eternally the same.

The same perspective is clarified again in terms of separateness and ubiquity, of difference and identity.

> The embodiment of Dao widely encompasses all. This means that it is everywhere. Being everywhere, it wondrously is beyond individual bodies and names, yet at the same time it is fully embodied in the myriad beings. This gives rise to the inherent principle of identity and difference.
>
> The principle of identity and difference, in its perfection, culminates in the absence of identity and difference. Identical and different, Dao in beings wondrously goes beyond all and is widely encompassing. Neither identical nor different, it wondrously goes beyond while at the same time actively encompassing all. As it goes beyond all, it realizes its fullest embodiment. This is wondrous complete pervasion. This is the Dao. (8b-9a)

The subtle vision of Sima Chengzhen thus formulates the differences and similarities in understanding the basic notions of the Daoist religion. With great philosophical exactness and in painstaking detail it formulates the logical and paradoxical dimensions of realizing the Dao. Sima's reading and explanation of the doctrine, ever theoretically subtle and in full command of various methods and faculties, yet never loses sight of the practical dimension, of the application of the doctrines in the lives and aspirations of Daoist adepts. Realization of Dao remains Sima Chengzhen's ultimate goal, even in his most intricate and paradoxical analyses of various doctrinal and theoretical aspects.

The Names of Laozi

A different approach to the same essential problem of Dao in the world and its accessibility to human beings is offered by Du Guangting in his *Guangsheng yi*, where he makes several notes on the deity Laozi and his names.

Historically, Laozi is the name of the philosopher associated with the *Daode jing* and its transmission to Yin Xi 尹喜, the Guardian of the Pass. His name means "Old Master" and has been understood as the polite title of the ritual master Lao Dan 老儋 (Old Dan), a teacher of Confucius later linked with the *Daode jing* (Graham 1990, 113). Once integrated into religious Daoism as a full deity and active personification of Dao, however, Laozi became more exalted and came to be called by different names.

Du Guangting mentions Imperial Heavenly Sovereign as his appellation when in heaven and Lord Lao as his title when teaching Dao on earth. In addition to these, the deity had 1,200 titles and 180 names. Among others, he was called the Father of Nonaction and the Mother of All Beings. However, in his deepest foundation he is like Dao itself: so enormous and so unfathomable that he cannot possibly be named (*Guangsheng yi* 2.2ab).

Moreover, the name Laozi itself took on a much deeper significance. From "Old Master," its emphasis was changed to "Old Child," a name given to the god by his mother upon birth because he had spent seventy-two (in later versions, eighty-one) years in the womb and was born with white hair like an old man (*Shenxian zhuan* 1; Kohn 1995b; Campany 2002). Du gives a much more sophisticated theoretical interpretation of the name.

> As to the name given to the sage, Laozi, "Old Child," it is usually assumed that it refers to the fact that he remained in the womb for eighty-one years and had white hair when

> he was born. The Holy Mother Goddess thus named him to show his wonderful nature to the world.
>
> In addition there are five theories regarding this problem:
>
> First, as the appearance of sages on earth is different from that of ordinary man, the Holy Mother wanted to call him "Old". But as he had only just been born, she also wanted to call him her "Child". Therefore she decided to combine these two words and call him Laozi.
>
> Next, the name "Old Child" was chosen to illustrate the nature of the sacred Dao as opposed to the profane. "Old" usually means aged, whereas "child" commonly denotes a young person. Normal people are first young, and gradually grow old, but Laozi started out being old and gained youth. Thus it was intended to clarify the fact that he lived and thereby returned to the root.
>
> Third, "old" refers to Laozi's position as supervisor of the many sages, whereas "child" indicates his creative power over the myriad beings. Laozi combines both names because he is the teacher of the sages and the creator of all beings. He is therefore called "Old Child." This name was given to him when he was born on earth. His real name Lord Lao, on the other hand, stems from times unknown in the past.
>
> Fourth, he is called Old Child to demonstrate his rejection of ending and his continuous return to the beginning. "Old" represents the end of life; "child", on the other hand, is its beginning. Normal people start at the beginning and gradually proceed toward the end. But Lord Lao rises from the end and gradually proceeds to the beginning. He wants to make all people practice Dao, reverse old age, and return to youthfulness. This is why he took the name "Old Child".
>
> Fifth, Laozi radiates the light of harmony to spread Dao among humanity. He is called "old", because he had white hair when he was born. He is "child" or "master," because this is a common appellation for philosophers. For instance, Kongzi, Mengzi, Zhuangzi, and Liezi all use their surname together with this suffix. Laozi, Heguanzi, Baopuzi, and Huainanzi call themselves after some special characteristic using the same word. (*Guangsheng yi* 2.16a; Kohn 1989c, 76-78).

With this detailed and multivalent explanation, Du therefore claims that the very name Laozi or "Old Child" symbolizes the full powers of the deity as the divine child, the creator, the returner, the eternal, the newly born. Both old and young at the same time, simultaneously transforming and eternal, divine and human in one body, the same being both growing and declining—Laozi in his human form combines and incorporates all the different aspects of life on earth, just as his name documents his power and his supernatural stature among humanity.

The god Laozi in Du Guangting's work, just as the doctrine of Dao in Sima Chengzhen's analysis and the concept of knowledge in Li Rong's discussion, is the subject of a detailed interpretation. The Daoist teaching, systematized into a coherent whole, is analyzed in one particular aspect with ever increasing subtlety, making the multifaceted complexity of the religion shine forth with concentrated power in a single aspect. The thinkers add dimensions of meaning and intricacy to one point to reveal the fullness and power of the entire artifice. Du Guangting, in particular, continues the tradition of earlier Tang thinkers while working in a politically less stable environment. Both in his analysis of Laozi's names and in his ritual and hagiographic work, he achieves an intensity of vision that penetrates and encompasses the religion to its very foundations.

Conclusion

To sum up, mystical thinking in Tang Daoism is highly systematic and systematizing, focuses on the scriptures and their exegesis, and uses commentaries, logical argument, definition of terms, and complex lists to clarify its meaning and its key issues. Coming to the fore at a time when Daoism is not only a well-developed religious system but also enjoys state support, Daoist philosophy plays an important role in the intellectual climate of the time and participates actively in its formation and development.

Like Daoism as a whole, the three representative thinkers respond to the call of the era in the concerns they address and the methods they utilize. Li Rong, poet and commentator on the scriptures, exercises his logical skills in epistemology to develop a better philosophical understanding of how one can know the Dao. Sima Chengzhen, a century later, uses logic to both obscure and illuminate the being and nonbeing of Dao in his students' minds. He addresses practical questions, remaining foremost and always the teacher of the unenlightened, but his approach is characterized by highly sophisticated questions and answers, paradoxes and logical twists. Du Guangting, finally, following both earlier masters in his extensive commentary and ritual works, adds a new component by actively integrating the myth of the highest deity into the philosophical discourse. Laozi and his different names, to focus on the example described above, come to represent yet another model of the reality of Dao in the world. In his lists and analyses, Du shows yet another way the true embodiment of Dao can be known by humanity.

The three thinkers, with their common concern with systemacity and the accessibility of the Daoist teaching, are at the same time the product of their respective ages. Daoist mystical philosophy, far from being an unworldly exercise of speculation and mere theoretical organization, emerges as a relevant activity in and contribution to the intellectual life of the time. It begins as a call for inherent order after the Six Dynasties' period of vigorous growth and proceeds, through the vagaries of the Tang's political and intellectual climate, to bring forth a large number of highly sophisticated and speculative materials.

Chapter Five

Modes of Mystical Experience: Enstasy Versus Ecstasy[1]

One form the accomplished mystic takes in Daoism is that of the immortal. The character for "immortal," *xian*, appears in two major forms: as 仙 or 仚, which both depict a man on a mountain (*Shuowen jiezi* 387); or as 僊, a word used in the *Shijing* 詩經 (Book of Songs) for "to dance with flying sleeves" and etymologically related to *qian* 遷, "to take off the ground" (Ōfuchi 1952, 35).

The connotations of the term vary with time and author, and it is not immediately clear what concrete ideas and religious beliefs the Chinese associated with *xian*. The texts before and during the Former Han dynasty together with numerous archaeological finds are generally accepted as describing actual beliefs of the time. However, since Wang Chong's 王充 *Lunheng* 論衡 (Balanced Discussions) at the latest, there is a critical awareness of the impossibility to bypass death entirely.[2] Immortals become increasingly a literary motif, while the religion begins to organize them according to type. More than that, immortality techniques are tested and developed, collections of recipes and descriptions of practices are found in increasing numbers.

In poetry, immortals are generally images of freedom, lightness, and beauty. In religion, they are long-lived and beyond death, they have magical powers and can control nature, they are the ones who populate the otherworldly hierarchy above. By the Song dynasty, the word

---

[1] An earlier version of this paper appeared as "Eternal Life in Taoist Mysticism" in *Journal of the American Oriental Society* 110.4 (1990), 622-40.

[2] In his "Daoxu pian" (ch. 7; Forke 1907, 332-250), he describes the ascent into heaven of Huangdi, Liu An, Lu Ao, Xiang Mandu, Wen Zhi, Li Shaojun, Dongfang Shuo and Wang Qiao. About Li Shaojun he remarks that "he parted with his body," and since humans do not have shells to cast off, he obviously must have died. About Wang Qiao he mentions that he did not eat and had no clothing and remarks: "How can frozen and starved people live any longer than others?"

"immortal" has been inflated to such a degree that it can refer to anyone who has done something extraordinary or who is in some way special. Stories frequently emphasize the magical powers, the joyful ease, and the trickster nature of immortals. In modern China, immortals are like fairies: beautiful, young, supernatural, living above the clouds. Still, the concept includes notions of the improbable, the fantastic, the crazy.

Overall, the ideas most closely related to immortality are longevity and flight, i.e., a permanence on earth and a freedom from all mundane strive. Two other important concepts are vital energy (*qi* 氣) and paradise, i.e., the concept that all life is made up from some primordial stuff which when used correctly will give magical powers and eternal life and the idea that beyond the range of human vision there are realms of permanence, of beauty, of a glittering radiance where the true ones make their home.

The earliest formulations of these ideals of immortality are found in the *Zhuangzi* 莊子 (Book of Master Zhuang) and the *Chuci* 楚辭 (Songs of the South); later authors go back to them again and again. The *Zhuangzi* is most frequently cited in its description of the "Free and Easy Wandering," an expression which refers to an attitude of spontaneity and instinct, freedom from circumstance and strive (Fukunaga 1946). The *Chuci*, in the "Far-off Journey" provides the archetypal description of the mystical excursion into heaven (Hawkes 1959; Fukunaga 1970). Important motifs, such as the lightness of the body, the act of flying into the sky (Murakami 1956, 185), the use of natural phenomena (thunder, wind, etc; Wen 1956, 175) as carriages, the identification of the writer with the powers of heaven, are all typical features of immortal existence (Van Gulik 1941, 33; Schafer 1973, 121). The ultimate freedom is then expressed as the loss of any conscious identity. A famous example for this is found in Zhuangzi's "butterfly dream" (Watson 1968, 49), an exceptionally clear description is found in the *Liezi*:

> After nine years I gave up speaking and thinking, I did not know the difference between benefit and damage, I did not know whether my master was really my master, nor yet that another was my friend.
>
> Outer and inner life had completely melted together. Thereafter the five senses also melted together, I could not determine whither the sensations came. My mind was frozen, my body free, flesh and bones seemed to have become rarefied.

> I did not know on what my body rested, nor did I know what was under my feet. I was borne hither and thither, like a leaf that falls from a tree, or like a dry chaff, without knowing whether the wind was riding on me or I on the wind. (Graham 1960, 36)

The mystical state here consists of a closing-in of knowledge, at the same time there is a feeling of freely floating along. This state is connected with mundane life in two ways: on the one hand, it is found in the conscious realization of Dao which pervades all universe in continuous change and as such is always very close by. "One could see it quite clearly if one used the soul for seeing instead of the eyes" (Van Gulik 1940, 89). On the other hand, it is a refinement of the body. Every individual can refine his material body through various techniques and meditations to such a degree that he or she can attain perfect lightness of the body and the ability to fly through the air (Zhou 1974, 144). Once a high degree of refinement has been attained, the body consists only of *qi*, the stuff of immortality.

Everything in nature has his or her own *qi*—so specialized that the term often seems untranslatable (Liu 1970, 70). The emanations radiating from beings are called *qi* as much as the matter from which they are made up originally. By treating the basic stuff of creation in the proper manner everyone can become finer and finer, until one is only the fine matter itself. This then causes people to fly and ascend into the higher regions of the cosmos (Maspero 1971, 479).

Not quite everyone who undergoes the training will eventually be successful. There are thus several different types of immortals: heavenly immortals who have attained permanent residence in paradise, sometimes even with their families; earthly immortals who have not quite overcome the attractions of mundane life and, despite their realization of freedom from it, decide to linger on a little longer; and immortals who leave this world by way of "deliverance from the corpse" (Robinet 1979; Cedzich 2001), that is to say, they leave their physical bodies behind when they ascend into the other world (Ware 1966, 192, 216). In addition to these three major groups there are child immortals, newly advanced immortals, and numerous other specific categories of divine beings (Zhou 1974, 112).

The background of the immortality complex and its historical development are rather shrouded in mystery. Generally there is evidence for a strong concern with long life around the fourth century B.C.E., when the philosophy of the Lao-Zhuang tradition first developed (Yü

1965, 87). The same period sees the origin of the *Chuci*, this southern and more shamanistically-oriented text. During the Han dynasty philosophy, longevity concerns and shamanism were joined into one complex then also incorporating cosmological, astrological, and medical theories. At this time, immortality was primarily understood as a mechanical process: one received divine materials from the immortals already residing in paradise, then transformed them for human use in a ritual procedure, applied them to oneself and thus could become an immortal oneself (*Shiji* 28). It was only necessary to get the immortal drug to open the gates of heaven (Zhou 1974, 14).

Toward the end of the Han, inner cultivation and physical techniques seem to have received more attention. In the 4th century then, strong evidence for a more magical approach to immortality is suggested in Ge Hong's 葛洪 *Baopuzi* 抱朴子 (The Book of the Master Who Embraces Simplicity, DZ 1185) (Murakami 1956, 39). The issue is complicated by the fact that the Han, being an age of unification and standardization, still retained a large variety of local ideas and practices, so that there are no unified concepts of life and death (Loewe 1979; 1982). Consequently it is hard to tell whether the concept of immortality was there originally, developed as a progressive advance, or should rather be described as a degeneration of earlier beliefs (Creel 1970, 10). The winged immortals depicted on Han mirrors and in Han tombs have invited wide speculation as to their origins and meaning in the graves (Seidel 1982). The biographies of immortals, it is generally assumed, were first descriptions of those pictures (Kaltenmark 1968, 266).

According to Yü Ying-shih, the fundamental human desire underlying the immortality complex is the wish for a prolongation of life, which is frequently expressed in prayers of the Zhou period (1965, 87). The *Shanhai jing* 山海經 (Classic of Mountains and Seas) mentions numerous places, peoples, plants of "no-death", death itself seems to have been understood as a curable disease (Bauer 1971, 155). The *Taiping jing* 太平經 (Scripture of Great Peace) draws a connection between one's good and evil deeds and the life-span one earns on earth (Yü 1965, 112). There was apparently, according to Yü, a strong desire to make this existence continuous, permanent, to prolong it as it is, to grow older and attain higher levels of wisdom, yet never lose the youthfulness and energy of the body. Old age, weakness, and diseases are early steps toward death, they have to be prevented in order to avoid the final stage. According to this understanding, the immortal state is a static solidity of body and mind.

Wen Yiduo, on the contrary, assumes that the Chinese originally held the concept of an immortal soul which would be freed by destroying (especially by burning) the body (1956, 159). Later this concept was developed to include the physical body. Thus, while immortality first implied the destruction of the body in order to free the inherent immortal soul, it later meant the preservation of the body, without however continuing the sufferings caused by it. Wen suggests that the concept of immortality is related to the migrations of the Jiang tribe from what is now Tibet in the west toward Shandong in the east, on grounds of the geographical location of the paradises in the eastern sea and in the mountains of the west. Originally, he suggests, the Jiang believed in the immortality of the soul, but developed a more physical approach to the problem after they mixed with the native inhabitants of eastern coastal China (Wen 1956, 153).

The important motif of ecstatic travel or flying through the air in immortality literature caused Guo and also Edward Schafer to see immortality as a flight from an unbearable situation in life. Flight is the symbol of a rejection of an insufferable surrounding (1963, 80). The search for solitude in the mountains, a concrete form of travel away from the world, tends indeed to be a measure of withdrawal from bad political and social circumstances. Kaltenmark thinks it quite possible that such mountain recluses would meet with aborigines in the mountains and learn not only a variety of medical and pharmacological methods from them, but also their understanding of nature and the world (1953).

These arts of the aborigines would then be related to the *fangshu* 方術, the various magical and therapeutically methods which came to the attention of the court during the Han dynasty (Kaltenmark 1968, 276). The role of the mediator between two worlds, typical for the immortal as the one who can fly and who can go back and forth between wilderness and civilization, suggests a shamanistic connection. Many of the classical techniques and attributes of immortals are moreover also found in the shamanistic religions of Central Asia (Bauer 1971, 151). According to this understanding, the immortal state is a free flight, a transcendence of spirit over matter.

While in the old texts it is not entirely clear whether immortality meant long life on earth, ascension into heaven after death, or the complete avoidance of earthly passing, it becomes clear through the study of the concrete methods Daoists applied to attain that desired state that immortality ultimately meant a combination of long life on earth and an ascension into heaven after death, but not the actual no-death of this physical body. In Daoist materials, "immortality" and "longevity" are therefore to a certain extent synonymous in the sense that one had to fully realize one's given life-span on earth and attain a mental state of feeling immortal to assure proper ascension after this body had fallen away.

Among immortality techniques one can distinguish physiological and psychological practices. Among the former, the ingestion of a cinnabar elixir has been meticulously studied by Michel Strickmann who suggests that ultimately "there was no belying the death that he [the adept] first had to die" (1979, 137). He points out that "in hagiography it is usually suggested that the successful immortal somehow managed to bypass death entirely. . . . some hagiographic accounts make willingness to follow a master in apparent suicide the crucial test of a disciple's resolution" (1979, 130). The elixir often was highly poisonous and would be swallowed upon receiving a summons from the immortals to take up a position in the heavenly hierarchy above. Immortality here is not the preservation of the physical body, but the attainment of a spiritual state in the other world.

Among the psychological methods, meditation techniques such as "guarding the One", "sitting in oblivion" (Kohn 1987a), ecstatic flight (Robinet 1976; 1989) and visualizations of body gods (Robinet 1979) are essential. In all these, immortality is not a bypassing of the death of the physical body, either. The body will eventually fall away like the skin of a cicada. The state attained is a mental equanimity toward death, a state of concentration in which one is either so internally harmonized that "life and death are one whole" or so far advanced beyond the world in ecstatic vision that one is more at home over there than down here. In either case, physical death—though occurring at some point—has become negligible.

The avoidance of physical death, it seems, was ultimately not an issue in the attainment of immortality. On the other hand, health and longevity (in the sense of living out one's allotted life-span) are important prerequisites for either the alchemical or the meditative transformation. What is more, the texts continue to describe the immortal state in terms of "eternal life," "eternity," or of attaining a life as long as that of the sun and the moon. The question thus arises: What is meant by these references to eternity? What is it that supposedly lives forever? It is not the physical body, nor is it some kind of immortal soul in the Christian sense. How exactly is the state of eternal life imagined? What are the necessary steps to its attainment?

Ecstatic Matching the Changes

Ecstatic visions of Daoist mystical attainment tend to emphasize more the psychological side of things than the materialistic. Typically they include statements such as "make your mind no-mind and go along with the changes." The final state here is a mental equanimity, a going-beyond of the mind over the various experiences of the body. The mind is made one with true spirit, with the functions of Dao; the adept of immortality survives in eternity as a spirit being. He or she rides on the changes and joins in the interplay of yin and yang.

The imagery of the ecstatic form of eternal life is strongly shamanistic: the flight into higher realms, the experience of an altered state of consciousness, the freedom from the limits of this world are all present in the descriptions. The process of attaining ultimate freedom is depicted as one of getting lighter and brighter, the higher one ascends, the purer the spirit becomes, the more light will be radiated by the immortal. The world view that underlies this model of eternal life is one of "becoming:" the universe is in a constant flux, nothing stands ever still or stops for a moment. Time is conceived as cyclical, eternity can only take place in an eternal return (Eliade 1959).

Many passages showing the ecstatic conception of eternal life are found in the *Zhuangzi*, famous for its central concept of "Free and Easy Wandering," which in itself bears expression of the free flight of the successful immortal (Fukunaga 1946). A concept close to "Free and Easy Wandering" and equally central is the notion of "non-dependence", a complete non-reliance on anything whatsoever (Robinet 1986). As the *Zhuangzi* has it, Liezi should have "mounted the truth of Heaven and Earth, ridden the changes of the six breaths, and thus wandered through the boundless " (ch. 1; Watson 1968, 32).

For Guo Xiang 郭象, the major commentator on the *Zhuangzi*, the central concept of the text is the "going along," the following of the current of things in a state of utter mental freedom, of ecstasy. In his work, he uses about fifteen different terms to express this concept, with slight variations in connotation: to accord with; to correspond to; to resonate with; to comply with; to depend on; to avail oneself of; to go along with; to let oneself go; to follow; to obey; to be content with; to resign oneself to; to frolic along; to follow and obey (Knaul 1985a, 23).

His interpretive tendencies become most obvious in his commentary on the famous story on the immortals on Mount Gushe in the first chapter of the *Zhuangzi*:

> there are immortals living on faraway Gushe Mountain, with skin like ice or snow, and gentle and shy like young girls. They don't eat the five grains, but suck the wind, drink the dew, climb up on the clouds and mists, ride flying dragons, and wander beyond the four seas. (1.25b-27b; Watson 1968, 33)

Guo Xiang says:

> This is a parable. The immortal is what we call today the sage. The sage, even though he may sit in court, in his mind is no different from the freedom of the mountains and the woods....
>
> He embodies the spirit, dwells in numinosity, and while pervading the principle of the universe reaches out to utmost wonder. Even though he may be quiet and relaxed within his hall, he mysteriously goes along with all beyond the four seas.
>
> Thus he can ride on the two forces [yin & yang] and control the six *qi*, he can join the mass of people and go along with the myriad beings. If there were no beings he did not follow, he would even float along with the clouds; if there were no shapes he would not use, he would even fly astride a dragon. He relinquishes his body and realizes spontaneity.
>
> Even though he is totally serene, he does not depend on anything, sitting in oblivion, acting in oblivion, doing everything in utter oblivion. . . . He can do this, because his spirit is concentrated.

Cheng Xuanying's 成玄英 subcommentary brings the light imagery out more strongly: "The passage states that the sage moves along with inner serenity, therefore he radiates in harmony with emptiness."

Another telling passage is the line in chapter 6: "Therefore the sage wanders in the realm where beings cannot impose upon him and is always there" (7.27a; Watson 1968, 81). Guo Xiang explains:

> The sage wanders in the realm of change, he frolics along with the flux of the daily new. As the myriad beings undergo ten thousand transformations, he changes with them thousand fold. As the transformations are limitless, so he is limitless with them. Who could impose upon him? He can

> perish in life and exist in death—when would he ever not be there?

Here eternal life is defined quite clearly as an ongoing floating movement in harmony with the changes. It is a going-along with the transformations in a free state of mind, come whatever may. Guo Xiang's sage is utterly one with the transformations of all beings; all states are the same to him, he can be non-existent while alive, he can be present while in death.

The all-pervading flux is central to Guo Xiang's thought; even when the *Zhuangzi* speaks of "preserving the body", he interprets it as a flowing along with its developments (14.12a). The *Zhuangzi* states:

> Let there be no seeing, no hearing... and the body will right itself.... When the eye does not see, the ear does not hear, and the mind does not know, then the spirit will protect the body, and the body will enjoy long life. (13.19a; Watson 1968, 119)

Guo Xiang comments:

> Forget to see and there will be spontaneous vision; forget to hear and there will be spontaneous hearing. Spirit will not be disturbed, the body will not go wrong. One has to let oneself go along with its spontaneous movement... All this means that one has to follow and obey one's inner nature in all its movements. Then one will enjoy long life.

This state of total harmony with the flux of existence is made possible through a complete mental unconsciousness, a forgetting of oneself in ecstasy, a freedom from self and others which will last as eternally as the changes continue to happen. "Whether beings come or go, he [the sage] is not aware of either," Guo Xiang insists (13.23b). In a similar manner he defines the state of complete oblivion: "Practicing forgetfulness, what would there remain unforgotten? On the inside unaware of one's body, on the outside never knowing there is a universe" (8.39ab).

Where Guo Xiang describes the ultimate state of immortality as a free floating in harmony with the changes, Cheng Xuanying uses expressions that point more toward a stability of mind and body, toward an arrest of all movements, cosmic or individual: "Let there be no outside seeing or hearing for the eyes and the ears, embrace and guard essence and spirit, then... you will become one with Dao" (13.19a).

This description represents what we shall call an enstatic view of immortality (see below). Here it is interesting to note that the same passage in the *Zhuangzi* gives rise to such variant interpretations, that apparently the state of inner unconsciousness is a prerequisite to both: the free flight and the mystical merging.

The *Xisheng jing* as a whole tends to be more on the enstatic side admonishing adepts to "preserve Dao", "guard the One", and "recover the root". Nevertheless, the commentaries occasionally mention ecstatic freedom as one of the results of the enstatic training in concentration and purity.

> Mystery and emptiness accumulate to fullness: life is eternal. (6.6b)
>
> Chong says: "'Mystery and emptiness' refer to Dao. One truly accumulates its wonderful energy until it completely fills one's body—then one will be able to fly into empty space and live forever.

As in the *Zhuangzi* and Guo Xiang's commentary, the complete loss of any kind of identity, be it physical or psychological, the complete ecstatic transcendence of the self, is the essential characteristic of the experience of eternal life.

A similar description is found in the *Neiguan jing* 內觀景 (Scripture of Inner Observation, DZ 641) of the mid-Tang:

> Lord Lao said:
> Dao highly values long life, so guard your spirit and hold on to your root. Never let essence and energy disperse, but keep them pure and always together. When body and spirit are aligned with Dao, you can fly to Mount Kunlun, be born in Former Heaven, continue living in Later Heaven, and forever pass in and out of the spaceless. (6b; Kohn 1989b)

Passing in and out of the spaceless, being alive either in Former or in Later Heaven—freedom, flight and ecstasy are the result of a preservation of essence and energy, of a merging, a union with Dao. Adepts no longer should directly lose their consciousness and identity to the flux, as Guo Xiang advises, but should first gather in and preserve the stuff that makes up the changes, i.e., Dao itself.

The clearest description of how adepts gradually attain perfect ecstatic freedom is found in Sun Simiao's 孫思邈 *Cunshen lianqi ming* 存神煉氣銘 (Inscription on Visualization of Spirit and Refinement of Energy, DZ 834), in a passage also contained in the *Dingguan jing* 定

觀經 (Scripture of Concentration and Observation, DZ 400) and in the appendix to Sima Chengzhen's 司馬承禎 *Zuowang lun* 坐忘論 (On Sitting in Oblivion, DZ 1036). Here immortality is attained by undergoing five phases of the mind and seven stages of the body. Where the former are an exercise in concentration, an enstatic stabilization of the mind, the latter are described as a gradual increase in movement, openness, joy, light, even ecstasy, until the successful adept of immortality takes up a position next to the Jade Emperor of the Great Dao (2b-3a).

The ecstatic experience of immortality is therefore described in terms of flight. It is a flowing, floating movement in accordance with the changes and transformations of the universe. It is a state of eternal becoming, of never standing still for even an instant. Adepts feel light in their bodies and radiant in their minds. All states they undergo give them nothing by joy, they are no longer limited to themselves, but have gone beyond the limits of individual body and mind. Heaven and Earth are one paradise to them, a realm of joyful pervasion without bounds.

Preserving Dao in Enstasy

The notion of "enstasy" in mysticism was coined by Mircea Eliade, the great historian of religion (Eliade 1958). It serves as an opposite to "ecstasy" and has all the characteristics that are opposite to our description of ecstasy above. The enstatic model of immortality therefore centers around the notion of "preserving", "embracing", "harmonizing", and "recovering". Rather than in terms of flux and going along, the final state is described in terms of fullness and stability, as an intense tranquility and restfulness which pervade the adept.

The imagery tends to emphasize union, oneness, merging—it is full of darkness and the shading of light. The immortal state of mind is not so much one of joy and freedom, rather it is characterized by innocence and utter simplicity. Eternity here is a state of purity in the sense of originality, of unsophistication. It is neither brilliant nor radiant. More like an uncut block of wood, it is not like a glittering gem. Time is conceived more as a linear movement which one arrests at a given point from which onward the body does no longer decay. One may also reverse time to the effect that one becomes younger and more energetic instead of older and weaker.

According to the enstatic outlook on immortality, Dao or the One is the deep underlying root or sources on the basis of which change takes place. It is the stuff from which all universal development springs. This source of the universe is what is truly permanent, it is "being" in its truest form. Unless this is recovered and preserved, unless one has made oneself completely one with this, eternity cannot be had. The underlying ground is static—so is the immortal state. The underlying ground is deep within, it is shrouded in darkness—thus one moves towards it by deepening, darkening, closing in. The basic idea of enstatic immortality is summarized in the *Neiguan jing*:

> Lord Lao said:
> Dao is free from life and death, but the body does undergo life and death. Thus we say that life and death are characteristics of the body, but not characteristics of Dao. The body only comes to life when it receives Dao. The body only dies when it loses Dao. Whoever is able to preserve and guard Dao will live forever and never perish. (5a; Kohn 1989b)

An early classical passage on this understanding of immortality is found in the words of Guangchengzi 廣成子 in *Zhuangzi* 11:

> Let there be no seeing, no hearing; enfold the spirit in quietude and the body will right itself. Be still, be pure, do not labor your body, do not churn up your essence, and then you can live a long life. When the eye does not see, the ear does not hear, then your spirit will protect the body, and the body will enjoy long life. . . . You have only to take care and guard your own body; the other things will of themselves grow sturdy. As for myself, I guard the One, abide in harmony, and therefore I have kept myself alive for twelve hundred years, and never has my body suffered any decay. (13.19a-21b; Watson 1968, 119-120)

Thus, there should be no more sensual activity, no more knowledge, but only a continuous guarding of the One, the underlying power of all existence. This will lead to a stability that lasts forever.

Cheng Xuanying in his subcommentary closely follows the literal message of the text and refrains from reinterpreting it along Guo Xiang's lines:

> Let there be no outside seeing or hearing for the eyes and the ears, embrace and guard essence and spirit, then the projections will not be confused, the mind will be in har-

mony with the body, and naturally you will merge with the true Dao.

Purify the spirit and calm your thoughts, make sure the body is not labored, don't get involved with outer projections of the mind. Essence and spirit should be always serene, the mind relaxed, the body at peace: then you can experience "long life and eternal vision" [*Daode jing* 59] . . . .

Preserve serenity and one-pointedness of mind, dwell always in the harmony of Dao, gather your energy and cultivate the body: even though the years of your life will be numbered, in the end there will be no days of old age and decay. (13.19a-21b)

The 5th-century *Xisheng jing* 西昇經 (Scripture of Western Ascension, DZ 726; trl. Kohn 1991a), too, subscribes fully to the enstatic model.

<u>21. Sympathy with Others</u>

Laozi said: To sympathize with others as a human being is not as good as sympathizing with one's body. To sympathize with one's body is not as good as loving the spirit.

Xu says: "... When the spirit is labored, it will leave the body; when it leaves the body, life will perish."

To love the spirit is not as good as harboring the spirit.

Li says: "Harboring the spirit means that there is neither attachment nor defilement without, that there is neither yearning nor worry within. When within and without are pure and at peace, the spirit will return naturally and never leave the body."

To harbor the spirit is not as good as preserving the body.

Li says: "Even though the spirit is perfect and wonderful, it is not established of itself. Rather, it needs the body to take refuge in, and only then it can revolve and function. Now, if you only harbor the spirit without guarding the body, then the body will decay and your physical frame will pass away. Then the spirit has nowhere to lodge. If you want the spirit to live forever, you must first guard the body. Guard the body by being at peace and pure, by joining Dao and Virtue, by pervading the dark and the subtle."

To preserve the body means to live forever.

Liu says: "Harboring the spirit is to value it highly... guarding the body is to keep it tranquil. The body is the habitation of the spirit, thus you have to guard the body

> to keep the spirit at peace.... When body and spirit are both complete, you can live forever." (4.13a-14a)

Both the spirit and the body have to be kept strong, they should be trained to guard each other so that no outside entity can interfere with the harmony and stability within.

This central state of harmony and stability is characterized by immobility, darkness, and a complete cessation of the functioning of the senses. It is attained through accumulation of energy and a calming of the mind. Let us first look at it as a state without any movement exemplified in the first section of the *Xisheng jing*:

> Without beginning or end, he exists continuously.
>
> Li says: "Where there is life there is a beginning; where there is death, there is an end. Dao, however, has neither beginning nor end... Truly and permanently be without movement and you will naturally be stable and live forever." (1.1b)

Next, the state is also characterized by a pervading darkness:

> If you don't step into opulence and brightness, you can live forever.
>
> Wei says: "Opulence refers to the transgressions and disgraces of life; brightness means knowing, seeing, and understanding everything. Don't get involved with these two, then you can attain the purity of a newborn baby, and approach Dao of eternal life."
>
> Li says: "Normal people tend to reject the black and approach the white, leave the dark and enter the bright. . . . Here the author encourages adepts to be dark and obscure, then they will begin to attain eternal life." (2.6b-7a)

More than that, the enstatic state is typically accompanied by a complete loss of all sensual activity:

> I don't see, don't hear, don't know: spirit does not leave my body, and I am forever at-one with Dao.
>
> Li says: Abandon sounds and sights and be pure and at peace, give up all distinctions and rest in non-action. When the spirit does not part from the person, then we say that it does not leave the body. When the body is in harmony with the spirit, one's life is joined with Dao. This means eternal life." (5.8ab)

The process of stabilizing is usually described as an assembly of energy or a recovery of essence and spirit:

> If you attain a state of permanent purity, tranquility, and non-action, non-being will be recovered naturally. Thus you go back to before you were born and no longer have a body. Nourish the body in non-action, then you will make your body and physical structure whole. Share in the abundance and fullness of Heaven and Earth: thus you will live forever. (4.12a-13a)

This description of the *Xisheng jing* is clarified in slightly different terms by the commentators:

> Wei says: "When Dao and the energy are recovered and return to the body, one will forget the body. When one forgets the body, then one's virtue will be in harmony with Heaven and Earth. Since Heaven and Earth are not alive for themselves, they can live long [*Daode jing* 7]. Therefore one will be complete in oneself, even if the body is not specifically protected, one will naturally continue to be alive, even if one's years are not particularly guarded."
>
> Xu says: "Heaven and Earth, essence and energy are full and stable—thus my life will last as long as the two forces."
>
> Li says: "Nourishing the body in non-action, being at peace in utter freedom from affairs, then one's merit reaches to the four extreme ends of the world, one's Dao is as full as to extend to the six realms of emptiness. This is called fullness and stability." (4.12a-13a)

The process leading to immortality in enstasy thus begins with a concentration of spirit and an energizing of the body. Both have to be nourished extensively so that health and long life will be perfected. Then deeper levels of immersion into Dao can be approached: the state of immobility, total darkness, and absence of sensual activity. Eventually a trance state, the total oblivion of self and others is reached. From here final realization takes place, the spirit man is born.

Practical instructions are outlined in the beginning of Sun Simiao's *Cunshen lianqi ming*:

> The body is the habitation of spirit and energy. As long as spirit and energy are there, the body is healthy and vigorous. But it dies as soon as spirit and energy are lost. Therefore, if you want to preserve your body, you first have to calm spirit

> and energy. Energy is the mother of spirit. Spirit is the mother of energy. Only when both are together, one will live forever.
>
> Now, in order to calm the spirit, you must first of all refine the primordial energy. When this energy resides in the body, spirit is calm and energy like an ocean. If this ocean of energy is full to overflowing, the mind is calm and the spirit concentrated. When this concentration is not lost, body and mind are gathered in tranquility. Tranquility then grows further into stability, and the body will continue to exist for years eternal. Dwell permanently on the source of Dao, and sageliness will naturally be perfected....
>
> With life fixated and the body eternal, both unite with true inner nature. Thereby one attains an age as old as the sun and the moon. (1a)

As a result of this process, one will become a spirit immortal or a spirit person. With this attainment, however, the enstatic mode is temporarily left and the ecstatic mode is entered. The state of dark immobility is relinquished in favor of a pervasion of all.

Section 7 of the *Zuowang lun* on "Realizing Dao" gives a description of what this means:

> [As a spirit man] one's spirit and inner nature are empty and fused into one. One's body no longer changes or decays. Once the body is united with Dao, there is no more life or death. When withdrawn from life the body is in harmony with the spirit, when apparent the spirit is in harmony with the body. Therefore the spirit man is able to tread on water and fire without suffering harm. He can stand in the sunshine or the moonlight without casting a shadow. Survival and destruction resting with himself, he passes in and out of the spaceless....
>
> Spirit merged with Dao—this is realizing Dao.... When a man embraces Dao, his body and bones will stay hard forever. Daily increasing in merit, one's disposition will change to unite fully with the spirit. By refining the spirit to a higher subtlety, one will then realize mystical union with Dao.

The *Xisheng jing* (26.2) says:

> "The spirit does not leave the body and I am forever at-one with Dao."
> Body unified with Dao means that one will survive forever!
> Mind unified with Dao means that all dharmas are pervaded!

Ears unified with Dao means that all sounds will be heard!
Eyes unified with Dao means that all sights will be seen!
(14b-15b)

This passage exemplifies the reversal from the enstatic to the ecstatic mode of immortality: when nothing is seen with one's physical eyes, then all is seen with one's eyes of the spirit or Dao. When the physical body is no more there as an individual entity, it exists permanently as the body of Dao. Oneness with Dao, the union with the underlying being of the universe leads to a freedom over all, to the ability to participate in the movements of existence, to be or not to be, just as life itself may be latent or active, hidden or apparent.

Another summary of the process, influenced more explicitly by Mahāyāna Buddhism, is found in the late-Tang text *Xuanzhu xinjing zhu* 玄朱心境註 (Annotated Mysterious Pearly Mirror of the Mind, DZ 574) which contains of two poems on "Guarding the One" with commentary. The first poem runs:

Attainment of the prime of the One
Is not a gift from Heaven.
Realization of Great Non-being
Is the state of highest immortality.
Light restrained, a hidden brilliance
The body one with nature:
There is true peace, won but not pursued.

Spirit kept forever at rest
In serenity and beauty: this is true being!
Body and inner nature, hard and soft
All is but cinnabar vapor, azure barrens.
One of the highest sages —
Only after a hundred years
The tomb is discovered empty.

The commentary explains that the One here stands for primordial energy, the beginning of the universe, the cosmic chaos Hundun. Becoming one with it means to enter into the formlessness of universal creation. This state is not naturally given, it has to be attained by practitioners, but not actively. Rather, they must restrain their light and hide their brilliance, i.e., assemble their yang energy within rather than waste it on the world without. The peace of mind and the permanence of the body which will eventually be found come about quite naturally in the end, they are "won but not pursued." Adepts keep their spirit at rest within, relax in serenity, and naturally develop a cosmic consciousness. In due course they will vanish to take up their residence in the higher realms: they have become fully part of the One. Much later they are recognized as true sages.

> Dao does nothing, yet nothing's left undone.
> Purity of mind does not come from knowledge and wisdom.
> What is knowledge? What is purity?
> Knowledge depends on wisdom. Purity is freedom in going along.
> Going along, not following: this is pervasion of mind.
>
> Pervade the One and all affairs are done!
> The One is the root, affairs are the branches.
> When affairs return to the One, the One is always there.
> It is there, yet nothing is—so we borrow a term and speak of "guard."
> By just "guarding" emptiness and non-being you can naturally live forever!

Arresting all natural processes in a state of mental and physical stability, in oneness, darkness, and unknowing, therefore first leads to a universal pervasion of all, to a freedom described in very similar terms as the purely ecstatic model of immortality discussed above. Yet this is not the ultimate goal. From pervasion of all on this earth, the immortal—then in a state of utter at-oneness with Dao—eventually ascends into heaven. The freedom thus won is again one of restfulness, not of change. A position in the heavenly hierarchy is a permanent situation, certain administrative tasks may come and go, but the administrator remains the same. Eternity here is a state of being, not of becoming, a linear permanence, not a cyclical return.

Both experiences of immortality, the ecstatic and the enstatic, can and must be undergone while still alive in this world. As the *Tianyinzi* 天隱子 (Writings of the Master of Heavenly Seclusion, DZ 1026) has it: "A spirit immortal is also a human being" (1a). While the subjective feelings of the immortals are variously of light or darkness, movement or immobility, ecstasy or enstasy, they are in all cases of eternity, cyclical or linear, of an everlasting existence. In both cases, man is transformed into god: one laughing and one serious, one moving and one staying, one boundless and one restrained.

What, then, exactly is the stuff from which the gods are made? What is the "eternal self," the truth of Heaven and Earth within man? If asked, what it is that survives into immortality, the texts invariable answer: the body. Yes, but which?

The Body That Lives Forever

The body in Daoism is understood as a replica of the cosmos, as a microcosm of the whole universe (Schipper 1978; 1982; 1994). This understanding which plays an important role in Daoist meditation and world-view is most clearly expressed in the origin myth where the creator becomes one with the world. The myth, which is by no means limited to China, has been told about Laozi as much as about Pangu, the cosmogonic deity of south China:[3]

> Laozi changed his body: His left eye became the sun and his right eye the moon. His head was Mount Kunlun, his hair the stars. His bones turned into dragons, his flesh into wild beasts, his intestines into snakes. His breast was the ocean, his finger the five sacred mountains. The hair on his body was transformed into grass and trees, his heart into the constellation Cassiopeia. Finally, his testicles joined in embrace as the true parents of the universe. (*Xiaodao lun*, T. 52, 144b; see Kohn 1995a)

What interests us here is the definition of the body inherent in this myth: the body consists of eyes, ears, hair, bones, limbs, intestines, i.e., a variety of physical limbs and organs, just what one would expect the body to be about. The body in Daoism therefore seems to be very much like what we commonly think of when we speak of "the body."

Now, the Chinese use different terms for "body" in variant versions of the myth: The *Xiaodao lun* 笑道論 (Laughing at the Dao, T. 2103, 52.143c-52c) of the sixth century says that Laozi transformed his *xing* 形 (T. 52. 144b), whereas the *Yuanqi lun* 元氣論 (On Primordial Energy) of the mid-Tang quoted in the *Yunji qiqian* (56.1b) claims that Pangu changed his *shen* 身.

Although the terms *xing* and *shen* are frequently used interchangeably, they do not mean exactly the same thing. The *Shuowen jiezi* 說文解字 (Explaining Phrases and Illuminating Characters) defines *shen* as the self, the personal body: it consists of twelve distinct parts, namely "scalp, face, chin, shoulders, spine, abdomen, upper arms, lower arms, hands, thighs, legs, and feet" (p. 392). The pictogram shows a human torso and two legs. The body appears as a conglomerate of members and bones. *Xing*, on the contrary, is defined as *xiang*

[3] The variant version about Pangu is told in *Yunji qiqian* 56.1b-2a.

象, "emblem," "idea," "image." It basically means the visual image that one has of something. This notion corresponds to our translation of *xing* as "form" or "shape." It means the body as one can see it, one's physical appearance.

The *Neiguan jing* agrees with the *Shuowen* definition. It says:

> That which structures and combines the hundred bones [spirits] is called personal body [*shen*].
> That which relays a complete visual impression of the image is called physical form [*xing*]. (4a)

Then, however, the texts become more specific. The *Neiguan jing* describes *shen* as having "arisen from emptiness and nothingness in accordance with karma and the course of destiny. An accumulation of essence, and an assembly of energy, it merely lives through the coming down of power and the descent of the spirit" (3b). This body is impermanent, it is only a temporary residence of the spirit, it is bound to return to dust and ashes (*Xisheng jing* 7). Here we learn that *shen* though, as a physical entity, though taking part in the forces of the cosmos, is not as eternal as Heaven and Earth, but comes to life due to some other agent, so far defined as "spirit," *shen*. The same characterization holds true also for *xing*.

In contrast to *xing*, *shen* is then defined in terms of afflictions. The *Zuowang lun* quotes the *Daode jing* which says: "The body is the reason why I have terrible vexations. If I didn't have a body, what trouble would I have?" (ch. 13)

The Tang thinker Li Rong 李榮 explains this as it is quoted in the *Xisheng jing*: "Having a body means having vexations and adversities. Frustrated by sight and hearing, tortured by taste and smell, one is subject to pain, irritation, heat, and cold" (2.9b). "As soon as there is a body the hundred worries compete to arise and the five desires [of the senses] hurry to make their claims" (4.5b).

Here we find *shen* defined as the conglomerate of the senses. He includes the various human sensations and feelings together with the evaluations attached to them and the passions and emotions arising from them. An inscription also entitled "On Sitting in Oblivion", dated to the year 829, the earliest extant version of the *Zuowang lun*, says:

> Laozi says: "If I did not have a body what vexations would I have?" But if one does not have a body and thus returns to

annihilation, shouldn't that be called the loss of the basis of eternal life?

Yet I answer: What you would call "not having a body" does not refer to not having this particular physical form. It rather means that the bodily structure is unified with the Great Dao, that one is never influenced by glorious positions and does not seek after speedy advancement.

Placidly and without desires, it means to forget that there is this body dependent on all kinds of things. (Wu 1981, 47b; *Daoshu*, DZ 1017, 2.7ab)

Shen is thus the "personal body" or the "extended self." It is more than the physical body, even though it does neither deny nor replace it. A purely psychological rendering of *shen*, such as, e.g., "identity" or "personality," will therefore not suffice. The personal body with its afflictions is evaluated critically by Daoists.

Xing, on the other hand, the shape one's body takes in the world, is understood very positively. It is an exact replica of the universe. The *Neiguan jing* describes how it literally incorporates various forces of the cosmos as it develops:

In the first month, essence and blood coagulate in the womb.

In the second month, the embryo begins to take shape.

In the third month, the yang spirit arouses the three *hun* souls to come to life.

In the fourth month, the yin life force settles the seven *po* souls as guardians of the body.

In the fifth month, the five phases are distributed among the five organs to keep their spirits at peace.

In the sixth month, the six pitches are set up in the six viscera nourishing the life force.

In the seventh month, the seven essential stars open up the body orifices to let the light in.

In the eighth month, the eight phosphor spirits descend with their true energy.

In the ninth month, the various palaces and chambers are properly arranged to keep essence safe.

In the tenth month, the energy is strong enough to complete the image. (1b; Kohn 1989b)

The text then goes on to assure us that "human nourishment of primordial harmony never ceases." The various gods of the universe reside securely in this replica of the cosmos—at least as long as they are not labored or driven out by the sensual afflictions that pester the *shen*.

How do the two types of body interrelate? The texts seem to suggest that the human body is a *xing* when it is first born. Only when a sense of personal identity is established through the senses and social positioning, it becomes a *shen*. For the translation this would mean that, at least in the mystical context, we should distinguish the "personal body" from the "physical body," the person from the physis.[4] The mystical quest therefore consists in the abandoning of the *shen* in order to retrieve the purity of the cosmic image which is the *xing*. Daoist mysticism would therefore consist in a "depersonalization," a change of body identity from person to physis, from ego to cosmos. As the *Neiguan jing* instructs the practitioners:

> Patterned on Heaven and symbolizing Earth, inhaling yin and exhaling yang, see how your body shares in the five phases and goes along with the four seasons. Your eyes are the sun and the moon, your hair is the stars and the planets. Your eyebrows are the flowery canopy, your head is Mount Kunlun. See that your body is network of passes and palaces. (6b)

The same pattern also applies to the word "mind", which as the ruler of the emotions is closer to our idea of heart, that is, as an emotional entity it is considered useless for cosmic purposes; in its aspect as a manifestation of the primordial force of the cosmos it resembles the idea of "spirit". Strictly speaking, *xin* should refer only to the normal mind, whereas *shen* should be used for the spirit and its functioning as the realized mind. When there is no more "mind", i.e., no more perception of oneself and the world through attainment of a mystical state, one speaks consequently of *wuxin*, "no-mind." However, even in such a state of no-mind some kind of perception is taking place. Now the perceiving agent is the spirit. Since spirit now functions as the mind, it becomes logically understandable that frequently *xin* is used to refer to both types of mind apparently without discrimination.

---

[4] The problem of translation is especially complex when the context makes it clear that either person of physis are meant, while the term used in the given instance infers the respective opposite. As shown above, the two terms for "body" are used interchangeably. To avoid confusion it is all the more important to have an underlying framework of reference.

The *Xisheng jing* (ch. 22; 4.14b) extends the mystical definitions of the body to cosmology. It correlates the two terms for body with words for "mind:" the personal body *shen* goes with the mind *xin*, the physical body *xing* goes with the spirit *shen*.

In the development of the cosmos, there was first only spirit, spirit was radiant light, it was pure, it was there alone. It developed, it wanted to perfect itself. For this purpose it embodied itself in *xing*, physical bodies, shapes, material beings. *Xing* in this cosmological system could almost be translated as "matter." It is, however, not entirely clear in the text, whether spirit brought forth physical bodies in order to perfect itself or whether *xing* was there as a cosmic force from the beginning. In any case, once spirit and physical bodies are joined they continue to develop: spirit perfects itself, it moves toward a new state of radiance and purity through, but ultimately free from, matter. In the course of this process, physical bodies as bodies become spiritualized, i.e., lighter, purer, more radiant. The end of the world, its purpose, is the perfection of spirit and physis on a higher level.

One form which the combination of spirit and matter takes is the human being. People therefore partake in both, they consist of pure spirit and pure physis. In their individualized form, spirit and physis (*shen* and *xing*) are then called mind and personal body (*xin* 心 and *shen* 神). Within man, however, spirit and physis tend to lose their cosmic quality and become personalized, that is, from the point of view of realization, they are defiled, spoilt for their true purpose.

This is not necessarily so: in essence the human mind and body are nothing but radiant spirit and pure physis incorporated in a human being. In empirical fact, however, they mostly are defiled by the vexations mentioned above. In this point the cosmological definition of the personal body differs from the mystical: the description of the abstract system allows for possibilities of inherent purity in the *shen* which the practical instruction does not see.

The mystical realization in Daoism consists therefore of two major stages: first, the de-personalization, de-mentalization of man, as the texts have it: make your personal body non-body and your mind no-mind (*Xisheng jing* 5.1a). Then follows the merging of this reduced and purified mind/body complex into the cosmic forces of physis and spirit: the traditional list includes the attainments of physis, followed by *qi*, spirit, and Dao itself. Dao relates to spirit as *qi* relates to physis:

it is made of the same stuff, but is of a finer quality.[5] The same ratio holds true for the relation of spirit to mind and physis to body. The cosmological system therefore consists of three major sets: Dao and energy; spirit and physis; mind and body. Differently put: Dao is the spirit is the pure mind; energy is the physis is the original body.

Immortality in Daoism is thus a physical state in paradise and a psychological state on earth. It may be described in ecstatic or enstatic terms, depending on whether the underlying world view understands the basic nature of the universe as either "becoming" or "being." In all cases immortality means an eternity, an everlasting life of the individual mind and body as they were meant originally: replicas of the universe, parts of primordial energy, spirit, and Dao.

---

[5] It might be added that *qi*, energy or breath, in Tang texts comes to be used as a substitute for *xing*, physis. This has mainly to do with the shift in interpretation from outer to inner *qi*, pointed out already by Maspero (1971, 498-506).

Chapter Six

Energetic Transformation: Mystical Experience in Internal Alchemy[1]

Unlike philosophical speculations and theoretical guidelines, descriptions of personal mystical experiences are hard to find in the Daoist tradition. Authors typically refrain from becoming too personal, and the overall tendency in the literature is to express the experiences of the mystic in generalized instructions and the listing of warning signs. This is different from Western religions, where the experience is at the pivot of it all and is described as overwhelming and ineffable, timeless and yet full of knowing certainty (James 1936), and where mystics have described its wonders time and again as they have their agonies when it eluded them for a period in the so-called dark night of the soul (Underhill 1911).

There is no strong emphasis on personal experience in Daoism. There are experiences, yes—the complete oblivion of all, for example, described often as "the body like a withered tree, the mind like dead ashes," and the ecstatic visions of the gods and palaces of the otherworld, to name the most common. But there are very few personal reports on the overwhelming and powerful nature of certain specific experiences that could be compared in impact and importance to their Western counterpart. This lack can be explained as a general feature of Chinese culture, where religious autobiography was not a major genre, and the earliest first-hand accounts of the troubles and delights of the quest for perfection only appear after contact with Western missionaries in the Yuan and Ming dynasties.

---

1 An earlier version of this paper was published under the title "The Subtle Body Ecstasy of Daoist Inner Alchemy" in *Acta Orientalia* 59.3 (2006): 325-40. More extensive presentations on internal alchemy are found in Kohn and Wang 2009.

Still, even before this period mystical manuals contain warnings and instructions regarding specific experiences. For example, the *Dingguan jing* 定觀經 (Scripture on Concentration and Observation, DZ 400), a Tang-dynasty text, says quite explicitly:

> If there are thoughts and fantasies during concentration,
> Manifold delusions and countless evils,
> Also specters and wicked sprites Will appear accordingly.
> But when you see the Perfected or Lord Lao,
> Divine wonders and amazing sights,
> This is an auspicious sign. (lines 27-28; Kohn 1987a, 138).

Similarly, the *Zuowang lun* 坐忘論 (Discourse on Sitting in Oblivion, DZ 1036) of the eighth century is very clear about the difficulties that adepts can expect to face and outlines the radiance of spirit and boundless joy they may eventually attain (see Kohn 1987a). Yet neither has quite the same importance, the same centrality as the mystical experience in the Western interpretation of mysticism. While Western mystics fixate on the experience, it seems, the Chinese concentrate more on the transformation of body and mind. The key to being a mystic, then, is not whether one has had a certain experience, but to what degree one's self is being transformed into cosmic dimensions, how sagely and non-acting one has become (Kohn 1992a).

The underlying reason for this difference in emphasis regarding experience is the nature of the worldview at the foundation of the two religious systems. Western traditions pose a transcendent divine agent, a God totally other; their mystics accordingly concentrate on rare visions of the deity, granted through his mercy, that are overwhelming, ineffable, and entirely out of this world. The Chinese tradition, on the other hand, sees its ultimate in Dao, a divine force so immanent that it is even in the soil and tiles, so much a part of the world that it cannot be separated from it. Oneness or union with Dao is the birthright of every being, not a rare instance of divine grace. It is natural to begin with, and becomes more natural as it is realized through practice.

The Chinese mystical experience of oneness with Dao, quite logically, is astounding only in the beginning. It represents a way of being in the world completely different from ordinary perception, sensually and intellectually determined. The longer the Daoist lives with the experience and the deeper he integrates it into his life and being, the less relevant it is. Thus, neither is the experience itself the central feature of the tradition, nor is there a pronounced "dark night of the soul," a desperate search for a glimpse of the transcendent divine.

The Body

Another major difference between the two traditions is the continued emphasis the Chinese place on the body in the transformation to a celestial being. Unlike in the West, where body and soul are radical opposites, body and spirit in Daoist mysticism, though clearly distinguished, are not seen as opposites. Rather, they represent different aspects of the same continuum of Dao and have to be purified in equal measure. As Max Kaltenmark puts it,

> Chinese terminology reflects subtle differences between states of a more or less ethereal quality, but of one and the same principle lying at the foundation of all the complex functions of man. The gross conditions of the body are as much included as are its finer essences and the higher mental states which make up holiness.
>
> This then is the reason why one can say that the Chinese do not make a clear-cut distinction between what we call body and mind. Their outlook is in general much more oriented towards life as an organic whole and ongoing process. (1965, 655)

The challenge for the mystic, then, is not to overcome the body in favor of the spirit but to transform the entire body-spirit continuum to a higher level and come to experience himself as the divine replica of the cosmos in oneness with Dao.

This perspective is again based on the worldview of the underlying oneness of everything in the Dao. In this framework, the human body is seen as an accumulation of cosmic, vital energy known as *qi* and evaluated in terms of its energetic workings rather than as a solid, ultimately fragile entity. *Qi* is at the root of everything that exists, whether natural or supernatural, human or nonhuman, animate or inanimate. It generally appears in the complementary forces yin and yang, which correspond to night and day, shadow and light, resting and moving, feminine and masculine, tiger and dragon, mercury and lead, and so on. They cannot exist without one another but continuously engender and develop in mutual interaction, moving in cycles of days and seasons, of inner circulation and outer rhythm. They are further subdivided into categories of lesser and greater and associated with the five phases (wood, fire, earth, metal, water), symbolic representations of their developmental patterns. In this more complex form, the phases of *qi* are then set into a relationship with the key organs of the human body, its senses, material constituents, psychological agents, and emotions.

Qi comes in two major forms, prenatal or primordial and postnatal or ordinary. Primordial *qi* is the cosmic parent of yin and yang, the power of the universe at its creation, the original purity of the cosmos in its most potent form. It is the ultimate neutral energy, the highest creative power, the most essential force of all existence. Everybody at birth receives a set amount of primordial *qi*, but even that amount is already miniscule compared to the intensity of the primordial power of the cosmos (Winn 2001). Postnatal *qi* is ingested through breath, food, and interaction with others. It mingles with the primordial reservoir deep within and most commonly diminishes it until the person becomes spiritually disconnected and physically weak, and eventually dies. Lack of primordial *qi* in this system is the reason why so many people feel alienated from God, nature, and each other, and why they tend to believe that the gross, dense, physical reality they see around them is all there is.

The Daoist endeavor consists in the recovery and replenishing of the tiny spark of primordial *qi* that is buried within all human beings. All *qi* continuously moves in the body in a smooth regular rhythm dictated by the cosmic patterns of yin and yang. It is in a state of ongoing flux, continuously changing, constitutes health or sickness, moods and tempers, and determines how we work, eat, and sleep. As and when the spark of primordial *qi* is ignited and strengthened, it will "gradually dissolve one's suffering and struggle and restore life to its innate state of grace and effortless, nonactive (*wuwei* 無爲) communication with heaven, earth, and all nature. Cultivating primordial *qi* is growing Heaven and Earth within" (Winn 2001, 14).

To do so, practitioners begin with cultivating *qi* as it appears in the body in its most tangible and concrete form—as *jing* 精 or essence. *Jing* is the indeterminate aspect of *qi*, also described as *qi* in transition from one determinate form to another (Porkert 1974). Put most concretely, *jing* is no longer the *qi* of the eggs in the omelet and not yet the *qi* of the eggs as assimilated in the body of the eater. As Michael Winn describes it, "*jing* is perhaps best understood in Western terms as primal matter. It is the raw fuel that drives the pulsating rhythm of the body's moment-to-moment cellular division and reproduction of itself" (2002, 20). Governed in the body by the kidneys and the Phase water, it is also closely related to the psychological power of the will or determination, the innate power to "seek pleasure, and to fulfill a specific destiny" (Winn 2002, 20). It is also the source of a person's charisma or magnetic power, of sexual attraction and an innate sense of wholeness. In its most concrete form *jing* in the body appears as sexual energy, i.e., semen in men and menstrual blood in women. Much of Daoist cultivation accordingly begins with the control and reorientation of sexual energy.

Eventually this *jing* is purified and made more subtle and transformed into *qi* that is then moved consciously around the body in various cycles. This *qi* in turn is further rarified into *shen* 神 (spirit), which is a third form *qi* assumes in the human body. *Shen* is understood as the inherent higher vitality of life, the power of consciousness, and the ability to think. It is closely associated with the individuality's outlook and personality and is said to reside in the central organ of the heart. It governs the emotions and has the most impact on the mystical transformation. Ultimately, spirit is also the goal of mystical attainment: the transformation of a baser *qi* being into an entity of pure spirit.

To achieve this, various methods of cultivation are employed, including formalized body movements, breathing exercises, ritual ceremonies, meditations, visualizations, and so on. It should be understood, however, that none of these practices—however beneficial they may be for health and long life and good fortune—are undertaken to obtain or acquire *qi*. Rather, *qi* is already there, and the practitioner already *is* part of nature's infinite *qi*-field. The task is not to change the basic set up of being human but to recognize one's true nature as part of Dao, to "understand the unconscious communication patterns that are always flowing between one's microcosmic (personal) *qi*-field and the impersonal (macrocosmic) *qi*-field" (Winn 2001, 13).

Internal Alchemy

The tradition within Daoism that makes most obvious use of this understanding of the body as a cosmic *qi*-field is known as "internal alchemy" (*neidan* 內丹). A complex system of techniques that integrated physical longevity methods, spiritual meditations, operative alchemy, and the intricate symbolism of the *Yijing* 易經 (Book of Changes), it can be traced back to the Tang dynasty (618-907) but came to flourish in the Song (960-1260), especially in south China, where it was practiced by various schools.[2] Internal alchemy describes mystical attainment in terms of three stages—transforming *jing* into *qi*, *qi* into *shen*, and merging *shen* with Dao in the form of interior spiritual entity known as the golden elixir or the immortal embryo.

Internal alchemical practice begins in the first stage with taking control of the *jing*, the sexual energy. For men, this means that they must avoid losing semen through ejaculation while women, through a series of meditations and breast massages learn to lessen and eventually stop the flow of menstruation. Instead practitioners retain their *jing* and reverse its flow, making it move up the spinal column "to nourish the brain." The brain, according to Chinese traditional medicine, is the Ocean of Marrow, and marrow is *jing* as manifest in the bones. Every time *jing* is lost through sexual activity, therefore, the brain, the bones of the head, and the skeleton of the body are weakened and become more brittle.

The *jing*, moreover, that travels up the spine is not the semen that would be ejaculated during sexual intercourse or lost in menstruation but its refined form, the *qi* from which the semen arose in the first place. At the top of the head, the reversed *jing* unites with other yin secretions of the body and, once it begins to overflow in the cavity there, descends again through the front of the torso to the energy center in the abdomen known as the lower cinnabar field. Circulated mentally in spiraling movements, the *qi* is stored here and forms the interior cauldron for the concoction of the elixir, the spiritual womb for the growth of the immortal embryo.

The process of *qi* circulation is known as the "microcosmic orbit" and still actively practiced today (see Chia 1983; 1985; Winn 2002).[3] Undertaken after preparatory meditations, chanting of sacred sounds, and the activation of the *qi* in the five organs, it is accompanied by

---

[2] For a general survey on inner alchemy, see Needham et al.1983; Skar and Pregadio 2000; Kohn and Wang 2009. Studies of specific texts and schools include Baldrian-Hussein 1984; Lu 1970; Darga 1999; Wilhelm 1962; Cleary 1992. For conceptual analysis, see Robinet 1989; 1995.

[3] There is a certain similarity between the microcosmic orbit and the Indian practice of Kundalini yoga in that both make interior energy flow backwards up the spine. However, in Daoism the goal is to circulate *qi* all through the body and gradually grow a spiritual self within, while in Yoga, the practice serves to open the energy centers in the torso and guide the energy upward in a linear (rather than circular) flow to eventually achieve union with an absolute self somewhere above the head. See Gyatso 1982; Short and Mann 1988; Winn 2002.

rhythmic breathing and the regular holding of breath. Also, the technique is practiced in synchronicity with the yin-yang patterns of the seasons and matched with appropriate visualizations, seeing for example the rising yang-*jing* as solar, and the descending yin-*qi* as lunar energies. Through this refinement, the *qi* in due course opens up to unveiling a kernel of grain or a pearl in the lower cinnabar field—the first concrete inkling of primordial *qi* within. Called the "mysterious pearl" or the "pearl of dew," this is the seed of the divine elixir from which the immortal embryo will eventually grow. It indicates the successful completion of the first stage.

During the second stage, the transformation of *qi* into *shen*, the immortal embryo grows over ten months in the lower and middle cinnabar fields (abdomen and solar plexus). It is nourished by the rhythmic ascent and descent of *qi*, which creates a great abdominal openness and allows the increasing sublimation of interior *qi* into spirit. Understood as a reversal of the cosmic process of creation, it involves reverting the five phases to the three primal forces (water, fire, and earth), and the coupling of the reversed energies of fire within water (yang within yin) and water within fire (yin within yang)—the latter often expressed with the help of the symbols of the *Yijing*. More primordial *qi* is assembled and the three cinnabar fields are turned into powerful alchemical cauldrons for its further refinement (Winn 2002,18).

This process requires the strongest meditative awareness yet—long periods of quiet sitting and deep inner stillness. After ten months of nurturing with primordial *qi*, the newly developed subtle body, the immortal embryo is ready to be born. For this, it is moved gradually upward along the spine until it reaches the upper cinnabar field in the head. From there it can leave the body through the top of the head, undertaking excursions to the celestial spheres as it pleases. The birth of the embryo into a free-moving spirit power signifies the adept's rebirth on a new level and a new yin body, an immortal being of softness, purity, and light.

The third stage, following this spiritual rebirth, is not described in great detail in the texts. They mention that the yin body is increasingly transformed into a body of pure yang, essentially through deeper absorption and meditative practice. Eventually it becomes pure, luminous spirit and is reintegrated into cosmic emptiness. In the course of this process, the adept acquires supernatural and magical powers that are, however, not considered of major importance by the tradition. The main objective is deliverance, achieved through the overcoming of individual identity and all body-mind duality.

The modern school of internal alchemy as taught by Mantak Chia subdivides this last stage into five levels:

> the birth of the immortal child through the absorption of higher forms of yin and yang, the sun and the moon, and by opening communication with the five spirit centers and the divinities of the four directions;
>
> the maturation of the immortal child through feeding of the true elixir of the sun, a series of meditations arranged according to one's astrological birth elements that involve the absorption of planetary power and ecstatic travels to the solar system;
>
> the crystallization of the primordial spirit by focusing on the center in the head and there absorbing and interiorizing various astral forces, such as the Big Dipper, the Polestar, and the four Great Star quadrants, eventually attaining the ability to travel freely around them;
>
> the merging of Heaven and Earth through opening a cosmic void within, where Heaven and Earth come together in primordial unity and where the physical body and personality of the adept fully dissolves into primordial *qi*;
>
> union with Dao, an event that occurs when virtue, destiny, and cultivation are complete (Winn 2001, 28-30).

Within this overall framework, then, two major sets of experiences can be described: the sense of energetic openness and interior subtlety as a being of pure *qi* when the microcosmic orbit is fully opened; and the mystical realization of the spirit being both within the body and in its travels through the otherworld.

The Microcosmic Orbit

An early description of the transformative experience of the microcosmic orbit is found in the *Xiwang mu shize* 西王母十則 (Ten Rules of the Queen Mother of the West; trl. Wile 1992), a work on women's internal alchemy of the eighteenth century (Despeux 2000, 397). The text notes that the *qi* refined through extensive breast massages will spontaneously begin to move about in the body. Once adepts become aware of this, they should actively guide it downward through the abdomen and divide it into two streams at the hips, spiraling it to the left and right in the course of thirty-six respirations. Getting warmer and more active, the *qi* begins to move up the spinal column, first slowly and hesitantly, then with increasing speed and vigor. To unblock hindrances along the spine, adepts click their teeth seventy-two times and take thirty-six deep nostril breaths before the practice. To prevent *qi* from staying in the genital area and flowing out of the body, they contract the muscles of the pelvic floor with some force and place both hands over the pubic bone, at the same time actively visualizing the upward flow of *qi*.

Once the *qi* has begun its upward course, practitioners raise both hands overhead, spreading and releasing the fingers at regular intervals twice thirty-six times, first slowly and lightly, then a bit faster. Next, they place their hands on their hips and shrug the shoulders thirty-six times, allowing the *qi* to pass through the Double Pass at breast level, the upper spine, and the Jade Pillow at the occipital bone. Any blockages found there can be further dissolved by clapping the teeth and concentrating on the nape of the neck. Once the *qi* has moved all the way up through the Niwan Palace to the top of the head, adepts move the lower lip above the upper to encourage the *qi* to descend along the front of the skull toward the nose.

They roll the tongue against the upper palate to establish a connection between the two central energy meridians in the torso, the Governing and Conception Vessels, thus allowing the sweet dew of the *qi* to descend further. It flows down naturally towards the Purple Gate near the heart, where it is held for a short period. Moving further down through the abdomen, it divides at the hips and is spiraled thirty-six times as before, then concentrated in the cinnabar field and rotated thirty-six times each to the left and the right (Despeux 1990).

This free flow of *qi* through the body brings with it a sense of ecstasy and an increased subtleness of bodily perception. It constitutes the reorganization of personal consciousness and bodily awareness on a subtler and more refined level. Practitioners gain a sense of being part of the flow of Dao rather than separate individual entities.

A first-person account of this experience of the microcosmic orbit has been transmitted from the early twentieth century, when Jiang Weiqiao (1870-1955), a learned and sickly young man who later became know as Master Yinshi, experimented with Daoist internal alchemy to cure himself of tuberculosis. To achieve his self-healing he set up a rigid schedule of meditation and physical exercises, establishing a daily routine that closely resembled monastic discipline. He got up around three or four in the morning and practiced "quiet sitting," as he calls his meditation, for an hour or two. Breakfast and a short hike, "always facing east, to absorb the energy of the rising sun" (Jiang 1985, 90), were followed by a rest and study period to culminate in another phase of quiet sitting around ten o'clock. After lunch he would spend some time pacing slowly around the room. Beginning at about three o'clock, he practiced the seven-stringed lute or went out for another walk. Dinner and another two hours of sitting in the evening concluded a busy day of self-healing.

In the course of a year, he managed to strengthen his *qi* and began to experience its strong power within:

> I had started my regimen on the fifth day of the third month of the year 1900. However, I had to endure many pains and hardships and I was remiss and idle in some thing or another practically every day.
>
> Later I learned how to leave things to nature, and my spirit became fresher and healthier every day. Before, when I had gone out for a walk I would make it for two or three miles, then had to rest for tiredness and exhaustion. After a few months of practice, once I got going I could walk on for ten miles and more and never feel the strain.
>
> Every time I sat down to meditate, I would focus my awareness on the cinnabar field in the lower abdomen. I could feel a cloud of hot power there. It came and went, rose and ebbed. I was quite amazed by it.
>
> Then, on the twenty-ninth of the fifth month, during the evening sitting, it happened first: All of a sudden there was this intense rumbling movement in the cinnabar field in my lower abdomen. I had been sitting in quiet meditation as usual, but this was something I really could not control. I was shaken back and forth helplessly.
>
> An incredibly hot energy began to rise at the bottom of my spine and climbed up further and further until it reached the very top of my head. I was startled and alarmed. (1985, 91-92; Kohn 1993b)

In traditional terms, this experience reveals the power of the primordial *qi* over all living beings and is a first sign of the practitioner's growing oneness with Dao, an initial step toward the dissolution of ego and the attainment of perfection. For Jiang Weiqiao, it was the first discovery of an energy that pervaded and nourished his body, a powerful, yet ultimately controllable agent, not a mystical divine force of universal creation. Later, as he describes it, the experience was repeated several times until the hot *qi* that rose along his spine no longer left the body through the top of the head but returned through the face and chest area to the lower abdomen. After undergoing the spontaneous establishment of the microcosmic orbit, he continued to use his power over the circulation of *qi* whenever he felt weak or sick, sometimes guiding it to flow freely, sometimes directing it to whatever part of his body felt unwell.

Another first-person report on the establishment of the microcosmic orbit is by Michael Winn, a long-term seeker of spiritual cultivation in the Indian and Chinese traditions. In the beginning of his quest, he studied Rajneesh's *Book of Secrets* and followed its breathing instructions to the point where he could slow his breath down to almost a complete standstill. Then:

> one day, after two weeks practice, I felt my breath stop completely. During a long pause between breaths, I entered a deep, peaceful state, and felt I no longer need to breathe air. Suddenly my whole body shook, then exploded into an intense orgasm and I watched myself catapulted into the space around me, with a clear vision of my body expanding rapidly through the walls of the room. After this initial explosion, I felt like a mushroom cloud above a nuclear blast, with the debris of my former consciousness blown to bits and slowly raining back down on my transparent body in blissful droplets. (2002, 7)

Here the opening of the *qi* body is not felt as a circulation of energy but rather as an explosion, a dissolution of the former, apparently solid foundation of self and body into tiny droplets of energy that were dispersed through space and slowly came back to settle in the personal sphere. Still, the event is very similar—the *qi* manifests violently with a rumbling and begins to move entirely on its own and without any conscious control of the practitioner. This control is only learned over time and exercised carefully in proper training.

Such training is undertaken in the contemporary Daoist practice of internal alchemy in a school known as The Healing Dao, of which Michael Winn is a leading practitioner today. Healing Dao was originally founded by Mantak Chia, a Thai of Chinese ancestry. Born in 1944, he was recognized early for his spiritual potential and began the practice of Buddhist meditation at age six. Later he moved to Hong Kong where he studied various *qi* techniques, such as taiji quan, aikido, and qigong. There he also met a Daoist master, known as the One Cloud Hermit, who taught him the secrets of internal alchemy over a period of five years. Developing his own system, in 1973 he founded The Healing Dao in Chiangmai, Thailand, and in 1978 brought it to the West.

According to Chia, practitioners begin their endeavor by becoming conscious of their organs and the *qi* flow within. Then they gradually learn to open the microcosmic orbit. About the experience accompanying this, he says:

> Most people have some sensations during their meditation. These may be warmth, heat, or tingling at the sacrum, Gate of Life, Third Eye, or tip of the tongue, or cold or numb areas. Some people feel an effervescence like champagne bubbles. You may experience mild electic-like shocks anywhere in the body; the body may shake rhythmically or suddenly jolt.
>
> Also, the hands, feet, or whole body may become unusually hot; in fact, you may feel strong sensations of heat anywhere in the body. Those who are visually oriented may see a light inside their heads, or points along the orbit may light up. If you have any of these sensations, you may conclude that *qi* is circulating. (Chia and Chia 1993, 478)

The reason for these various sensations in the body is that "we have begun to absorb *qi* from Heaven, Earth, and the Higher Self, and our channels are widening to absorb additional bursts of *qi*" (1993, 484). This is considered very beneficial and an important step on the way, leading to a sense of self and body that is no longer limited to ordinary consciousness but grows into a dimension of subtle energetics and cosmic connection. The mystical dimension of existence here is opened through the physical experience of the body and the reorganization of self in terms of *qi* flow and the perception of subtle energies. Experience is determined entirely by the body—but the body is transformed into a more subtle, more cosmic, more divine entity.

The Immortal Embryo

This transformation of the body is further intensified in the second stage of the alchemical process, when the inner seed of the elixir, created by the systematic circulation and collection of *qi*, blossoms forth and gives rise to the immortal embryo. Over ten months of intense meditation, this spiritual alter ego of the practitioner grows to completion, and a primordial light begins to shine through the entire body. Adepts then enter a state of deep absorption, lying immobile as if dead, appearing pale in complexion, and apparently not breathing at all. They need a helper at this time who watches over them day and night for however long the state persists, which may well be up to six days. All noise and shouting that might startle them must be avoided, lest the tenuously growing spirit embryo be injured and the adept be afflicted by madness or demonic forces. When they come out of this absorption, nostril breathing begins very subtly and the divine light opens up. One can then call out to them in a low voice. They slowly begin to move and will gradually rise, get dressed, and take some nourishment, still remaining vigilant since the process is not yet over. Rather, the most important part is still to come: the exiting of the spirit into the celestial realm (Despeux 1990).

The first exiting of the spirit embryo is known as "deliverance from the womb." It is the adept's celestial rebirth and is accompanied by the perception of a deep inner rumbling, like a clap of thunder. Then the celestial gate at the top of her head bursts free and opens wide, and a white smoky essence can be seen hovering above her. The spirit passes through the top of the head and begins to communicate actively with the celestials, transcending the limitations of the body. Before this exiting procedure, adepts actively move the immortal embryo from the middle to the upper cinnabar field, using rhythmic breathing and/or the recitation of sacred sounds.

As long as the adept has not entered a state of very deep absorption, the embryonic spirit is not yet fully detached from the *qi* circulating in the body and cannot leave. Once absorption is attained, on the other hand, and the spirit has begun to move on its own, the adept easily maintains concentration and may experience various strong internal states. For example, she may have a vision of a shower of heavenly flowers, perceive divine perfumes, or see an image of a seven-storied pagoda. According to Wu Chongyu of the Ming dynasty, "leaving the state of great absorption is accompanied by different phenomena in every individual. Some see a shower of celestial flowers, others see wind and clouds." The *Dadan zhizhi* 大丹直指 (Pointers to the Great Elixir, DZ 244) of the late thirteenth century similarly has:

> As your perfect *qi* rises, your ears will hear the sounds of wind and rain. Then inside your head there will be the sounds of harps and gold and jade. In your heavenly Pond [mouth], the Metal Liquid [saliva] will gush forth like a cool stream. Some will flow up into the brain, some will congeal into pearly dew, some will enter into the gullet. Its flavor will be sweet and delectable.

> Later, inside your head you will hear the sounds of flutes, zithers, harps, and chimes. Or you may hear the call of the crane, the cry of the monkey, or the chirping of the cicada. . . . When the spirit reaches its exit point, you will hear a huge clap of thunder. (Eskildsen 2001, 150)

After its first exit, the spirit learns to come and go freely and communicate widely with the otherworld. In the beginning, it moves rather slowly and does not travel far from the body, then, supported by further meditative exercises known as "nursing for three years," it gradually gets used to its new powers, moves about faster and travels further afield until it goes far and wide without any limitation. As the spirit enters into these cosmic ventures, the adept exhibits supernatural powers: she can be in two place at once, move quickly from one place to another, know the past and the future, divine people's thoughts, procure wondrous substances, overcome all hazards of fire and water, and has powers over life and death. Known as "spirit pervasion," this indicates the freedom achieved by the spirit and also manifest in the practitioner.

Few first-person accounts are found on this part of the practice. Michael Winn mentions that he, at some point in his intensive training, found his sleep needs drastically reduced and experienced different spiritual powers, "ranging from bursts of telepathy and foreknowledge of the future to experiences of the entire universe collapsing into a single point" (2002, 8).

He also reports on a dramatic experience of cosmic merging in a situation of what the Daoist tradition calls "dual cultivation" or partner practice:

> We had sat naked for a few minutes, facing each other in cross-legged meditation position to tune in. We were both suddenly overtaken by a powerful energy field with extremely intense and unusual vibrations. Not a word was spoken, as our mental, emotional, and speech faculties were completely suspended, but we later confirmed having an identical experience.
>
> One aspect of our consciousness began experiencing a very yang orgasm, expanding out of the bedroom faster than the speed of light, whizzing through galaxies, exploding supernovas, and then beyond. Another part of us was orgasmically imploding inward with opposite and equal force,

> grounding and concentrating the great intensity in our physical bodies. (2002, 26)[4]

Here the energy fields of the two practitioners merge in an explosive and powerful manner, moving both outward as their spirits travel into the planetary vastness of the otherworld and inward as the body is opened to cosmic emptiness and primordiality. The experience is overwhelming and transcendent, yet firmly grounded in the energetics of the body, the result of years of practice and the cultivation of subtle forms of *qi*.

However, even this high level if mystical attainment is not the ultimate goal of internal alchemy, which is only reached after further meditative practice, known as "wall gazing." This technique is adopted from Chan Buddhism, whose first patriarch Bodhidharma is said to have realized full enlightenment by sitting in a cave and gazing at a wall for nine years. In this very final phase of the process, the adept whose body is already transformed into pure light has yet to fully overcome its limits and melt utterly into cosmic emptiness. The process takes nine years or 3,000 days, a number symbolic of highest yang and great completion.

A poem attributed to the great lady adept Sun Buer 孫不二 (1119-1182) describes it as follows:

> All your tasks already well fulfilled,
> Just sit down in a corner, concentrate the spirit,
> Feel your body rest on purple clouds,
> Your whole being calm, floating on weak waters.
> The *qi* forces melt together, yin and yang unite,
> Spirit, Heaven, Earth all are only one.
> Concluding the great work, you see the Gate of Jade
> Emerging from the mists—and heave a deep, long sigh.
> (Chen 1934; Cleary 1989)

The deep meditative absorption in this stage, perfected over long years of practice, involves the attainment of complete purity, tranquility, and nonaction. Mind and spirit are no longer of this world but illuminate the infinite, and the adept is fully integrated into the

---

[4] A similar experience, reported by an outside observer, is also described in Shi 2002. Here a Daoist master demonstrates partner practice for a visitor, inviting a Buddhist nun to join him. They remain fully clothed, but streaks of light energy begin to flash to and from their bodies, creating a *qi*-field of movement and bliss.

heavenly spheres. Eventually he or she sheds her earthly form and ascends upward, mounting a cloudy chariot or riding on an immortals' bird. She receives formal empowerment from the palaces above and becomes an acknowledged member of the heavenly host. Received by the divine ladies at the court of the Queen Mother, she is led to the immortals' paradises and attains the ultimate state of mystical achievement.

Conclusion

The mystical experience in Daoist internal alchemy, the most recent and still practiced form of Daoist cultivation, can therefore be described as a form of subtle body ecstasy. Practitioners learn, through breathing, gymnastic, and meditative exercises, to open themselves to a level of experience that is not accessible to ordinary, dualistic, outward-oriented consciousness. They realize on an experiential level—as opposed to the purely theoretical or intellectual understanding of concepts and doctrines—that the universe consists of various fields of *qi*, primordial, postnatal, yin, yang, fire, water, five phases, and so on.

Feeling the *qi* in its different levels within, refining sexual energy (*jing*) into *qi* and *qi* into spirit (*shen*), they systematically reorganize their experience to a wider, more inclusive, more open, a strongly cosmic level. Doing so, they essentially reprogram their conception of the universe with its various signs, metaphors, and symbols towards an energetic perception, a mode of communication with nature in its own way, a *qi* based way of being in the world. In the course of this transformation, moreover, they discover internal levels of existence they never suspected and learn to interact with beings of the supernatural plane—ghosts, demons, gods, immortals, and various planetary entities. Their universe expands both within and without, and they become denizens of the larger universe, flowing streams of *qi*, pure aspects of the Dao.

Their experiences, moreover, although not commonly described in personal narratives are extraordinary and supra-sensual, raising the individual's consciousness to intense levels both within and without. What, then, do they teach us about the nature of mystical experience? As seen from the Daoist tradition of internal alchemy, mystical experience is transcendent of ordinary consciousness and common perception, not transcendent in the Western sense of experiencing something totally other but transcendent in that it goes far beyond the world to a deep, underlying level of existence that is always there, always accessible, always present, but not usually perceived.

Mystical experience, moreover, is immensely physical and takes place firmly on the basis of the body. This body, however, is not a clod-like lump of material solidity but a replica of the universe, an entity of flowing, subtle energies that are activated through systematic cultivation and take on a life of their own, superseding and eventually replacing the individual's personal consciousness. Mystical experience means the dissolution of self and body and mind into the larger cosmic flow of Dao, the recovery of the universal power of primordiality, the attainment of a state at the original creation of all.

Mystical experience according to the Daoist tradition is also very much determined by culture. It is consciously and actively created through a series of exercises that apply physical movements, breathing techniques, and specific guided meditations. While the very highest level of total dissolution is something that happens on its own and cannot be controlled, all other stages and experiences along the way are systematically prepared and learned. This, again, is why there are so few personal narratives: people know what to expect and when to expect it, they are guided kindly but firmly by a master who knows the body energetics and can give helpful support at all stages. It is accordingly no accident that the two first-person reports on the establishment of the microcosmic orbit cited above were written after the *qi*-flow opened up unexpectedly and without a teacher's guidance. The practitioners were surprised and amazed and wondered what they had stumbled into—experiencing mystery not unlike their Western counterparts but with access to a tradition that could map their route and provide them with support and reassurance.

Mystical experience in the Daoist tradition, to sum up, is therefore more like a well-prepared, cosmic peak experience in the sense of Abraham Maslow. According to him, peak experiences are special moments of complete happiness, fulfillment and meaning. Transcending the ego and giving people a sense of unity with all-that-is, they may come about through love, creativity, art, or being in nature, and are characterized as times of greatest maturity, individuation, and selflessness, moments of perfect health and unity (Maslow 1964, 73). They are common to humanity but differ in degree and interpretation. Although arising of their own accord, they can be invited to occur. The more an individual accepts peak-experiences positively and acknowledges them as a meaningful part of life, the more frequently they recur. The higher the frequency of peak-experiences, the more positively they are felt and the more the individual's consciousness moves into what Maslow calls Being-cognition, the psychological equivalent of the selfless cosmic consciousness of the mystic, a state of openness and freedom and a sense of rightness and oneness with the cosmic flow (Maslow 1964, 83).

Daoists in the tradition of internal alchemy, therefore, use the worldview of intermingling, flowing *qi*-fields to create an environment that invites peak experiences of varying strength and intensity, from the smooth and open *qi* circulation in the microcosmic orbit through the sense of spiritual presence in the creation of the immortal embryo to the ecstatic excursions into the far reaches of the universe. Daoists learn to be open to the *qi* reality within and without, they train to flow along with it, and they attain mystical transcendence both within this world and within this body.

Chapter Seven

Sages and Perfected: Mystics in the World[1]

A popular Japanese movie shows an enlightened master traveling to an inner city where he seeks shelter in a slum. He shares a house with a prostitute, a thief, and a beggar, slatternly and aggressive people who fight over every little chore. The master, without criticizing or even raising his eyebrows, defuses their conflicts by simply taking over whatever task is at hand and provides a nicer environment for them by cleaning up. He is there without imposing, merely helping and supporting, lending an ear when desired, staying away when not wanted. Over a period of several months, the household gains a modicum of internal harmony and gradually the moral quality of its members changes: the beggar takes on part-time work, the thief becomes honest, and the prostitute starts waitressing. Once they are set, the master fades away, moving on to help other suffering beings.

The story, while fairly modern and popular in a Japanese Zen environment, yet contains a key to understanding certain key characterisitcs of the intrinsic interaction of mysticism and morality in traditional Chinese religion. First, the enlightened master, one who has realized Dao and is pure in his deepest being, is incognito; he goes unrecognized and does not make a show of his attainments nor does he present any rules or teachings. Second, he is completely humble, able to there when most needed yet leaving when unwanted.

Third, his transformative power comes not from formal rules, lengthy lectures, or vocal criticisms but from his actions, his taking on whatever is needed without fuss. He does not pass judgment on the world

[1] A first version oft his paper appeared under the title, "The Sage in the World, the Perfected Without Feelings: Mysticism and Moral Reponsibility in Chinese Religion," in *Crossing Boundaries: Essays on the Ethical Status of Mysticism*, edited by G. William Barnard and Jeffrey J. Kripal (New York: Seven Bridges Press, 2002), 288-306.

and does not consciously set out to change it; simply by being who he is and where he is, the world transforms. Fourth, his mere presence, through the aura and atmosphere he generates, creates a morally better world, a world where people live in greater harmony, higher honesty, and better cheer.

The reason why the master can be who he is and do what he does is found in the underlying worldview of traditional China, which also applies to Daoism and Chan [Zen] Buddhism. According to this, the world is fundamentally good and inherently harmonious. Created in a series of transformations without a radical break from the pure, formless Dao, it manifests itself in a wondrous and mysterious combination of manifold forces and beings that ideally work together to constitute a perfect cosmos—as and when each realizes its nature as originally part of Dao.

This cooperation of all things and beings in the universe is a given, but any particular individual can realize its pure Dao-nature to a lesser or higher degree. The master in our story, or any kind of mystic or realized person in this system then is one who has realized his or her Dao-nature to perfection, is naturally who he was meant to be and can radiate the purity of the underlying cosmic goodness to all around him. The members of the slum household, on the other hand, have not realized their true potential, have become removed from the inherent harmony of Dao and thus developed patterns of disharmony and immorality. Still, because they too are part of the system as a whole, which is ultimately one, they are immediately affected by the condensed power of purity embodied in the master and transform, over time and without consciously wishing or even noticing it, to a higher degree of goodness and harmony.

The goodness of the cosmos, moreover, is not necessarily a moral goodness, a goodness that can be expressed in a set of rules and enforced by laws and other restraints. The goodness of the cosmos goes beyond human morality because it is cosmic and natural, and both cosmos and nature are cruel and unjust at times, they do not have a set of values that can be defined or to which they can be held. At the same time, the goodness of the cosmos is intuited by human beings as a sense of wellbeing and inner harmony which, if it is to be achieved with their limited sensory and intellectual faculties, can and is expressed in moral rules. Morality is thus a part of the cosmic harmony which the mystic embodies, and his being in the world increases the moral quality of life around him. Nevertheless, the mystic is not *per se* moral, but rather transmoral or supramoral, going beyond the demands of human society in a spontaneous sense of cosmic oneness.

The various traditions of Chinese religion all share this fundamental vision and show a strong socio-political and thus also moral concern in their conviction that ideal human beings, those who have fully realized the true nature of the cosmos as understood by them, have a direct impact if not actually a political function in the world. The most important traditions, then, are Confucianism and classical Daoism in ancient times (500-200 B.C.E.), religious Daoism in the middle ages (200-900 C.E.), and Neo-Confucianism of the Song through Ming dynasties (960-1644). Each have a vision of the ideal human and his life in the world: the sage, the perfected, and the immortal.

The Sage

The sage (*sheng* 聖), in the literal interpretation of the character, is the king of ears and mouth, one whose senses are perfectly attuned to the moving of the cosmos, who can recognize and understand signs that others hardly notice and who will elucidate them for others. Thus, as Ken DeWoskin says,

> The consummately refined sensory skill of the sage was his hearing; it was perhaps the most important means by which his sagacity was made apparent to the world. He had the ability to hear the faintest tones, distinguish the finest interval, and judge the subtlest qualities of timbre. (1982, 34)

Not only can the sage hear the inaudible sounds of the depth of the universe, he also knows its intimate signs. As the *Lüshi chunqiu* 呂氏春秋 (Spring and Autumn Annals of Mr. Lü) has it: "The knowledge of the sage reaches for millennia into the past and the future—he is not guessing at things; he always has reasons for what he says" (20.22a).

The sage as one who knows thus serves the world by bringing hidden realities to the surface, revealing the supersensory, the subtle realities of things. He does so by means of the senses and gives verbal explanations, but his intuitional oneness goes beyond both senses and words in a kind of mystical union which enables him to recognize the true patterns inherent in the world and be one with them.

The notion of the sage is a key concept in ancient Confucianism, Neo-Confucianism, and philosophical Daoism. In the first, he is ideally identical with the ruler, the key mediator between Heaven and humanity and bringer of order not only to himself and a selected few but to the empire at large. As a ruler, he puts his task before any personal needs, and may appear harsh or inhuman in his actions while ultimately working for the larger good of the world.

A classical example here is the sage-ruler Yu, the first emperor of the legendary Xia dynasty, who lived at the time of the great flood. Working with a large crew around the country, chiselling through mountains and plains to allow the billows to flow off into the ocean, he passed his own home three times: the first time he heard his infant son, newly born during his absence, wail; the second time he saw him play in the mud; the third time he spoke to him, now ten years old, refusing his wish to join his father. All three times Yu passed but did not stop, being aware of his personal concerns but not giving in to them and behaving with impersonal distance to those his dearest. Apparently uncaring and even immoral, he was yet true to himself as part of the larger workings of the cosmos in his great task of controlling the flood. While he had become almost inhuman to the people around him, he was yet the representative of something higher and bigger, something that went beyond the moral or humane concerns of the world (Ching 1997, 56-62)

Just as "Heaven and Earth are not humane, they treat the myriad beings as straw dogs [things without value]" (*Daode jing* 5; Chan 1964, 141), so the sage, at one with Heaven and Earth, is not humane and often treats people roughly. He is the "apogee of human relationships" who has developed the roots of goodness, which all people have within them, to their limits (*Mengzi* 4a2; Fung and Bodde1952, 1:125). He is thus moral in his basic attitude toward life but transmoral when it comes to the realization of his higher, cosmic purpose. Because the sage goes beyond ordinary morality, he is not bound by the rules of society. As the medieval thinker Sun Zhuo 孫桌 explains, the sage may even kill because his actions are performed in a state of oneness with the cosmos, of no-mind, i.e., without personal, clinging, self-interested intention. Whatever a sage does will therefore not leave the same violent impact that it would have if committed by a lesser man. His perfection of humaneness is at the same time the complete obliteration of humaneness, "his greatest filial piety is the complete forgetfulness of filial piety" (Link and Lee 1966, 169).

Not every sage, however, is a ruler. According to the ancient Confucian system, he could also be philosopher, one who thinks through the principles of the cosmos and explains them to others. These then write his ideas down—which is why the writings of the philosophers, as the teachings of the great Confucius himself, often appear short and disconnected (Fung and Bodde 1952, 1:2). In addition, there may also be people without any special social function who have the inborn quality of sagehood, the so-called "inner sages" who stay withdrawn and private, and those who are not born sages but, as all human beings part of the unity of the cosmos, have begun to develop their sage potential. All these have an impact on their surroundings because it is part of their inner nature to pursue and perfect self-cultivation. This is first spelled out in the "Daxue" 大學 (Great Learning) chapter of the *Liji* 禮記 (Book of Rites), describing the effects of personal investigation and cultivation:

> When things are investigated, knowledge is extended. When knowledge is extended, the will becomes sincere. When the will is sincere, the mind will be rectified. When the mind is rectified, the personal life will be cultivated. When the personal life is cultivated, the family will be regulated. When the family is regulated, the state will be in order. When the state is in order, there will be peace throughout the world. (Sect. 1; Chan 1964, 86-87)

Any effort at self-cultivation thus increases the inherent sage potential within the human being and thereby contributes to the greater goodness of the universe. This vision of the sage as the active practitioner of self-cultivation later became the key notion of Neo-Confucianism, which actively encouraged the pursuit of sagehood by any educated person and saw the utterly moralized cosmos as its highest goal. Here sagehood was at least as much a matter of effort as of inherent potential; and the mystical improvement of the moral quality of one's life became an active part of the goodness of the cosmos, the more inhuman or radical aspects of the cosmic power being relegated in favor of moral values. The conjunction of mysticism and morality in the Chinese tradition is most obvious here (see Taylor 1978; Ching 1976; Chan 1967).

The subtle and not necessarily moral impact of the sage, on the other hand, is described in more detail in the ancient Daoist tradition. The *Daode jing*, although it too tends to see the sage as ruler, yet remains open about his role and places a higher emphasis on his transformative power, in whatever position he may find himself. Thus it says:

The sage in all affairs rests in nonaction,
And practices the teaching of no words.
The myriad beings are active through him—
He does not turn away from them.
They live through him—
He does not take possession of them.
The sage acts in the world, but does not depend on it,
His task accomplished, he does not stay with it.
And because he does not stay,
It remains. (ch. 2)

Here the sage is one who is unobtrusive, inactive, and independent, free from all possessions or attachments and without a formal teaching or program of action (see Ching 1997, 214-18). Because he is all these things, which match him to the natural forces of Heaven and Earth, "the sage is whole" (ch. 22) and his accomplishments are thorough and long-lasting, have a deep and permanent effect on the society around him. Part of these effects is that he imposes some of the same qualities on the people, "causing them to be unknowing and free from desires, so that the smart ones will not dare to impose" (ch. 3). He is "always there to help the people, rejecting no one and no creature" (chap. 27), never puts himself forward in any way yet finds himself a nucleus of social and cosmic activity. As the text has it,

Not presenting himself, he is radiant.
Not thinking himself right, he is famous.
Not pushing himself forward, he is meritorious.
Not pitying himself, he is eminent. (ch. 22)

Not only unobtrusive and withdrawing, the sage also has his particular transformative power because of his transmoral nature which refuses to make ordinary judgments. Thus he can say of himself:

The good, I treat with goodness;
The bad, I treat with equal goodness.
Thus my virtue is full of goodness.
The honest, I treat with honesty;
The dishonest, I treat with equal honesty.
Thus my virtue is full of honesty. (ch. 49)

This, as interpreted in the fifth-century *Xisheng jing* 西昇經 (Scripture of Western Ascension, DZ 726), indicates a fundamental voidness of moral judgment:

Laozi said: Whether one of the hundred families does anything good, I don't know. Whether one of the hundred fami-

> lies does anything evil, I don't know. Whether anybody practices loyalty or good faith, I don't know. (ch. 37)

The philosopher here refuses to say whether anything is good, evil, or virtuous by common human standards, yet the same passage also has him say that "Dao of Heaven is supported only by good people," indicating that there is a level of goodness, honesty, or virtue that is transmoral and at the root of cosmic functioning. In other words, the goodness of the hundred families is a different goodness from that of the Dao. The Dao is supported only by good people, but this value judgment is not based on what is commonly described as good and evil in the ordinary world of everyday life.

The sage goes beyond the standards of social existence, he does not "know" whether anybody is doing anything good or bad at any given point. But he is sure that the accumulation of good will lead to good while that of evil will lead to evil, the basic law of the cosmos being at work throughout and observable by everyone. As people then are influenced by the sages among them or improved by the practice of self-cultivation, the moral goodness of everyday life gradually contributes to the greater goodness of the universe. The sage, himself beyond moral standards in his oneness with Heaven and Earth, thus nevertheless is a strong pillar of morality within the world and for those around him.

The Perfected

Another mystical figure of traditional China is the perfected, realized one, or true person (*zhenren* 真人), who is first described in the *Zhuangzi* and later becomes important in the medieval Daoist religion. The major characteristic of this figure is his complete lack of feelings, which makes him an equal of Dao. Although "Dao gave him a human face and Heaven gave him a human body, he does not let [feelings of] likes and dislikes enter and harm himself" (ch. 5) but preserves his essence and attains long life and a peace of mind that matches Heaven and Earth. More interested in the inner workings of the perfected mind than in the social and political impact of the sage, the *Zhuangzi* gives a psychological description how the perfected remains free from worries and the ordinary emotions of life:

> The perfected does not fight if he has little, does not grow proud if he has much. He never plans his affairs. He is able

> to make a mistake and not feel bad about it, attain success and not claim credit for it, climb into high places and not get nervous, enter water and not get wet, enter fire and not get burned. All this is because his knowledge is part of Dao itself.
>
> The perfected sleeps without dreaming and wakes without worrying. He eats without delighting in the taste and breathes very deep. . . . He does not know how to delight in life or loathe death. He comes into the world without pleasure and goes again without refusal. (ch. 6; Watson 1968).

This quality of the perfected comes from his mind being utterly concentrated and empty, from his attainment of a kind of mystical union described as complete forgetfulness: "I smash up my limbs and body, drive out perception and intellect, cast off form, do away with understanding, and make myself identical with the Great Dao" (ch. 6). There is no sense of ego-identity left in this person, thus he is without feelings, similar to the mystics described in other religious traditions who are said to place their faith in something higher than themselves, go along with life, and never be afraid of death. Utterly equanimous in all situations, they have freedom and peace within, trust in the deity and compassion for all creatures without. Never striving for anything, never regretting anything, they encompass a personality that is beyond common humanity and fully at-one with the universe. Larger than life, they represent the complete realization of life; one with the deity, with Dao, they are more than mere humans. More than human, they are also no longer moral agents, because being free from feelings they have no conscience or other inner root where moral rules could take hold.

As the perfected are mainly recognized by their inner psychological state, they may appear in any form and social status and express their perfection in a variety of different ways. The classical description found in the *Zhuangzi* is in terms of the superb skills of a master craftsman, as for example Cook Ding's carving of an ox. He says of his skill:

> What I care about is only Dao, which goes beyond skill. When I first began cutting up oxen, all I could see was the ox itself. After three years I no longer saw the whole ox. And now—now I go at it by spirit and do not look with my eyes. Perception and understanding have come to a stop, and spirit moves where it wants. I go along fully with the natural make-up. (ch. 3; Watson 1968, 50-51)

Here the forgetfulness of the perfected mind is realized in a highly practical, everyday skill, so that the craftsman no longer sees his work object or is even conscious of himself wielding his tool. Instead, having given up perception and self-definition in favor of the all-pervasive Dao, he lets himself be carried along by its currents and moves fully in tune with nature itself. Thus his carving is perfect, his knife never slips. The same applies also to the art of woodworker Qing who only goes out to cut wood for a new bell-stand after having purified himself for a week:

> When I have fasted [in mind and body] for three days, I no longer have any thought of congratulations or rewards, titles or stipends. When I have fasted for five days, I no longer have any thought of praise or blame, skill or clumsiness. And when I have fasted for seven days, I am so still that I forget I have four limbs and a form and body. By that time, the ruler and his court no longer exist for me. My skill is concentrated and all outside distractions fade away. (ch. 19; Watson 1968, 205-06)

The perfected without feelings is thus a figure of high mental purity who applies his forgetfulness of self in all he does but specifically in the daily arts and techniques of his trade. His actions and convictions are entirely unmoral, the only thing that counts is his oneness with Dao and the degree to which cosmic power flows through him. Nevertheless by exercising his perfection within everyday activities, he makes the world a truer and more harmonious place, thus contributing again, not unlike the sage, to a greater goodness among ordinary people.

The quality of the perfected as an energy center of cosmic power also makes him long-lived and even immortal, able to join the course of the stars and fly ecstatically off to the heavens. As Guangchengzi 廣成子 says in the *Zhuangzi*:

> I enter the gate of the inexhaustible and wander in the limitless fields, form a triad with the light of the sun and the moon, partake in the constancy of Heaven and Earth. What stands before me I mingle with, what is far from me I leave in darkness. All other men may die, but I alone remain! (ch. 11)

This inner sense of oneness with Dao and eternal participation in the cosmic flow further characterizes the perfected as a being without relations, one who has "seen his aloneness" and is without opposite, "standing beside Heaven and Earth and at-one with all" (ch. 1). He is not by choice or in any way socially active nor even very conscious of the society around him, whose occasional intrusion he either indulges tolerantly or rejects impatiently; he does not evaluate anyone or anything nor expects to be judged, his actions being nothing but expressions of the pure flow of the Dao.

People encountering such a perfected, on the other hand, will see someone whose movements are like natural processes, who appears not to be doing anything actively by himself but to be carried along fully by the Dao. Free from self, free from merit, free from fame (ch. 6), he leaves no traces or teachings behind and cannot be used as an example by later generations. He neither changes anything in the world through the way he lives nor does he act upon others, his deeds being as fleeting and as invisible as Dao itself. People will also see him as a gentle, maybe slightly mad person who rests in tranquility of mind whatever he does. He will, as the *Zhuangzi* commentator Guo Xiang puts it, "mystically accept all that he encounters and never rouse his mind," "never experience any opposition in the world," but "go along perfectly with the mildness and severity of heat and cold and never let them enter upon his mind" (*Zhuangzi zhu* 4.156; 2.68; 6.231; Knaul 1985a, 30).

At the same time, he may also look like a cautious and reasonable person who never uses his powers of mind unless forced to do so. His ability to enter water and not get wet, enter fire and not get burned, then, is not so much a magical feat or even an expression of the power of the concentrated mind but the result of natural caution. As Guo Xiang says, the perfected would "naturally walk on dry land without, however, purposely avoiding water; he naturally would be far away from fire without, however, intentionally running away from it. Even though he might not feel heat as heat, he would never run towards a fire . . . or plunge into water, or endanger his life in any other way" (ch. 6). Still, if it came to the crunch, he would emerge unscathed, being utterly free from fear and totally concentrated in mind.

Not seeking anything out, whether good or bad, the perfected would yet commonly encounter useful and positive situations in life, always stepping into good fortune and never being befallen by calamities (ch. 17). One with nature, he would never harm any living being, so that when "he steps among wild beasts, they are not disturbed; when he comes across wild birds, they do not fly away" (ch. 5). Fully in harmony with the inner nature given to him through Dao, he follows the natural life course laid out for him and never encounters anything that is not appropriate or cannot be handled. His whole existence, unknowing and without self, is blessed and fortunate, he is at one with himself as part of the eternal Dao.

The social relevance of such a person, beyond morality in his thinking and acting and not responsible in society or for it, even if he has a position or skill to maintain, lies first in the inner harmony he spreads by just being who he is and second in his being a model of perfection for others, from whom they can—not by active instruction but by outside observation—gain inspiration on how to be at one with Dao and fully realize one's existence on earth. If that happens, as Guo Xiang says, "if everyone follows his so-being and rests in utmost accordance [with the Dao], then wise and foolish, aggression and love, noble and humble, coming and going, ruler and minister, up and down—all will be perfected to the utmost. Then there will be no more suffering under heaven!" (ch. 11; Knaul 1985a, 31). The perfected without feelings, a transmoral being of cosmic consciousness, thus can serve as an inspiration to others, as an example of how life without suffering can be possible. Inspired by him and following his attainments, all people can find perfection, which in turn will create a perfect society on earth.

The medieval Daoist religion, in a further development of this ideal, locates the vision of social perfection in the heavens, where the perfected and immortals reside next to the gods in a celestial assembly that is free from the strife and suffering of the common world. Attainment of mystical union and the perfected consciousness on earth is then, after the body has been shaken off or transformed into pure heavenly energy, continued in an eternal existence among the celestials, from where inspiration can be given to humanity through the appearance of mysterious signs or direct revelations of knowledge and scriptures. The perfected in heaven, like their counterparts on earth, thus can have an impact on the purity and moral wellbeing of human society, but their own quality, as part of Dao, is beyond morality and whatever transformations they may work among humanity is by subtle example or mysterious indication only, never by active guidance, rulership, or teachings as might be given by the sage (see Robinet 1984; Kohn 1992a, 108-16).

The Immortal

The most important mystical figure of religious Daoism is the immortal, an ideal that developed after the model of shamans and mountain recluses. The character for "immortal" (*xian* 仙) accordingly shows a man next to a mountain or, in an older version, a figure dancing with flying sleeves. Immortals appear on the scene only in the late Zhou and early Han dynasties when concepts of the immortality of the soul were expanded to include physical forms of long and even eternal life, various indigenous tribes were found to possess arts of making the body stronger and lighter, and contacts with other cultures enhanced the belief in a magical paradise of pure power where wondrous figures live that nourish on energy and can appear and disappear at will (see Yü 1964, 87; Wen 1956, 159; Kaltenmark 1953, 12-16; 1969, 76; also Hayashi 1975).

Immortals are characterized by their reclusive nature, which makes them inhabitants of deep mountains or far-off islands, by their close relationship to animals, documented in depictions of feathered or furred figures on Han-dynasty mirrors, and by their complete control over physical functions of the body, which includes not only the practice of gymnastics and breathing exercises but also magical powers of multi-location and invisibility. They are described in several early hagiographic collections, notably the *Liexian zhuan* 列仙傳 (Immortals' Biographies) and the *Shenxian zhuan* 神仙傳 (Biographies of Spirit Immortals; trl. Campany 2002), and come in two major types, earthly and celestial. The former are reclusive and often eccentric practitioners of longevity techniques who have withdrawn to the mountains but may on occasion reappear to exorcise demons or effect faith-healings; the latter reside in heavenly paradises and descend every so often on a whim to bring a bit of magic to the world.

Morality enters the realm of the immortals on two levels: as a prerequisite for immortality training and as an aspect of accomplished immortals' activities. Although again, as the sages and perfected, inherently transmoral beings, immortals have yet to prove certain moral qualities in their character before being accepted as worthy disciples and allowed to undergo training. Several stories, both in ancient and late medieval literature, document this fact. The most popular and detailed among them is the biography of Lü Dongbin 呂洞賓, leader of the Eight Immortals, who was subjected to ten tests. For example,

> Once Lü, at the time of the New Year, was leaving his house to be accosted by a beggar demanding alms. He handed over all [the presents] he carried, cash and gifts in kind. But the beggar remained dissatisfied and threateningly demanded more, using the most abusive terms. Yet Lü kept a smiling face and again and again apologized to him politely.
>
> Then again, Lü was looking after some sheep in the mountains. A hungry tiger came upon them, with the result that the flock scattered in all directions. Lü interposed his own person between the tiger and the terrified sheep. The tiger gave up the chase and crept away. (*Zengxian liexian zhuan* 13a; see Yetts 1916, 794; Kohn 1993a, 130)

These two tests, representative for the entire series, focus on Lü's degree of attachment to material things and social customs as well as on his fear of death and his compassion for helpless creatures. The aspiring immortal thus must be generous with his possessions and independent of social approval, has to have courage in the face of death and other threats or beguilements (one tests also has Lü encounter a sensuous beauty), and be willing to sacrifice himself on behalf of weaker beings. These moral virtues, which are not only Daoist but also Buddhist and were actively demanded in the later school of Complete Perfection (Quanzhen; see Hawkes 1981, 160; Eskildsen 2004) yet are not required for their own sake or to develop a particularly moral type of person but were seen as indicative of the personal determination necessary for the utter overcoming of body and self on the path to otherworldly immortality. Moral values, although necessary in the beginning of practice as a sign of inner strength, are therefore not central to the ideal but have to be put aside and overcome together with all other aspects of ordinary life and common features of being human.

On another level, morality in the form of compassion for others forms one aspect of immortals' activities in the world. Both before and after their ascent into heaven, they appear among mortals and support them by healing diseases, exorcising demons, providing instructions for long life, or merely adding an increased sense of beauty to the world. Numerous stories document these activities, including one in the *Liexian zhuan* about a man known as Lord Horsemaster who cured animals far and wide and once even relieved a celestial dragon of an atrocious tooth-ache; another in the *Shenxian zhuan* about the so-called Gourd Master who failed the tests of full immortality but managed to become a strong demon-dispeller on earth, reducing frightful monsters to quivering jelly wherever he went; and one again about the wonderworker Zuo Ci 左慈 who could procure the most wonderful foodstuffs from far-off places within an instant (Kaltenmark 1953, 47; Campany 2002, 279-92).

In their eccentric way relieving human suffering and making the world a more enjoyable place, immortals yet also use their magical powers to escape restraints and make fun of imperial officials, thus holding up a mirror of joy and laughter to earthlings striving so hard and taking themselves so seriously. Again the wonderworker Zuo Ci provides a good example. He has angered the ruling warlord, and guards come into the palace to throw him into prison.

> But as the guards were approaching to arrest him, Zuo Ci simply walked straight into a wall and vanished without a trace.
>
> The warlord hired a number of men to capture him. One of these saw him in the marketplace. On the point of seizing him, suddenly all the people there were transformed into Zuo's exact likeness. No one could tell which one was he.
>
> Later some of the hired men found him on the slope of Southtown Hill. Again they pursued him, and he fled among a flock of sheep, turning into an animal himself. . . . Suddenly one old ram bent its forelegs, stood upright like a human being, and said in a human voice: "What a fluster you are in!"
>
> "There!" the men cried excitedly. "That ram is the one we want!"
>
> But as they made a dash for him, the entire flock of several hundred turned into rams. They all bent their forelegs, stood upright like humans, and cried: "What a fluster you are in!" (Kohn 1993a, 299)

This exclamation of the magical rams sums up the relation of the immortals to the world very nicely. From the perspective of the unlimited freedom of the heavens, all worldly striving and ambitions appear just so much nervous fluster and tension, an expenditure of energy that ultimately leads to no purpose or end. Thus immortals, like sages and perfected beyond the scope of ordinary human life, hold up a mirror to the world from the perspective of a transmoral state that is at one with Heaven and Earth. They illustrate how one can live with the larger universe as one's home, free from involvements, obligations, and social relationships, yet not unfriendly or harmful.

Themselves part of the essential goodness of the cosmos, immortals in their turn too increase the goodness of the world but not as the sages through serious personal, political, or philosophical influence, nor as the perfected through inspiring others with their humility, simplicity, and forgetfulness. Rather, immortals are whimsical and unpredictable, appearing literally out of the blue and doing a good turn to an utterly amazed community or again rendering social institutions ineffectual and making the threatening postures of warlords and demons look ridiculous. They increase the goodness of the world by helping humanity in their eccentric way, by making people laugh at themselves and gain a healthy distance to their plight. The happiness radiating from them spreads into the world and allows people to be more whole, more cheerful, and better human beings.

Not only a mythical ideal represented in fanciful stories of old, in the late middle ages the ideal of immortality was institutionalized in the Daoist religion, and practitioners came to temples and monasteries to undergo a regimen of both physical and spiritual practices that would turn them into immortals. Their goal was to gain first mystical oneness in a state of utter forgetfulness on earth and eventually ascend to the heavens of the otherworld as celestial beings. Transformation from an ordinary mortal into a wondrous part of Dao was thought to occur in three major steps: a renewal of the body through the practice of gymnastics, breathing, and herbal diets; a calming of the mind through the attainment of one-pointedness; and a complete change of one's entire existence in a process again described in seven stages.

According to the latter, practitioners first find their body has grown light and their mind luminous, and they themselves are in a perpetual state of joy and exultation. Next, they begin to look youthful and begin to see the world in a new way, deep and mysterious. Third, they attain a high longevity and ecstatically travel to the far ends of the earth, divine servants at their back and call. Fourth, they become one with pure energy and gain the magical power to appear and disappear at will. Fifth, they become pure spirit, changing in utter spontaneity, completely boundless and with the power to move mountains and oceans. Sixth, the changes become even more pervasive, and adepts are perfected beings who pervade all existence and change according to occasion. Seventh, finally, they whirl out of all to reside in the heavens next to the divine emperors at the source of the Dao.[2] As this inside description of the transformation into an immortal shows,

[2] This description follows the *Cunshen lianqi ming* 存神鍊氣銘 (Inscription on the Preservation of Spirit and Refinement of Energy, DZ 834) by the seventh-century Daoist physician Sun Simiao. See Kohn1987.

there is nothing moral about the process, neither in its foundations nor in its results.

The change that occurs within the person, body and mind, is one from a limited, individualized entity into a boundless, cosmic part of the universal flow of the Dao. It dissolves individual consciousness to the point of complete forgetfulness and transforms the apparently solid body of the practitioner into a stream of energy that flows freely throughout the universe. A person like this while still alive will behave either like the perfected in an unobtrusive, gentle, and benevolent fashion, or again—if his skills include healing and the management of demons—as a shamanic healer or exorcist. In all cases he will stand aside from society and remain beyond its rules and judgments, secure in his being part of Dao and thus able to point out the absurdities and pettiness of ordinary life. After death, or rather after ascent into the heavens, such a person will remain part of the heavenly realm of Dao and from there come back to give help or inspiration to human beings on earth. The goodness he has found through his transformation in either case serves to make the cosmos truer and the world a better place.

Conclusion

Traditional Chinese religion, to summarize, knows three major types of mystical figures as characterized by its different historical traditions. All three have in common that they are one with Dao, the underlying flow of the universe, the cosmic law that creates and carries all, and as such stand beyond morality in a position that can be described as transmoral or supramoral. All characterized by their aloneness, their lack of family relationships and personal conscience, they are like the cosmos and nature and do not have a set of values that can be defined or to which they can be held. Nevertheless because the cosmos and nature both partake of the fundamental goodness of Dao, each of these figures also in his own way contributes to the realization of goodness—and thus also moral goodness—in the world, exerting an active moral influence on the human community.

On the background of this commonality, the three figures play different roles and are described differently in the literature. The sage, to begin, transforms society through political, personal, or philosophical impact. Among the three he is the most clearly socially responsible, but he too is like Heaven and Earth in that he is not humane in his personal relationships but places the cosmic needs first. Also, a sage is a natural phenomenon, one cannot become one by mere practice but has to be born with either inherent sage abilities or with a strong urge for self-cultivation.

The perfected, second, realizes the pure goodness of the cosmos in the forgetfulness of his mind, the purity of his mental concentration, and the high quality of his skills in the world. He is the least socially concerned or active, typically staying aloof from society and moving along in his own pure world of the Dao. Still, anyone with a certain amount of effort can attain this mental state, and the perfected serves thus as a model or inspiration for others. A strongly social component only enters the ideal in the thought that the more people realized the mental purity of the perfected the better society will become until it reaches the spontaneous, unknowing perfection of the Dao.

The immortal, the ideal figure of religious Daoism third, has reached a celestial state that is both mental and physical after undergoing a long and very hard training that completely changes his personal and bodily nature. As a result of this training he has attained magical and shamanic powers, such as, healing, exorcism, multi-location, invisibility, and so on. He uses these powers to improve the world but not in a political or social way. Instead he holds up a mirror to people, showing them the futility and absurdity of their petty efforts, laughing at them but also with them and presenting them with a model of pure, unadulterated happiness and laughter.

The three different figures thus vary in their roles and relations to society—the sage being central in society, the perfected being marginal, and the immortal being entirely outside. Nevertheless they each have some social or moral responsibility that comes from their cosmic purity as realized in their minds and lives. The sage therefore allows people to rest with him and depend on him; he sees and hears the signs of the cosmos and makes them accessible to the human community. The perfected is moral in that he never harms any living beings but is overall gentle and mild to everyone he encounters. The immortal, finally, aside from being subjected to moral tests at the beginning of his training, serves the community by providing healing and exorcism and by showing how life can be happy and full of laughter.

Within this overall picture, certain critical questions arise about the nature and social activities of these three figures, questions that are inspired by the Western scholarly mind but that, at least to a certain extent, have also been asked by the tradition itself.

To begin again with the sage. Ideally, both in ancient Confucianism and Daoism, the sage is also the ruler and by definition a transmoral being whose acts may appear bad by common standards but serve a higher cosmic purpose. As a sage-ruler, this figure has the closest link to the cosmic patterns and can govern the world in utter perfection. The problem arises when the ruler is not as much of a sage as he may think but is in fact a tyrant who thinks of himself as a sage and assumes that every little personal whim of his is an expression of cosmic harmony. Thus, while even great rulers typically levy taxes and corvee labor so they can undertake great construction projects to the benefit of the people, these may easily be taken too far and make the population's burden too heavy. How, then, does one know whether the ruler's demands and projects are part of cosmic goodness or part of a personality gone astray with power?

The tradition, which sees this problem clearly, answers that the cosmos itself is the guardian of its purity. In other words, if harvests are bountiful and the rains come at the right times and in the right measure, the ruler's activities are in harmony and thus cosmically good, however morally questionable they may appear. If there are earthquakes, floods, droughts, famines, and epidemics, on the other hand, Heaven and Earth are harmed by the ruler's activity, and we have a tyrant on our hands. The sage, if successful, thus must be humble and withdrawing, never see himself as a sage but always let the cosmos work through him. He may or may not be in a position of ruler, but wherever he is, moral rules do not apply to him, yet the overall quality of harmony in his surroundings prove him right. Someone deeming himself a sage and doing harm to his surroundings must be stopped, even to the point of revolution and rebellion against the state.

The figure of perfected contains two problems—a personal and a social one. First, one the personal level, a human being without emotions and completely detached from his or her surroundings, is no easy man to live with by any standard but remains encapsulated in himself. The more people like that are being produced, moreover, the more sterile the society becomes, with "love" turning into a dirty word and any form of attachment, even among kin, being scorned. As a result, perfected in larger numbers would be like trees, standing next to each other and swaying similarly in the same cosmic wind but without any close contact or personal relationships.

The tradition has not seen this point all that clearly, but it has raised the problem of oblivion and forgetfulness in an active social context—again in a rather humorous way. A story in the *Liezi* documents this. Here a man known as Huazi has attained a state of complete forgetfulness:

> He would receive a present in the morning and forget it by evening, give a present in the evening and forget it by morning. In the street he would forget to walk, at home he would forget to sit down. Today he would not remember yesterday, tomorrow he would not remember today. (ch. 3; Graham 1960, 70)

His family, naturally concerned and inconvenienced by this behavior, consults with various specialists until a Confucian, a highly socially minded practitioner, manages to snap him out of it. Huazi, however, is far from pleased.

> "Formerly, when I forgot," he says, "I was boundless; I did not notice whether Heaven and Earth existed or not. Now suddenly I remember, and all the disasters and recoveries, gains and losses . . . of twenty or thirty years past rise up in a thousand tangled threads. . . . Shall I never again find a moment of forgetfulness?

Aside from the personal and familial difficulties of the perfected personality, the expansion of the ideal of forgetfulness and spontaneity to wider circles of society also raises the specter of social determinism. If everyone and everything has its particular natural place and function in the world, who is to say what this is? The prostitute in the initial story may have been meant to be a waitress by the cosmic principle, yet what if she decides after a few years of waitressing to start her own coffee shop? Is she, although, not immoral in her course of action, going beyond her predetermined position and thus creating disharmony?

The tradition again has seen this problem and answered it with the notion of luck: if all goes well in what she does, she is on the right track; if there are obstacles galore, she is overstepping the cosmic bounds. The real danger, however, lies not so much in her own perception of what she is or should be but in an outside restraint being put upon her, such as was in fact exercised by East Asian rulers, most notably in the *mibun* system of Tokugawa Japan, established under Confucian influence. Anyone born into a particular family or social position could, according to this system, not move from it, a carpenter's son had to be a carpenter even if his talents lay in the field of tailoring or acting. Social determinism sponsored by the belief in the original goodness of the cosmos that manifests itself in who and what people are is thus one of the dangers of this system, where the transmoral nature of the perfected can and has become socially harmful.

As regards the immortal, finally, the key problem is not so much his or her action in society but the more theoretical issue of individual will in such a celestial figure. If anyone has become completely one with Dao and lost his or her personal identity to the larger flow of the universe, where then should any personal intention or will come from, even the will to laugh and make fun, to leave the world or be eccentric in it? On the other hand, if there still is a personal intention in these figures, if they have a will, then why should they not have a conscience and thus a root of morality within them? This question was not seen and thus not discussed by the tradition, to whom immortals appeared like the wind and the rain, cosmic forces whose movements one could not predict and which yet seemed to come and go with a will of their own. Like the wind and the rain, immortals have an impact on the world but are in themselves far beyond its concerns, so that they seem to be laughing at the human plight which looks miniscule and petty from their heavenly perspective.

Part Two

Translations

Chapter Eight

The Ultimate

There is no absolute, transcendent deity or creator god in Chinese religion; rather, the world is understood to depend on an underlying principle, an inherent blue-print, a natural way (Dao) that makes things be what they are. This understanding is expressed in highly abstract and rather philosophical terms in Neo-Confucianism, where the key ground of existence is described as the Great Ultimate, from which then spring the two forces yin and yang and the five phases of the cosmos.

In Daoism, Dao is at the center of belief and practice, in the religion mythologized as the deity Laozi, himself at one with the origin, formless and substanceless, the dynamic motor of creation. Both visions contain already the seed of mystical realization—perfect adaptation to the patterns of the cosmos to recover the Great Ultimate in oneself, and obedience to the rules and teachings of Laozi to find oneness with the Dao.

The Dao

From *Daode jing* (Book of the Dao and Its Virtue), translated many times (see LaFargue and Pas 1998).

There is a being, in chaos yet complete
that preceded Heaven and Earth.
Silent it is, and solitary;
standing alone, it never changes.

It moves around, yet never ends.
Consider it the mother of all-under-Heaven.
I do not know its name.

To call it something, I speak of Dao.
Naming its strength, I call it great.

Great—that means it departs.
Depart—that means it is far away.
Far away—that means it will return.

Therefore Dao is great,
Heaven is great,
Earth is great,
the king, too, is great.

In this enclosure,
there are these four greats,
and the king rests as one of them.

The king follows Earth,
Earth follows Heaven,
Heaven follows Dao,
But Dao follows only itself. (ch. 25)

Look at it and do not see it:
call it invisible.
Listen to it and do not hear it:
call it inaudible.
Touch it and do not feel it:
call it subtle.

These three cannot be better understood,
they merge and become one.
Infinite and boundless, it cannot be named
but belongs to where there are no beings.

It may be called
the shape of no-shape,
the form of no-form.
Call it vague and obscure.

Meet it, yet you cannot see its head.
Follow it, yet you cannot see its back.
Grasp Dao of old and control existence now.
Know the beginnings of old and have a thread to the Dao. (ch. 14)

Lord Lao Before Creation

From *Youlong zhuan* 猶龍傳 (Like unto a Dragon, DZ 774; dated 1086), 1.1b-2a and *Yunji qiqian* 雲笈七籤 (Seven Tablets in a Cloudy Satchel; DZ 1032; dated 1023), 102.2ab.

Laozi is Lord Lao. He is the body of the Dao, the first ancestor of primordial energy, the deepest root of Heaven and Earth. The Great Dao, mystery and wonder, sprang forth from spontaneity, was born in the unborn, lived before there was any before. Raised in emptiness and pervasion, educated by the Heaven and Earth trigrams, he is called All-Highest. He is the Dao of order and perfection. His spirit sojourns in the subtle and the remote. He cannot be named. He says of himself:

I am born prior to the shapeless,
Grow before the Great Beginning and
rise on the verge of Grand Initiation.

I wander in the prime of Great Immaculate and
Float freely through the Dark Void,
In and out of the hidden and mysterious.

I contemplate Chaos as yet undifferentiated
And view the clear and turbid in union.
The Three Luminaries do not yet shine,
The myriad beings do not yet have shape.

Only I can sojourn in the garden of the blurred and vague,
Wander through the fields of open vastness!

Lofty, I stand alone!
Great, I am without equal!
I see the invisible.
I hear the inaudible.
I touch the unattainable.

Thus I am called Chaos Primordial
And from here take my beginning.
I watch light radiate from the indistinct
And gaze at the subtlety of the shapeless.

Observing the image of the vague,
Seeing the infinity of Chaos,
I stride over the vast barrens of the universe
And pass through all different types of beings.

The chief I am of all creation—
Utterly alone and without relation!
Dispersing, pure energy;
Congealing, a man!

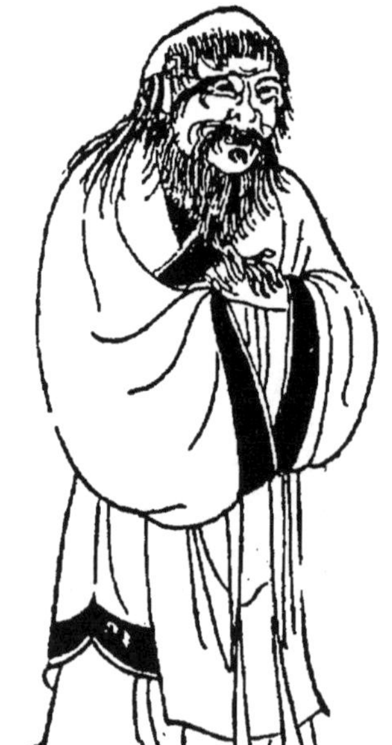

Laozi, the Dao

From *Laozi bianhua jing* 老子變化經 (Scripture on the Transformations of Laozi, Dunhuang manuscript S. 2295; dated ca. 200 C.E.). Text edition and French translation in Seidel 1969, 131-36 and 60-73.

Laozi rests in the great beginning,
Wanders in the great origin,
Floats through dark, numinous emptiness. . . .

He joins serene darkness before its opening,
Is present in original chaos before the beginnings of time.
Beyond harmony of the pure and turbid,
Moving along with great initiation,

He resides in the ancient realm of obscurity and vastness. . . .
Alone and without relation,
He has existed since before Heaven and Earth.
Living deeply hidden, he always returns to be:

Gone, the primordial;
Present, a man!
How vague and obscure!
Heavenly, he transforms to the turbid.

Soon his spirit assumes a form
In the womb of Mother Li.
He grows a body for an excellent destiny,
Resting in her belly for seventy-two years.

Then he appears in the country of Chu.
His mouth square, his lips thick,
With the three and five on his forehead,
showing the sun horn and the moon crescent.

His nose has a double rim;
His ears have three openings;
His soles show the character for "five;"
His palms have the signs of heaven.

His nature is free from desires,

His behavior follows nonaction.
A counselor aiding heaven,
The Three Sovereigns rely on him.

Observing him,
Look at constant change,
At the original source of all.

After living for a long time,
When the state declined
And the king's way collapsed,
He left the country of Chu.

North toward Kunlun
He strode on a white deer
And has not returned to this day.

Laozi is
The utmost essence of spontaneous nature,
The true root of the Dao,
The father and mother of the teaching,
The foundation of Heaven and Earth,
The starting point of all life.

He is the ruler of the gods and spirits,
The first ancestor of yin and yang,
The soul of the myriad beings.
Forever strong in numinous emptiness,

He transforms with the turns of life.
Circling around the eight poles,
He supports the earth and suspends the sky.
He moves along with the sun and the moon
And circulates with the stars and chronograms.

Breathing the Six Jia cyclical energies,
He joins the Heaven and Earth trigrams.
Controlling the changes of the four seasons,
He rules the alterations of heat and cold.

In his hand he holds the staff of the immortals
And the jade tablet inscribed with characters of gold. . . .

Laozi can be
Bright or dark,
Gone or present,
Big or small,
Rolled up or stretched out,
Above or below,
Vertical or horizontal,
Last or first.

There is nothing he cannot do ,
Nothing he will not accomplish.
In fire, he does not burn,
In water, he does not freeze.

He meets with evil without suffering,
Confronts disasters without affliction
Opposed, he is not pained,
Harmed, he is not scarred.

He lives forever and does not die,
Merely dissolves his bodily form.
Single and without counterpart,
Alone and without dependence,
He is yet joined with all and never separate.
Always remaining deep in nonaction,
He yet cannot but follow the world.

Creation and History

From *Santian neijie jing* 三天內解經 (Inner Explanation of the Three Heavens, DZ 1205, dat. 420). Also translated in Bokenkamp 1997.

[1a] The living body of human beings was originally endowed by Heaven above and patterned on Earth below.

Once there were the sun and the moon, there was the distinction between darkness and light.

Once there were heat and cold, there were the energies of birth and death.

Once there were thunder and lightning, there were the periods of emergence and entering.

Once there were the wind and the rain, there were the phases of movement and rest.

Accordingly human beings have:

> dispositions either wise or ignorant,
> inner natures either good or bad,
> energy either hard or soft,
> life-expectancy either long or short,
> positions either high or low,
> ranks either venerable or humble,
> conditions either fortunate or unlucky,
> times either destitute or successful.

Without humanity, Heaven and Earth would not have been established. Without Heaven and Earth, humanity would not have come to life. Heaven and Earth without humanity are like a human body uninhabited by spirit, without which the body could never exist. Similarly, if there were spirit but no body, spirit would have no place to reside.

Thus, what establishes all is Heaven, what works in all is the Dao. Human inner nature and the life-expectancy granted by spirit merge with Dao and become one with Heaven.

[1b] Therefore the three forces—Heaven, Earth, and Humanity—completed their virtue and became the ancestors of the myriad beings.

> Heaven cannot but nurture life!
> Earth cannot but raise living beings!
> Human beings cannot but cultivate energy and nourish life!

In the same way:

If Heaven abandons its mystery and prime, there are the occurrences of sudden changes and eclipses.

If Earth goes against its yellow splendor, there are the disasters of tornadoes and earthquakes.

If human beings turn their backs on utmost Dao, there is the harm of scattering and collapse.

Essential *qi* flows to the top, while the mass of essence flows to the bottom. Above and below interpenetrate each other, like shadow and echo follow shape and sound.

If human affairs go wrong down below, their calamitous reverberations destroy all ordered plans above. Then there are sudden changes and eclipses of the sun and the moon, the stars and chronograms are in the wrong positions. All this comes when human affairs are out of their proper order.

Due to changes of this kind, people since lower antiquity have had their life-expectancy shortened and distorted, their corpses and bones exposed to the wolves, their longevity never lived out to the full.

All this was because in their cultivation they lost the true origins; in their marriages they did not stick to the proper classifications. Thus they disturbed their energy and it became disordered and turbid. They developed faith in the false and abandoned the true. With the original Dao so distorted and falsified, the masses were ignorant and utterly confused. None knew where their misfortunes were coming from.

[2a] Also, they slaughtered and cooked the six domestic animals in order to pray and implore emptiness and nothingness. They sang songs and danced to the beat of drums, pursuing Dao with offerings of wine and meat. Thus they thought to pursue life and reject death. Yet this false Yao soon made their heads ache and their feet itch. Human affairs did not accord with each other, prayers and implorations were distorted and went awry. Thus it happened that people began to lose their lives in early death.

Oh, how very painful is life in this time! Therefore today I have put together the "Essential Explanations of the Three Heavens" to show them to all those not awakened. My readers, you must stick to them diligently and keep them well hidden! Never must you transmit them foolishly or lightly. If you transmit them to the wrong person, misfortune will be visited upon your children and grandchildren.

The Dao, when it first arose from its source, came from what has no before. Dark and obscure, vast and open, it had no prior cause. In emptiness it was born as pure spontaneity, to then transform and change and bring forth the Elder of Dao and Virtue. Born even before primordial energy, he is the Lord residing in the midst of the Dao. Thus he is the Elder of Dao and Virtue.

Following this, there were the mystery and prime of Great Clarity, the Highest Three Heavens, the Great Dao of Non-Ultimate, the Highest Lord Lao, the Highest Elder, as well as the Lord Emperors of Heaven, the Nine Old Ones, the Lords of the Immortals' Capital, the Elders of the Nine Energies, and many more.

The energy of Dao then developed tens of thousands of layers, and there were the lords of the 1,200 celestial offices. [2b] The Jade Emperor of Great Clarity ordered the people of the world to write down the verses and scriptures of Great Clarity. These properly speak of the perfected in all the heavens.

After this, in the midst of darkness and obscurity, emptiness and pervasion were born. In the midst of emptiness and pervasion, great nonbeing was born. Great nonbeing transformed and changed into the three *qi*: mysterious, primordial, and beginning. Intermingling in chaos, the followed each other and transformed to bring forth the Jade Maiden of Mystery and Wonder (Xuanmiao yunü).

After the Jade Maiden had been born, the chaos energies congealed. They transformed and brought forth the Old Master [Laozi]. He was born the left armpit of the Jade Maiden. At birth he had white hair, thus he was called the Old Master. The Old Master is Lord Lao.

Through the transformations and changes, energy was first formed, then Heaven, Earth, Humanity, and all living beings arose. Revolving along with creation, Lord Lao transformed and was born to refine his body and energy.

Even in the beginning Lord Lao had already dispersed and spread the three *qi*: mysterious, primordial, and beginning. Even before the light and the turbid were separated, when all was in chaos and indistinct like the yolk in an egg, he had followed the transformations and spread them out.

Thus the mysterious energy, clear and pure, rose up and became Heaven. The beginning energy, thick and turbid, coagulated downwards and became Earth. The primordial energy, light and subtle, flowed everywhere and became Water. Thereupon the sun and the moon, the stars and the constellations were properly arranged.

[3a] Lord Lao then harmonized these three *qi* and formed the nine countries. In each country he placed nine people, three men and six women. In the time of Fu Xi [Prostrate Sacrificer] and Nü Gua [Snake Woman], all people received surnames and personal names.

Then Lord Lao brought forth three ways to teach the people of the world. First, the Middle Kingdom was of yang energy, pure and orderly: he gave it the Great Way of Nonaction to worship.

Next, the eighty-one barbarian countries on the periphery were of yin energy, aggressive and awesome: he made them worship the Great Way of the Buddha and imposed strict regulations on them to control their yin energy.

Third, the southern countries of Chu and Yue were of both yin and yang *qi*: he gave them the Great Way of Clear Harmony for their worship.

At this time, the rule of the Six Heavens flourished and the three ways of teaching were practiced. Under emperor after emperor Laozi emerged and became the country's teacher. Under Fu Xi, he was the Master of Luxuriant Efflorescence. . . .

Under Tang of Yin, he was called Xizezi. [3b] He went on changing without end. Sometimes his family name was Li and he was called Hong, also known as Jiuyang [Ninefold Yang]. Then again he was called Dan or Boyang [Elder Yang]. He was also known as Zhong or Boguang [Elder Radiance], as Zhong or Ziwen [Master Pattern], as Zhao or Bochang [Master Senior]. In addition he had the names Yuan or Boshi [Elder Beginning], Xian or Yuansheng [Prime Born], De or Bowen [Elder Pattern].

In one day he transformed nine times. Or he changed twenty-four times. In thousands of transformations, myriads of changes, he followed the world along, sinking and floating with it. Immeasurable he was! Uncountable his changes!

Thus arrived the time of King Wuding of the Shang dynasty. Laozi returned to the womb in Mother Li. During the pregnancy of eighty-one years, he continuously recited a sacred scripture. Then he parted her left armpit and was born. At birth he had white hair. Therefore she called him Laozi, Old Child. The Scripture of the Three Terraces we still have today is the text Laozi chanted in the womb.

As regards his return to the womb in Mother Li, it must be understood that he himself transformed his body of pure emptiness into the shape of Mother Li. Then he took refuge in his own womb. There was never a real Mother Li. Unaware of this fact, people nowadays say that Laozi took refuge in the womb of Mother Li. Such is not the case.

[4a] Thus arrived the time of King You of the Zhou dynasty. Laozi knew that the dynasty was doomed to decay. With disheveled hair and feigning madness, he excused himself from the Zhou and left.

Traveling in an oxcart, he reached the pass in the Zhongnan mountains and met Yin Xi, the Guardian of the Pass. He transmitted to him the *Shangxia zhongjing* 上下中經 (Central Scripture of Above and Below) in one scroll and the "Scripture in Five Thousand Words" [*Daode jing*] in two scrolls, three scrolls in all.

When Yin Xi received these texts, his Dao attained perfection. Laozi with the eyes of Dao saw far west into the barbarian countries. He observed that they were aggressive and violent and very hard to transform.

Thereupon he entered Kashmir together with Yin Xi. His spirit transformed into Megha the Great and as such he subdued the barbarian king. For him he wrote scriptures of the Buddha way in as many as six thousand and four myriad words.

The king and his country all worshiped and served him. Kashmir is located about forty thousand miles west of the Chinese home country. When its entire region followed his great law, Laozi went further west and entered India. This is another forty thousand miles after Kashmir.

The queen of India was called Qingmiao [Clear Wonder; Māyā]. When she was taking an afternoon nap, Laozi ordered Yin Xi to stride on a white elephant and change into a yellow sparrow. In such shape he flew into the mouth of the queen. [4b] To her his shape appeared like a shooting star coming down from heaven.

In the following year, on the eighth day of the fourth month, he split open her right hip and was born. He dropped to the ground and took seven steps. Raising his right hand toward heaven, he exclaimed: In the heavens above and on the earth below, I alone am venerable! The Three Worlds are nothing but suffering. What can be pleasant in them? He later realized that all birth is essentially suffering and became the Buddha. From that time onward, the Buddhist way flourished anew in these areas.

In lower antiquity, times were excessively heartless. Witches and evil practitioners turned up everywhere to do profitable business. Shamanistic rituals were performed and devils worshiped. Truth and heterodoxy were no longer properly distinguished.

Lord Lao thereupon revealed the *Taiping jing* 太平經 (Scripture of Great Peace) to Gan Ji 干吉 in Langya. To Li Wei in Sichuan he gave orders to assist the Six Heavens and inspect right and wrong.

Heavens and Emperors

From *Taishang lingbao wufu xu* 太上靈寶五符序 (Explanation of the Five Talismans of Highest Numinous Treasure, DZ 388), ch. 1.

[11b] The Heaven of Nine Qi belongs to the green, sprouting energy of the east. The energetic vapor of this heaven is like the first sprouting of grass in the spring; its radiance is like the first peeking-forth of the rising sun. Underneath it is the abyss of morning florescence; above it is the Palace of Flowing Glow. In its chambers reside jade maidens dressed in green; in its halls live the perfected all-highest kings. The jade maidens ride on the beasts of the nine mountains; the perfected kings ride on the divine dragons of the nine luminants. Above, this heaven guides the energy of the nine heavens; [12a] below, it directs the flow of the nine springs.

With its help, nourish on the two forces to live forever; guard yin and yang to pervade all. Through it, Heaven reaches its primordial energy, governed by the Great Ultimate; Earth protects its mountains and peaks, ruled by the god Goumang. The spirits revolve emptily in the terraces of serenity; human beings nurture their five organs in the space guarded by lips and teeth. Increase it, and you will have no limits; visualize it, and you will have no end. Thereby you can go through ten thousand kalpas and yet begin again; reject decline and decay and recover your youth. Like the Peng-bird you can soar through the nine empyreans, ascend upward to the mysterious grottoes, visit the numinous officers of Great Perfection, and become the ancestor of the immortal administrators. Great indeed is the long life won through the green, sprouting energy of Lingbao, from the effort of the Heaven of Nine Qi.

The Heaven of Three Qi belongs to the vermilion, cinnabar energy of the south. The energetic vapor of this heaven is like scarlet clouds being illuminated by a white sun; its radiance is like the shining glow of dark jade. Underneath it is the wide pond of the red spring; above it is the Vermilion Palace of long life. In its chambers reside jade maidens dressed in deep vermilion; they live on the three mountains of Great Yang. [12b] In its halls live the elders of primordial energy, who ride on three-horned unicorns. Above, this heaven guides the numinous transformations of the Great Clarity, mysterious and primordial [energy]; below, it directs the creation and organizations of the Heaven of Three Qi.

It orders those among the myriad beings who are not yet ready to revolve fully along with heaven; its essence belongs to the south and the summer. People who nurture this essence in their cinnabar lips and thus pluck it for themselves will have no end; raising it thus, they will live forever. Doing so, one can repulse old age and return to infancy; turn away from decrepitude and become fresh once more. One can stop the falling leaves of autumn and return one's radiant flourishing to the myriad springs. Thus following the holy dragon one can look over the empty barrens and soar up to the far end of the clouds, letting completely go of one's mind and voiding all thoughts, in a transformation entirely free from all dirt and defilements. Great indeed is the long life won through the vermilion, cinnabar energy of Lingbao, from the effort of the heaven of the three *qi*. . . .

The Five Emperors of Numinous Treasure

NOTE: These names are taken from the heavenly writings put together by Yu of Xia and assembled on the southern slope of South Mountain in Guaiji. [15a]

The East is known as the numinous awesome worship.
He is called the Azure Emperor.
His spirit is that of [the cyclical signs] *jia* and *yi*.
His dress is all green.
He rides on an azure dragon.
He hoists green banners.
His energy is that of wood.
His planet is Jupiter.
His following spirits number 900,000.
Above he matches the energy of spring.
Below he brings forth the myriad beings.
The South is known as the red whirlwind bow.
He is called the Red Emperor.
His spirit is that of [the cyclical signs] *bing* and *ding*.
His dress is all red.
He rides on an red dragon.
He hoists vermilion banners.

His energy is that of fire.
His planet is Mars.
His following spirits number 300,000.
Above he matches the energy of summer.
Below he raises the myriad beings.

The Center is known as the containing pivot string.
He is called the Yellow Emperor.
His spirit is that of [the cyclical signs] *wu* and *si*.
His dress is all yellow.
He rides on an yellow dragon.
He hoists yellow banners.
His energy is that of earth.
His planet is Saturn.
His following spirits number 120,000.
Above he matches the energy of earth.
Below he supports the nine heavens.

[15b] The West is known as the radiant soul treasure.
He is called the White Emperor.
His spirit is that of [the cyclical signs] *geng* and *xin*.
His dress is all white.
He rides on an white dragon.
He hoists white banners.
His energy is that of metal.
His planet is Venus.
His following spirits number 700,000.
Above he matches the energy of fall.
Below he gathers the myriad beings.

The North is known as the hidden lord department.
He is called the Black Emperor.
His spirit is that of [the cyclical signs] *ren* and *gui*.
His dress is all dark.
He rides on an black dragon.
He hoists black banners.
His energy is that of water.
His planet is the Pole Star.
His following spirits number 500,000.
Above he matches the energy of winter.
Below he stores the myriad beings.

Chapter Nine

Language

Language is an important means of communication and of central value in a properly functioning society. In Confucianism, the doctrine of "rectifying the names" (*zhengming* 正名) describes how any term used should indicate just what it means and nothing else, and how anyone taking on a given social role should live up to that role to the fullest. Language here is thus a means, not an obstacle, to mystical realization. Not so in Daoism. Here worlds are an empty cultural convention, whose meaning shifts with the times and circumstances and which do not have any value on their own. They detract from, rather than help to understand, reality as it is. Mystical practice, as a result, includes a critical understanding of the ultimate relativity of all verbal utterings and the eventual overcoming of language in a state of no-mind and no-speaking.

True Words are Not Beautiful

From *Daode jing* (Book of the Dao and Its Virtue)

The Dao that can be dao'ed
is not the eternal Dao.
The name that can be named
is not the eternal name.

Nameless:
the origin of Heaven and Earth;
Named :
the mother of the myriad beings.

Always free from desires:
you can see its wonder.
Always cherish desires:
you only observe its outcome.

They grow together
yet with different names,
both part of the mystery.
Mysterious and more mysterious:
the gate of all that's wondrous. (ch. 1)

The Dao:
eternal, nameless, simple;
Small, yet subject to neither Heaven nor Earth.

Kings and lords maintain it,
the myriad beings come to them.
Heaven and Earth are in harmony,
sweet dew falls.

People do not order it,
it is everywhere equally.
First you control it,
then names appear.

Once there are names,
knowledge must arise of when to stop.
Know when to stop,
and you will never perish.

Compare how Dao is in all-under-Heaven
to the converging of rivers and valleys
toward the great streams and endless oceans.
Great Dao:
overflowing, left and right!

The myriad beings rely on it to be born,
it never turns them away.
Its merit, so perfect,
yet it claims no fame for its existence.

It garbs and nurtures all,

yet claims no position as their chief.
Always free from desires:
Call it small!

The myriad beings return to it,
yet never make it their chief:
Call it great!

To its very end it does not think itself great.
Thus it perfects its greatness. (ch. 32)

True words are not beautiful.
Beautiful words are not true.

A good man does not argue.
Who argues is not a good man.
A wise man has no knowledge.
Who knows is not a wise man.

The sage does not accumulate,
The more he does for others,
the more he gains himself
The more he gives to others,
the more he has himself.

The way of Heaven is:
always benefit, never harm!
The way of the sage is:
always work, never compete! (ch. 81)

Oral Instructions

From *Xisheng jing* 西昇經 (Scripture of Western Ascension, DZ 726). Earlier translation in Kohn 1991a.

1. Western Ascension

Laozi ascended to the west
to open up Dao in India.
He was called Master Gu;
skilled at entering nonaction,

Without beginning or end,
he exists continuously.
Thus steadily ascending,
he followed his way and reached the frontier.
The guardian of the Pass, Yin Xi,
saw his [sagely] *qi*.

He purified himself
and waited upon the guest,
who in turn transmitted Dao and Virtue
He arranged it in two sections.

Laozi said:
I will tell you the essentials of the Dao:
Dao is naturalness.
Who practices can attain [it].
Who hears can speak [about it].
Who knows does not speak.
Who speaks does not know.

Language is formed when sounds are exchanged.
Thus in conversation, words make sense.
When one does not know the Dao,
words create confusion.

Therefore I don't hear, don't speak;
I don't know why things are.

It can be compared to musical sound.
One becomes conscious of it by plucking a string.
Though the mind may know the appropriate sounds,
yet the mouth is unable to formulate them.

Similarly Dao is deep, subtle, wondrous.
Who knows it does not speak.

On the other hand,
one may be conscious of musical sounds, sad melodies.
One then dampens the sounds to consider them within.

Then when the mind makes the mouth speak,
one speaks but does not know.

2. The Depth of Dao

Laozi said:
Dao is deep and very profound;
an abyss of emptiness and nonbeing.
Though you may hear its doctrine,
in your mind you don't grasp its subtlety.

Why is this so?
The written word does not exhaust speech,
and by relying on scriptures and sticking to texts
your learning remains on the same [intellectual] level.

Rather, you must treasure it:
recollect it within,
meditate on it,
consider it carefully.

The Dao of naturalness will not wait for you.

13. Scriptures and Precepts

Laozi said:
All that is said in scriptures and precepts,
all that is prescribed in laws and statutes
is powerful,
awe-inspiring,
openly declared.
It is not as good as the wondrous and subtle.

The full is not as good as the empty;
the numerous is not as good as the rare.
The exuberant and multiple will die an early death;
to be hectic is much worse than to come a little late.

All that flourishes must decay;
all that prospers must decline.

The sage gives up all knowledge
and acts in nonaction.
He speaks by saying nothing;
he things by never undertaking.

How do we know this?
The even is not as good as the odd.
The many is not as good as the few.

What kind of wisdom is harder to follow?
What kind of kindness is harder to attain?
The meaning of this makes sense to few.

To know without knowledge:
this is the pivot of Dao.

Emptiness ends and nonbeing begins:
what use is it to be a flying immortal?

The great Dao is vast and open;
nothing is not structured or surrounded by it.

If you understand that,
you see that right ultimately returns to wrong.

Carefully examine all the words of the scriptures:
Who knows can pursue.

14. Deep and Wonderful

Laozi said:
Words of Dao are deep and wonderful;
precepts and scriptures are similarly esoteric.
Heaven, Earth, and all beings are born from the One.

If you understand that,
you know the difference between emptiness and reality.
If you don't understand that,
you look at it and see no difference.

As long as your will is fixed on existence,
your nonaction is ailing.
You are entangled by existence
and have endless years without end.

Words of Dao are subtle and deep;
while you haven't understood them,

just try to grasp their basic meaning
and observe the precepts without fail.

First lessen all desires;
then never let your intention run loose.
Leisurely stay in a tranquil place;
practice meditation in a quiet chamber.

The cinnabar scriptures of ten thousand scrolls
are not as good as guarding the One.
Yet, the scriptures are not irrelevant;
they do after all contain reality and emptiness.

Whenever they speak of being,
there is always also nonbeing,
but you cannot as yet distinguish this.

Whenever they speak of nonbeing,
there is always also being,
but you cannot as yet decide on that.

Therefore,
just practice according to instructions,
coming and going with the rhythm of the world.

Teachings in the name of Dao
can be true or bogus,
just as fortune can be good and bad.

There are public and private situations of shame:
who understands this can see the delicate dividing line.

Why divine the past and foresee the future?
Better to just remain simple.

37. Good and Evil

Laozi said:
Whether one of the hundred families does anything good,
I don't know.
Whether one of the hundred families does anything evil,
I don't know.
Whether anybody practices loyalty or good faith,

I don't know.
Accumulate goodness
and good *qi* will come to you.
Accumulate evil
and evil *qi* will come to you.

Thus the sage says:
I embrace the beginning of the world,
preserve the mother of the world.
The more the myriad beings follow this,
the more they strengthen the life of their selves.

My thinking is always free from knowledge;
how would I ever know
whether one or the other action is good or evil?

By accumulating goodness,
the spirit light helps perfection.
The Dao of Heaven is supported only by good people.

Serene Intention

Laozi said:
My Dao means utter serenity.
When the intention dies,
tranquility is born
and life is recovered.

More and more life gradually immerses me,
all excitement and agitation are stopped completely.

I am full of the undifferentiated source of Dao,
enveloped by primordial *qi*.
Its root is increasingly deepened.

The four limbs are stiff;
There is no-mind within.
I reach the innermost flourishing of the myriad beings,
the nonultimate to which all nature returns.

I can do so because
I am empty, free from desires.

Calling the Gods

From *Daode zhenjing xujue* 道德真經序訣 (Introductory Explanation to the Perfect Scripture of Dao and Virtue, S. 75, P. 2370; 5th century)

Begin by burning incense and straightening your robes, then greet the ten directions with three bows each. Concentrate your mind inside and visualize Master Yin [Xi], the Master on the River [Heshang gong], and Laozi, the Great Teacher of the divine law. Then open the text and recite the following in your mind:

> Mysterious, again mysterious,
> the origin of Dao.,
>
> Above,
> virtue joins chaos prime.
> Heaven's truth:
> wonderful, yet how far, alas!
> Coming closer,
> the Great Lord of Niwan.
>
> In my room,
> the Seven Treasures come together,
> doors and windows open of themselves.
>
> Utter in my purity,
> I strive for deeper truth,
> Riding on bright light,
> I ascend the purple sky.
>
> Sun and moon shine to my right and left,
> I go to the immortals, find eternal life.
> All seven ancestors rise, are reborn in heaven,
> The world, how true:
> the gate to virtue and to Dao.

Finish this mental recitation, then click your teeth and swallow the saliva thirty-six times each. Visualize the green dragon to your left, the white tiger to your right, the red bird in front of you, and the dark warrior in your back.

Your feet stand between the eight trigrams, the divine turtle and the thirty-six masters bow to you. In front of you, you see the seventeen stars, your five organs give forth the five *qi*, a network pattern streams across your body.

On three sides you are joined by an attendant, each having a retinue of a thousand carriages and ten thousand horsemen. Eight thousand jade maidens and jade lads of Heaven and Earth stand guard for you.

Then repeat the formula, this time aloud, and begin to recite the five thousand words of the scripture. Conclude by three times grinding your teeth and swallowing the saliva.

Scriptural Exegesis

From *Heshang gong zhangju* 河上公章句 (Verses and Sayings of the Master on the River, DZ 682), chs. 6 and 10. Earlier translation in Erkes 1958. The translation of the original follows the commentary's interpretation. The more common version is added in brackets.

Chapter 6: Image Complete

Nourish the spirits and you will not die. [The spirit of the valley does not die.]

"Valley" means "nourish." If one can nourish the spirits, one does not die. The "spirits" are the spirits of the five organs. The spirit soul in the liver, the material soul in the lungs, the spirit in the heart, the intention in the spleen, and the essence in the kidneys. If the five organs are exhausted or harmed, the five spirits will leave and one dies.

This is called the mysterious and the female. [t is called the mysterious female.]

This means that the Dao of no-death lies in the mysterious and the female. The mysterious is heaven; in the human body it is the nose. The female is earth; in the human body it is the mouth.

Heaven feeds people with the five *qi*, which enter the organs through the nose and settle in the heart. The five *qi* are pure and subtle, they cause people to have sentience and spirituality, intelligence and perception, sound and voice, as well as the five kinds of inner nature.

They are represented in the spirit soul, which is male and leaves and enters the human body through the nose in order to interact with heaven. Therefore, the nose is the mysterious.

Earth feeds people with the five tastes, which enter the organs through the mouth and settle in the stomach. The five tastes are turbid and heavy, they cause people to have body and skeleton, bones and flesh, blood and pulses, and the six kinds of emotional passions. The are represented in the material soul, which is female and leaves and enters the human body through the mouth in order to interact with earth. Therefore the mouth is the female.

The gates of the mysterious and the female are called the root of Heaven and Earth.

"Root" means "prime." This means that the gates of the nose and the mouth are whereby the primordial energy that pervades Heaven and Earth comes and goes.

It goes on forever. [Endless flow of inexhaustible energy.]

Breathe through nose and mouth softly or hard. In either case, do so without interruption and very subtly, hardly knowing whether the breath is coming or going, is there or not there.

Use it and never be strained. [Use it, and it will never be exhausted.]

In using the breath you should be open and relaxed, never rushing or straining.

Chapter 10: Can You?

Sustaining vital energy and the material soul, and thereby embracing the One, can you prevent it from leaving? [Can you balance your life force and embrace the One without separation?]

"Vital energy and material soul" is the same as "spirit and material souls." People sustain the two kinds of souls and thereby obtain life. They should love and nurture them, realizing that joy and hatred cause the spirit soul to vanish while haste and alarm make the material soul leave. The spirit soul resides in the liver, the material soul in the lungs. Indulging in wine and sweet delicacies harms the liver and lungs. Instead people should keep the spirit soul tranquil so that their will can be set on the Dao, and they will be free from trouble. They should maintain the material soul in a state of peace so that they attain long life and can extend their years.

The second part means that if one can embrace the One and cause it never to leave from the body, one will live forever. The one is the first product of Dao and Virtue, the essential energy of Great Harmony. Therefore it is called the One. The One pervades everything in the world. Heaven attains it to become clear; Earth attain it to become solid; princes and kings attain it to become upright and just. Entering people, it forms their mind; emerging from people, it forms their activities; spreading through people, it forms their virtue. All this is simply called the One. What it ultimately means in practice is that one makes the will one and not two.

Concentrating on the breath and attaining softness, can you be like an infant? [Can you control your breath, quietly, like a baby?]

Concentrating firmly on essence and breath without letting it be disturbed, your whole physical being will adapt to it and become soft and pliant. On the inside be without yearnings and worries, on the outside without ambitions and affairs: then the spirits will not leave.

Purifying and cleansing your mysterious perception, can you be without error? [Can you clarify your dark vision without blemish?]

You should purify your mind and make it clean and pure. With the mind resting in mysterious union, perception can know everything. Therefore the text speaks of mysterious perception.

Then you will be free from lasciviousness and wrongdoing.

Nurturing the people, governing the country, can you be without action? [Can you love the people and govern the country without action?]

Regulating the body means nurturing energy and breath; this will make the body whole. Governing the country means nurturing the people; this will put the land at peace.

Regulating the body means inhaling and exhaling essence and breath without allowing the ears to hear it. Governing the country means spreading virtue and compassion without letting the people know it.

As the Gate of Heaven opens and shuts, can you be like the female? [Can you open and close the Gate of Heaven without clinging to earth?]

The Gate of Heaven is the constellation Purple Tenuity in the North Culmen. It opens and shuts, begins and ends in accordance with the five phases. In regulating the body, the Gate of Heaven is the nostrils. To open it, breathe hard; to shut, it breathe softly.

In regulating the body, you should be like the female, quiet and tranquil, soft and weak. In governing the country, you should be in accordance with the world's transformations and never take the lead.

Brightly penetrating the four quarters, can you be without knowledge? [Can you brighten the four directions without knowledge?]

This means that Dao is as bright as the sun and the moon, penetrates all directions, and fills the world even beyond its eight ultimate poles. Therefore it is said: "Look for it and do not see it; listen for it and do not hear it." Manifest everywhere in the ten directions, it is radiant and shines brilliantly. Yet nobody knows how Dao fills the world.

It generates and nurtures them. [Give birth and cultivate.]

Dao gives birth to the myriad beings and nurtures them.

It generates but does not possess. [Give birth and do not possess.]

Dao gives birth to the myriad beings but it does not take possession of them.

It acts but does not depend on them. [Act without dependence.]

Dao acts widely everywhere but never depends on or expects any reward.

It raises them but does not control them. [Excel but do not rule.]

Dao raises and nurtures the myriad beings but it does not control them or hold them back, thereby turning them into mere tools.

This is called mysterious virtue.

This means that Dao and its virtue in their mysterious union cannot be seen, yet wish to make people know Dao.

Chapter Ten

The Self

The self in the Confucian tradition is an integrated whole, consisting of body and mind working closely together and largely controlled by the conscious mind. Realization of the self in an experience of awakening is therefore a meditative state of thought-observation that culminates in a conscious awareness of self and surroundings. Inner harmony is found through the raising of consciousness, through the intensification and expansion of the conscious self.

In Daoism, on the contrary, there is no such integrated self, and the conscious mind plays a much lesser role. Here the body is predominant, but even that is not one integrated organism but a network of palaces and passages where various gods and demons make their home—determining the individual's character, disposition, and chances of realization.

The divine residents number in the thousands, but their most important representatives tend to be located in the three energy centers (cinnabar or elixir fields) of the body, in the head, chest, and abdomen. Here are the three worms, demon-parasites that make people indulge in sensory pleasures, cause them sickness, distress, and death, and also the three Perfected Ones, pure gods of Dao who raise people to the state of the immortals.

Mystical practice means to see the self as determined by these divine forces, then take measures to expel the three worms and entice the three Perfected Ones to stay. Realization is not the conscious awareness of self and surroundings but the complete transformation of the body into an abode of the celestials, the self into a heavenly hall.

Souls and Demons

From *Chu sanshi baosheng jing* 出三尸保生經 (Scripture on Preserving Life by Removing the Three Worms, DZ 871, dat. 9th. c.), 1b-2b, 7a-8b.

The three spirit souls are located beneath the liver. They look like human beings and wear green robes with yellow inner garments. Every month on the third, thirteenth, and twenty-third, they leave the body at night to go wandering about.

At this time, lie down with your feet up, your head supported by a pillow, and your legs stretched out straight. Fold your hands over your heart, close your eyes, and hold your breath. Clap your teeth three times. Now visualize a red energy in your heart about the size of an egg. It emerges from the heart and rises into the throat, from where it spreads a wondrous radiance that envelopes your entire body to grow into a glowing fire all around it. You should feel the body getting quite warm. At that point, call out their names:

> Spirit Guidance—come to succor me!
> Inner Radiance—come to nurture me!
> Dark Essence—come to protect my life!
> Swiftly, swiftly, in accordance with the statutes and ordinances!

The Seven Material Souls

If you do this, the three spirit souls will be at peace. Disasters cannot arise and all nasty specters will be subdued. Your body calm, Dao will be perfected, and you will be forever free from suffering and toil.

The seven material souls consist of the energy of yin and of evil. They are basically demons. They can make a person commit deadly evils, be stingy and greedy, jealous and full of envy. They give people bad dreams and make them clench their teeth, incite them to say "yes" when they think "no."

Their names are: Corpse Dog, Arrow in Ambush, Bird Darkness, Devouring Robber, Flying Poison, Massive Pollution, and Stinky Lungs. They cause people to lose their vital essence in sexual passion and get dissipated by hankering after luxury and ease. Through them, people will completely lose all original purity and simplicity.

Exerting demonic influences on the mind, their deepest motivation is to diminish living beings. Dark and shadowy, full of destructive poison, their reason for being is only to harm people. They constantly lead people astray from the road of perfection and light and make them enter into the realm of confusion and darkness. They cherish evil and have no patience for the good, work toward death and have no concern for life.

They encourage people to give free rein to egoistic cravings and indulge in the turbid pleasures of the sense, making them rot and their vital energy leak out. Thus they cause people's speedy demise in the hope to feed on their ancestral sacrifices. Only by refining inherent primordial energy into cinnabar and by keeping the essence of perfection well contained within, can one make yang dominant and yin dissolve and be free from their harm.

To this end, every night at bedtime, recite the following incantation:

> Holding the numinous seals
> of the Three Sovereigns and the Great Ultimate,
> I swallow cinnabar and nourish on energy,
> Expelling all that is not auspicious!
> Swiftly, swiftly:
> in accordance with the statutes and ordinances!

Doing thus, your sleep will be peaceful and secure, and your body will stay healthy and strong. No specters, wiles, disasters, or nasty currents will dare to come close.

In addition, there are three demonic worms in the human body:

The Three Worms

The upper worm is called Peng Ju, also known as Shouter. He sits in the head and attacks the cinnabar field in the Niwan Palace. He causes people's heads to be heavy, their eyesight blurred, their tears cold. He makes mucus assemble in their noses and their ears go deaf. Because of him, people's teeth fall out, their mouths rot, and their faces shrink in wrinkles. He deludes people so that they desire carriages and horses, crave for fancy sounds and sights, and glower over evil and filth. Together with the Green Worm, he bores holes to rot people's perfected primordial energy. He causes their bodies to be bent, their hair to turn white, and their lives to be short. He makes them deluded and drowsy, then goes off to record their sins, reporting their names to the celestial officers of Highest Prime. . . .

The middle worm is called Peng Zhi, also known as Maker. He enjoys deluding people with the five tastes and makes them greedy for the five colors. He lives in the human heart and stomach and attacks the Scarlet Palace and the Central Heater. He causes people's minds to be confused and forgetful, so that they are full of troubles, dry in saliva and low in energy, follow evil and see things upside-down, go wild with depression and burn up with vexation. He makes their mouths dry and their eyes white, drills cavities into their teeth and wreaks havoc with them day and night.

Because of him, people's five organs and six intestines are beleaguered with disease, their sleep is plagued by nightmares, and they have dreams of intercourse with demons that robs them of their vital essence. Their urine in tinged with blood, they have nocturnal emissions, vomit frequently, and often cough up phlegm. They hear a buzzing in their ears and sweat for no apparent reason, being confused and flustered by all sorts of affairs.

In addition, he makes people's vision murky and dim in broad daylight, then gives them scary nightmares in the depth of night—terrifying them into an early death with the hope to gorge himself on their ancestral sacrifices. . . .

The lower worm is called Peng Qiao, also known as Junior. He lives in people's stomachs and legs and attacks the lower parts of the body. He makes energy leak from the Ocean of Energy and thereby invites a multiplicity of ills. Attracting the robbers of human intention, he makes people hanker after women and sex.

Vigorously encouraging their dissipation and lust, he makes people empty of energy and exhausted through their attachment to things. There is no stopping or catching him. He makes people interact with demons at night, when they let their vital essence flow out, thus turning their backs on life and embracing death.

Physically he makes people's bone marrow wither, their muscles stiff, their flesh shrivel, their thinking tired, their bodies empty of energy, and their hips heavy. Because of him, people have no strength in their thighs and knees and feel a constant urge to pass water. Getting every fuller of pathogenic energy, they gradually develop a serious disease. Even suffering from the five exertions and seven injuries [see p. 12 above], they remain deluded and confused, full of defilements and attachments.

Body Gods

From *Huangting waijing jing* 黃庭外景經 (Outer Radiance Scripture of the Yellow Court, DZ 263), verses 3-15, including commentaries by Liang Qiuzi 梁丘子 in *Xiuzhen shishu* 修真十書 58 (DZ 263; 4.869-78) and Wuchengzi 吳成子 in *Yunji qiqian* 12. For related materials, see Kroll 1996.

Above there is the Yellow Court; below, the Primordial Pass.

The Yellow Court is in the head. It encompasses three palaces known as the Hall of Light, the Grotto Chamber, and the Elixir Field. Enter between the eyebrows toward the back of the head. After one inch, there is the Hall of Light; after two inches, there is the Grotto Chamber; after three inches, there is the Elixir Field. These three constitute the Upper Prime.

The Yellow Court is paired with the Grotto Chamber. Together they bring forth an infant god, who is their resident perfected. Always visualize him! Be careful not to lose the image.

The infant turns into a perfected in the Hall of Light. Then he is called Master Elixir. Here, to know the perfected means to concentrate on the Hall of Light as its residence.

Practice breathing and daoyin, close your eyes and turn your vision inward, calm your mind and concentrate your thoughts. Merge with chaos in the limitless! Let essence revert upward and circulate in the Niwan [Elixir Field]. This will bring about the Perfected Master Cinnabar.

In the Hall of Light, the infant and the Master are a like lord and minister. Further behind, in the Grotto Chamber, they are like father and mother. In the Elixir Field, they are like husband and wife.

According to another explanation, the Yellow Court is the spleen. It is located one inch above the Great Storehouse [stomach in the abdomen, about three inches above the navel]. The spleen is the seat of the God of the Center, the Yellow Lord Lao. He rules from here.

The Primordial Pass is three inches below the navel. The Gate of Primordial Yang is suspended before it. When essence here is completely clear, it reflects the entire body. Never slacken in your practice of this Dao.

* * *

The Yellow Court is the eyes. The father and mother of the Dao both nourish the immortal embryo. On the left, there is the Numinous Yang, also known as Splendor Brightness. On the right, there is Great Yin, also known as Mystery Radiance. All three together build the right virtue, they support each other as they develop.

Behind there are the Dark Towers; in front, the Gate of Life.

The Dark Towers are the kidneys. Like overturned cups standing on their rims, they are three inches off the navel, big on top and small below. They contain another universe, with their own sun and moon. The Gate of Life is below the navel.

* * *

The Dark Towers are the kidneys. They are related to the eyes through the qi circuits. The Gate of Life is the navel. It is about three inches in size. When the sun rises and the moon sets, yin and yang are balanced. Breathe the primordial breath in and out to nourish the numinous root.

Breathe in and out and through the stove; qi enters the Elixir Field.

To breathe out means to expel the breath; to breathe in means to draw it in. The stove is the nose. This is the essential method to expel the old and draw in the new. The vital qi then enters between the eyebrows and after three inches reaches the Elixir Field in the head. Thus one draws in the breath through the nose and enters it into the Elixir Field.

* * *

Breathing out is expelling; breathing in is drawing in. Through respiration the primordial breath can enter the Elixir Field. The Elixir Field is three inches below the navel, the gate of yin and yang. This is where ordinary people produce offspring. Daoist use it to preserve their lives.

The clear fluid in the Jade Pond waters the Numinous Root.

"Clear fluid in the Jade Pond" refers to the mouth where the saliva assembles. The Numinous Root is the tongue. One should always keep the teeth together, rinse with saliva, and accumulate it to water the tongue.

* * *

The mouth is the Jade Pond, the Palace of Great Harmony. The saliva is the clear fluid, always beautiful and fresh. Saliva collected in the throat makes the sound of thunder and lightning. The tongue is the Numinous Root. Always keep it well watered.

All can practice this, all can live long.

Practice this day morning and night without slackening. Then you can attain long life.

* * *

By practicing this day and night, one will subdue the deadly forces, kill the Tree Corpses and expel all evil demons. Body and flesh will blossom; the true qi will return. When all evils have lost their power, one will live long and radiate a brilliance.

The gods of the Yellow Court wear red robes.

Concentrate and visualize mother and child in the spleen. See how they enter the spleen from the stomach, wearing red.

* * *

The tiny pupils in the eyes are a couple. The right is the king, the left is the queen. Wearing red garments, the proceed to a banquet in the palace at the rear of the Elixir Field. Visualize them morning and night, never relax your effort!

The Pass Gate has a strong lock; keep its doors in place.

The gate of the lower Elixir Field has to be locked. Don't open it wantonly.

* * *

Close your eyes and look inside. There is nothing that is not seen. Close your mouth and curl your tongue. This is feeding on the mother. Keep the jade flower in the throat. You will never suffer any trouble. All this is due to qi. The teeth are the doors, the tongue is the lock that keeps them in place.

The Dark Towers communicate with loftiness and eminence above.

The kidneys are located at the gate of the Dark Towers, i.e., the building of the Earth Administration. They are the storehouse of vital qi. Above they are connected with the ears. The ears are on the sides of the head, they are lofty and eminent.

* * *

Dao knows of three primordial points where compassionate intention arises. The lower of these is the steadiness of the mysterious spring in the Dark Towers [testicles]. The middle one is the pair of Dark Towers of the kidneys. The upper one is the pair of Dark Towers of the ears. The latter watch over the Golden Gate and the Jade Entrance. They also communicate with Heaven, in the same way as Lady Jiao plays the zither and the flute, holding and suppressing the notes *gong* and *shang*.

In the Elixir Field, essence and qi are subtle.

The Elixir Field is located three inches beneath the navel. It is about three square inches in size. Its qi is subtle and wondrous. Visualize it, and it is there; forget about it, and it is gone. It changes and disappears. Thus we say it is subtle.

* * *

The Elixir Field is the first chamber, opposite the Hall of Light. Its essence and *qi* are subtle and hard to distinguish. Thus we say it is subtle.

The Jade Pond with its clear fluid develops opulence.

The Jade Pond is the mouth. The clear fluid is the saliva as it accumulates there. "Develop opulence" means that saliva is collected at the root of the tongue like a pond. Thus it is opulent.

* * *

In the mouth, there is saliva. It rests and moves. Only when collected on the tongue, in its white kind, is it rich and greasy like fat. Rinse with it and maintain it fresh: This is the way to long life.

The Numinous Root is stiff and strong—grow old but never weak.

The Numinous Root is the tongue. Always keep it rolled up and the teeth strongly together. During the practice never let the tongue get tired or dry. Always visualizes its god, and you will live long but never grow weak.

* * *

The Numinous Root is the tongue. It governs the four directions and harmonizes the five tastes. It expels stench and invites fragrance. Bite the teeth together and preserve your qi, thus you can live by swallowing saliva.

In the Middle Pond, a deity resides, clad in red.

Constantly visualize the infant in the heart. He is clad in red garments, finely ornamented, and resides in the middle Elixir Field. All exhaustion and bad fortune, all sloth and agitation, through him are made to go.

* * *

Ruojing in the throat is the god of the Prime. Beneath middle harmony, the towers show the partition of the way. With his reddish glowing dress, this god becomes a friend.

Three inches below the Field is where the gods reside.

This refers to the spleen, situated in the abdomen. Beneath the upper burner is the Numinous Root of the navel. This is where the gods reside.

* * *

The palace of the Hall of Light is three square inches in size. The gods reside in the very center of the eye. The eyebrows are their flowery canopies; the five colors are their couches.

The Cosmic Self

From *Huming jing* 護命經 (Scripture of Protecting Life, DZ 632, dat. ca. 1120).

Sovereign Heaven brings me forth
Sovereign Earth raises me
Sun and moon irradiate me
Stars and planets shine on me

All immortals assist me
The Ruler of Fates champions me
The Great One joins me
The Jade Star calls on me

The Three Offices protect me
The Five Emperors guard me
The Northern Polestar joins me
The Southern Culmen upholds me
The Northern Dipper helps me
The Three Terraces assist me

Golden Lads come to serve me
Jade Maidens hasten to obey me
The Six Jia gods guide me
The Six Ding gods escort me

The gate of Heaven opens for me
The door of Earth lets me through
Mountains and marshes allow me in
Rivers and streams let me pass

Wind and rain accompany me
Thunder and lightning follow me
The Eight Trigrams honor me
The Nine Palaces shield me

Yin and yang venerate me
The five phases tally with me
The four seasons complete me
The life star perfects me—

The mysterious ledgers of Great Clarity
Rise and fall between the Three Offices,
Up and down, back and forth,
Without end, without break.

The food of gold and juice of jade,
Once looked for, is found with ease.
In void Brahman, before the sun and moon,
I swear a pledge with heaven.

Oh, sacred Huan, Piao, Xing, Kui, Bi, Shuo, Fu—
Stars of the Dipper:
Whatever I seek shall be attained!
Whatever I turn to shall find success!
Whatever I do shall be in harmony!
Whatever I wish shall come to pass!

Through changes and transformations of all kinds,
I shall join Dao in harmonious perfection
What spirit would not come to serve me?
What command of mine would not be obeyed?

Before me is the red bird,
Behind me the dark warrior,
To my left, the green dragon,
To my right, the white tiger.

Above me hangs the Flowery Canopy,
Below I step on the Kui Star of the Dipper.
The divine Dao illuminates all,
Its majesty banning evil in the ten directions.

All who love me shall live in peace,
All who hate me shall meet with disaster!
All who plot against me shall die,
All who detest me shall perish!

Numinous lads and spirit maidens—
Destroy all evil with your diamond bolts!
All three thousand six hundred of you,
Always remain by my side!

Raising banners, holding talismans,
You go everywhere with me!
As the Highest Lord protects the capital,
So Heaven grants gives me good fortune everywhere.

Entered in the golden register and jade ledgers,
And equipped with the twenty-four talismans,
May I match the cycle of the stars!

Swiftly, swiftly, in accordance with the statutes and ordinances!

Chapter Eleven

Training

In accordance with their overall orientation toward society and the celestial, Confucianism and Daoism differ in their mystical training. To become a Confucian master, one needs to develop and perfect social virtues, such as humanity, righteousness, propriety, and wisdom, to live a life of harmony and social goodness, serving to perfect the principle of the Great Ultimate in the world.

In Daoism, the goal is otherworldly, and one accordingly leaves the world behind as a monk or nun, wanders through the country without firm home or position and lives in simple thatched huts instead of solid houses. One studies the scriptures for inspiration, concocts medicines for health and long life, and spends one's time in deep meditation. The training lies more in person-centered cultivation than society-centered goodness, final attainment being more an inner state of celestial nature than a life of social harmony.

The techniques applied to reach mystical oneness range from exercise, breathing, and guiding of *qi* to an extensive variety of meditations: the observation of different colored light in the body that illuminate and strengthen the energies and spiritual presence of the organs; the visualization of celestial gods or goddesses and becoming one with them through absorption or sexual union; and the concoction of an alchemical elixir from inner-bodily fluids and energies that is mythologized as the mating of dragon and tiger, yin-girl and yang-boy. In all cases, the Daoist methods emphasize the celestial nature of self and realization, guiding the adept to a more cosmic state of being.

Spiritual Radiance

From *Xiwangmu baoshen qiju jing* 西王母保身起居經 (The Queen Mother's Scripture on Treasuring the Spirit When Rising and Resting, DZ 1319, dat. 4th c.).

The *Taisu danjing jing* 台素丹景經 (Great Simplicity Scripture on Cinnabar Radiance) says: Rub both hands together to generate *qi* and heat, then rub your face with them. This opens the body and lets people look radiant and glossy. It prevents wrinkles and discolorations. Over five years you will gain a complexion like a young girl.

The *Danjing jing* says: Rub both hands together to generate heat, then rub your face and eyes. [6a] Guide the hands to stroke the hair like grooming or combing it, also crossing the arms and using the hands on opposite sides. This will prevent the hair from getting white.

The chapter on "Essential Radiance Massage" in the *Dadong zhenjing* 大洞真經 (Perfect Scripture of Great Pervasion) says: When you get up in the morning, always steady your breath and sit up straight, then interlace the fingers and massage the nape of your neck. Next, lift the face and look up, press the hands against the neck while moving the head back. Do this three or four times, then stop. This will cause essence to be in harmony, the blood to flow well, and prevent the entering of wind or bad *qi*. Over a long time it will keep you free from disease and death.

> Next:
> bend and straighten the body;
> extend the hands in the four directions;
> bend backward and stretch out the sides;
> shake out the hundred joints.
> Do each of these three times.

Also, when first getting up, take a cloth and rub the forehead, the four sides of the head, and the area behind the ears. Let all these places get warm and moist. Then stroke the hair like grooming it and, finally, massage the face and eyes. [6b] This makes people's eyes bright and prevents wayward *qi* from arising. Also, the body will never be dirty or defiled. At the end of the practice, swallow the saliva thirty times to guide the inner fluids.

The *Xiwang mu fantai anmo yujing* 西王母反胎按摩玉經 (Queen Mother's Jade Scripture on Massages for Returning to the Womb) says: The main aspect of long life is the cultivation of eyes and ears. If you keep seeing mixed things, your eyes will darken; if you keep listening to things widely, your ears will close up. These are diseases that come from the inside of the body and are not unwanted guests brought in from without.

People say how hard it is to hear of Dao. But is not hard to hear or Dao, it is only hard to practice it. No, it is not hard to practice Dao, it is only hard to follow through with it.

If the eyes and ears are disturbed and confused, your imagination cannot let go of difficulties and problems, then, even if your feet step into an immortals' pavilion and your hands take hold of a dragon's porch, it will do no good.

Rather, practice the massage. To do so, always pick yang days. The first of the month is a yang day; the second is a yin day. [7a] Every day, in the morning and evening, close your eyes, face your birth direction, then rub the hands to generate heat and rub the eyes to the right and left, as well as the ears under the opening. Brush the hands back to the center of the next. Repeat nine times. Now, visualize a cloudy vapor in the eyes in three colors: purple, red, and yellow. Each sinks down and enters the ears. After a long time, recite the following incantation:

> Oh, Eye Lads of the Three Clouds,
> Perfected Lords of Both Eyes:
> Be radiant and light in bringing forth essence,
> Open and pervasive as imperial gods.
>
> Oh, Great Mystery of Cloudy Righteousness,
> Jade Numen of the Expanded Chapters:
> Preserve and enhance my two towers [ears],
> Open and spread my nine gates [orifices].
>
> Let my hundred joints respond and echo
> And my various fluids return to the Niwan Palace.
> Allow my body to ascend to the jade palaces above
> And let me rank among the highest perfected.

After concluding this incantation, swallow the saliva three times. This concludes it. You may now open your eyes.

Practice like this on every day in the morning. There is no need to also do it in the evening. If you continue to do this for three years, your ears will be keen and your eyes bright.

[7b] Also, when you groom your hair, do so facing your birth direction. Then chant the following incantation:

> To the Great Emperors spreading numen,
> Five Elders reverting spirit,
> The gods Niwan and Xuanhua:
> Preserve my essence and let me live long.
>
> As my left holds the shadow of the moon
> And my right pulls the root of the sun,
> May my six harmonies become clear and pure
> And the hundred deities deliver their grace. . . .

[8b] Also, in sitting and sleeping, always have your nostrils face your birth direction. Do it also when eating and drinking. If you cannot face your birth direction, use the northeast or northwest. They are also good, because they are the gates and passages of the spirit and material souls.

Also, when rising from sleep, always begin by rocking the body to the right and left and by rotating the neck, each twelve times. After this, sit up straight and raise both hands to support heaven. Hold this for a while, then use your palms to massage your cheeks up to the ears. Do this for some time, then chant:

> As I roll forwards and point backwards,
> Let me become the honored guest of the Heavenly Emperor.
> As I rub my left ear and right cheek,
> Let me life long and reach great transcendence.
> As I raise my head and swallow my qi,
> Let the Great One reach its ultimate.
> As I bend into a hanging moon or dragon form,
> Let the Ruler of Fates climb in his carriage. [8b]
> As I drink and eat the embryonic prime,
> Let the Double Towers of Kunlun appear.
> As I bend and drop to both knees,
> Let the Perfected join my will.

After this incantation, inhale deeply and hold the breath. Visualize a red energy ball, red and silky, in your navel. Allow it to emerge from the navel and enter into your nostrils. Repeat this three times. Doing this concludes the sequence of self-massages. It allows people's hundred passes to be open and flourishing and helps them live long without getting sick.

You can also visualize a purple energy in the center. To do so every day, close your eyes and lie down to rest your body and calm your breath. Lie as if asleep, so that other people won't even know you're not sleeping. Then in inner vision reach out to the four directions. Let your eyes and ears penetrate beyond ten thousand *li* [miles]. If you do this for a long time, you can even see yourself as far out as ten thousand *li*. If done powerfully, using essence and mind, you can even see as far as a million *li*. Doing this, you will always hear the music of gold and jade in your ears together with the soft rustling of leafy bamboo. It is wondrous indeed.

The Five Sprouts

From *Fuqi jingyi lun* 服氣精義論 (How to Absorb *Qi* and Refine Integrity, YJQQ 57; DZ 277, 830; dat. 730s). German translation in Engelhardt 1987.

[2b] What makes the body complete is being rooted in the organs and lungs. What keeps the spirit at peace is being focused on essence and *qi*. Although the body is equipped with the spirits of the five directions, once their images are set, the bone structure begins to decline and the *qi* gets less. This leads to a general state of decay.

Thus ingest cloudy sprouts to enrich the body fluids and inhale misty radiances to nurture your inner numen. It will help your protective and defensive *qi* to preserve their purity and harmony; and assist your appearance and complexion in driving off all withering and fading. As you practice this over a long period, you can match the wondrous [Dao] and accumulate [positive] responses. Your spirit begins to flow freely and you can join the Five Elders [of the five directions]. You may even ascend to the nine [kinds of] perfected and be ranked among them. Records in the classical texts describe how to view the fluid pathways [in the body] and what to pay most attention to in cultivation studies. They set things out most suitably and in great detail.

[3a] Each day at dawn recite the following secret incantation:

Green Sprout of the East:
Be absorbed to feed my [internal] green sprout [liver].
I drink you through the Morning Flower [root of upper teeth].

The incantation said, pass your tongue along the outside of the upper teeth, lick your lips, rinse your mouth by filling it [with saliva], and swallow. Do this three times.

VermilionCinnabar of the South:
Be absorbed to feed my [internal] vermilion cinnabar [heart].
I drink you through the Cinnabar Lake [root of lower teeth].

The incantation said, pass your tongue along the outside of the lower teeth, lick your lips, rinse your mouth by filling it [with saliva], and swallow. Do this three times.

Lofty Great Mountain of the Central Wusi Position:
Be absorbed to feed my [internal] essence and qi.
I drink you through the Sweet Spring [root of the molars].

The incantation said, pass your tongue over the back of the throat to pick up the Jade Spring, lick your lips, rinse your mouth by filling it [with saliva], and swallow. Do this three times.

Radiant Stone of the West:
Be absorbed to feed my [internal] radiant stone [lungs].
I drink you through the Numinous Liquid [saliva inside the lips].

[3b] The incantation said, pass your tongue over the inside of the upper teeth, lick your lips, rinse your mouth by filling it [with saliva], and swallow. Do this three times.

Mysterious Sap of the North:
Be absorbed to feed my [internal] mysterious sap [kidneys].
I drink you through the Jade Sweetness [saliva on tongue].

The incantation said, pass your tongue over the inner side of the lower teeth, lick your lips, rinse your mouth by filling it [with saliva], and swallow. Do this three times.

When the requisite number of times is reached, inhale through the nose to fullness, then release the breath slowly. Do this five times or more, and the perfect Dao will be accomplished.

According to Master Yi, the incantation to the Sweet Spring runs:

> White stones craggy, hard to cross,
> Deep spring gushing, pure Jade Broth,
> Drink it, live long,
> Extend your destiny far out.

This reflects the method of the five talismans of Numinous Treasure. In the scriptures of Highest Clarity, there is yet another recipe, that of the cloudy sprouts of the Four Ultimates. The method is holy and secret. Do not transmit it lightly.

[4a] Whenever you absorb *qi,* first practice the five sprouts to open the five organs. Then use the following common correspondences for the best results.

The east is green, flows in the liver, opens the eye orifice, and matches the body's meridians.

The south is red, flows in the heart, opens the tongue orifice, and matches the body's blood.

The center is yellow, flows in the spleen, opens the mouth orifice, and matches the flesh.

The west is white, flows in the lungs, opens the nose, and matches the body's skin.

The north is black, flows in the kidneys, opens the ear orifice, and matches the body's bones.

Within this system, the lungs are the flowery canopy [overall shield] of the five organs. They come first because they are located above the heart and facing the chest. They have six leaves, and their color is like silk, shiny pink. The lung meridian, moreover, issues at the point High-Low [Gaoshao]—located at the inside tip of the index finger of the left hand, in the low spot about two millimeters from the nail.

[4b] The heart is located beneath the lungs and above the liver. It matches the area one inch below the pigeon tail. Its color is like silk, shiny red. The heart meridian issues at the point Central Balance [Zhongheng] at the inside tip of the middle finger of the left hand, right at the low spot about two millimeters from the nail.

The liver is located beneath the heart and behind the small of the back. It has four leaves on the right and three leaves on the left. Its color is like silk, shiny violet. The liver meridian begins at the point Great Growth [Dadun]—located on the third knuckle of the big toe of the left foot.

The spleen rests above the navel, positioned horizontally closely next to it, and is covered by the belly. Its color is like silk, shiny yellow. The spleen meridian begins at the point Hidden Whiteness [Yinbai]—located at the tip of the big toe of the left foot, on the corner of the nail, like the tip of a scallion leaf.

The left and right kidneys face the navel area in front and rest on the pelvis. Their color is like silk, shiny purple. The left kidney is known as Kidney Proper [Zhengshen]; it corresponds to the five organs. The right kidney is known as Gate of Life [Mingmen]; it is where males store their semen and where females become pregnant. The kidney meridian, moreover, issues from the point Gushing Spring [Yongquan]—located at the central indentation in the middle of the left foot.

[5a] Whenever you wish to absorb the *qi* of the five sprouts, always meditate on them entering your organs and allow their fluid to spread and flow freely, each according to the organ over which it presides. You can also circulate the sprounts through the entire body and thereby cure all sorts of diseases. For example: To absorb the green sprout, meditate on its *qi* entering the liver, then envision the green *qi* inside it as bountiful and life-giving while you see its green fluid as blending and permeating the organ. Keep your attention there for a long time, then move on to envison the *qi* in the Great Growth point on the foot and through further circulation and absorption allow it to reach into the liver meridian, from wehre it can flow through all the channels of the body, reaching up even as far as the eyes. Like this, absort the *qi* of all five directions.

The best time to do this is after the chou hour [1 a.m.–3 a.m.]. Make sure you wash and rinse properly, don your cap and robe, then enter a separate chamber. Burn incense and kneel upright to face each direction in turn. Calm all thinking and purify the mind. Then, with full attention, carry out the practice.

Internal Alchemy

From *Nei riyong miaojing* 內日用妙經 (Wondrous Scripture of Interior Daily Practice, DZ 645; dat. 12th c.)

Now, as regards daily practice,
Keep your food and drink firmly regulated
And sit alone in silent meditation,
Never allowing even a single thought to arise.
As the ten thousand affairs are all forgotten,
You can concentrate on the spirit and firm up your intention.

Keep the lips close to each other
And the teeth lightly touching.
Your eyes don't see a single thing,
Your ears don't hear a single sound.
Thus your mind is unified and focused within.
Now harmonize your breathing into a regular rhythm,
Let it become subtler and subtler, issuing lightly,
Almost as if it wasn't there at all,
And without even the slightest interruption.

Then naturally
The fire of your heart will sink down
And the water of your kidneys will rise up,
And in the cavern of your mouth
Sweet saliva will arise of itself.
Then the numinous perfected will support your body,
And spontaneously you know the path to eternal life.

During all the twelve double-hours of the day,
Always maintain purity and tranquility.
The numinous terrace [of your heart] is kept free from all affairs: this is purity.
Even a single thought does not arise in your mind: this is tranquility.

The body is the residence of the energy,
The mind is the lodge of the spirit.
When intention stirs, the spirit is agitated;
When the spirit is agitated, the energy disperses.
In the same way

When intention is stable, the spirit remains firm;
When the spirit is firm, the energy gathers together.
The perfected energy of the five phases
Thus gathers together and forms a pinch [of pure stuff].

Then naturally in the body
A sound can be heard stirring. [1b]
Walking, standing, sitting and lying down
Be constantly aware
Of a movement in the body like wind blowing,
Of a rumbling in the stomach like thunder booming.

Eventually harmonious energy penetrates everywhere,
And its essential oil trickles to the top.
Then with ease you can drink from the pure pinch
And your ears will begin to hear the tunes of the immortals.
They are melodies never plucked on strings,
Sounding spontaneously without any clapping,
Reverberating of themselves without any drumming.

Spirit and energy then combine
Like forming a boy child in the womb.
If you can spot them in your interior realm,
Spirit will start speaking to you
From the true residence of emptiness and nonbeing,
Where you can reside at ease with all the sages.

Next, refine the combination in nine transmutations
And you will produce the great [cinnabar] elixir.
You as spirit will leave and enter freely,
And your years will match those of Heaven and of earth.
The sun and moon will join to shine on you,
And you are liberated from all life and death.

Everyday you do not practice this
You lose something of your power.
So, during all twelve double-hours of the day,
Always maintain purity and tranquility.

Energy is the mother of spirit,
Spirit is the son of energy.
Like a chicken hatching an egg,

So you should concentrate on the spirit and nurture your energy—
Then, how can you ever be far from the Wondrous?

Mysterious and again mysterious—
In the human body, there are seven treasures.
Use them to support the state and cherish the people,
Grow them from the fullness of your essence, energy, and blood.

Essence is quicksilver (silver);
Blood is gold (gold);
Energy is jade (lapis lazuli);
Marrow is crystal (crystal);
The brain is numinous sand (agate);
The kidneys are jade rings (rubies);
And the heart is a glittering gem (cornelian).

Keep these seven treasures firmly in your body
Never letting them disperse.
Refine them into the great medicine of life—
And among the ten thousand gods
Ascend to the immortals.

The Inner Elixir

From *Wuzhen pian* 悟真篇 (Awakening to Perfection, DZ 142), 5.2a-17a, by Zhang Boduan 張伯端 (ca. 983-1082). French rendition in Robinet 1995, 244-51.

The inner medicine reverts to join the outer,
And as it opens up, so does the outer.
In the harmony of alchemy, the same types go together,
In warming and nourishing, both are used the same.
Inside, there is true celestial fire,
A radiant inner furnace, ever crimson.
To the outer furnace add and lessen with great care—
No more wondrous effort than finding the true seed.

This path is most spiritual and sagacious
Endangered only by your small endowment, making concoction hard.
Blending lead and mercury is not done in a single morning,
Yet soon the first stings of the mysterious pearl emerge.

A man determined to refine the drug
Cares not to live in village or at court.
To him effort is easy, the medicine not far,
But others, told of it, would merely laugh.

The first showing of the white tiger is most precious:
It's the flowery pond, the spirit water, the true gold.
Knowing this highest good benefits one's deepest source,
Can't be compared to the quest for ordinary medicines.
If you want to cultivate it to the ninth transmutation,
First purity the self and control your mind,
Then collect it just at the right time, keeping it firm in raising and in sinking,
And giving it the right increase of fire—however serious the danger.

The Herdboy and the Weavermaid aspire to be joined,
So do the turtle and the snake, as is their heavenly nature.
The moon-toad and sun-bird, too, mix their beauty at new moon,
While yin and yang sustain each other in continued cycles.
Basically this is the wondrous activity of *Qi* an-Heaven and Kun-Earth;
Whose profound origin no one can understand.
Yin and yang in separation only fall into error—
How could they ever reach the immensity of Heaven and of Earth?

If you want true lead to retain mercury,
Keep near the center and do not leave the house.
When wood and metal are separated,
They cannot come together without a go-between.
Wood, inner nature, loves metal's obedience and righteousness;
Metal, inner passion, loves wood's goodwill and benevolence.
They devour and consume each other, getting very close,
And for the first time the man finds himself pregnant.

The yin girl "two and eight"—where does she belong?
The yang boy "three and nine"—where is his residence?
They call themselves fluid wood and essential metal,
Joining with earth, they form three families.
Then, relying on Lord Ding fire to be refined,
They feel passionate joy as husband and as wife.
Never daring to stop the Chariot of the River,
They are transported to the heights of Kunlun paradise.
The crimson sand, seven times revolved, returns to its root;
The golden fluid, nine times reverted, goes back to its perfection.
Stop relying on temporal division and formal hexagrams,
Just make sure the five phases are in proper order.
At the origin, one pince of mercury,
Flowing everywhere through space and time:
The yin and yang values are complete and easily join spirit
Entering and leaving, so close to the mysterious female.

The male has female substance deep within,
Bearing yin yet embracing the essence of yang.
The two joined in harmony, the medicine is found;
Transforming material and spirit souls to numinosity and sageliness.
Trust in Dao: a grain of golden cinnabar
Swallowed by a snake makes it into a dragon,
Picked up by a chicken makes it into a phoenix
That soars into the clear world of yang perfected.

Once Heaven and Earth go beyond Bi and Tai, the equinoxes' hexagrams,
Once morning and night acknowledge Tun and Meng,
The hexagrams before Qi an and Kun, Heaven and Earth,
The different spokes join at the hub, water returns to source,
And you find its wonder in right addition and subtraction.
Attain the One, and all affairs are done!
No more divisions into the four directions.

Diminish and again diminish, watch over past achievements.
The treasure of life must not be fooled about with.

At the winter solstice, the first yang arrives,
the another every thirty days and through the year.
Within the month, at full moon Fu "return" emerges,
While after new moon *Qi* an "Heaven" is fulfilled and Gou "Meeting" appears
The day, too, is divided into hot and cold,
And yang is born in Fu "Return" just about at midnight,
While the first yin appears in Gou "Meeting" at noon.
So know your times, morning and evening, to refine the perfect medicine.

Without knowing the rhythm of the five phases and four emblems
You can't distinguish cinnabar, mercury, lead, and silver.
Never having heard about cultivating cinnabar and regulating fire,
How can you call yourself a hermit?
Unwilling to ponder your mistakes,
You entice others on erroneous paths
And lead them forever to wrong pass ways—
How can you bear to live with such a cheating heart?

Only after doing more than 800 virtuous deeds,
Accumulating as many as 3,000 hidden merits,
Only through treating others as yourself, enemies as friends,
Can you begin to join the spirit immortals in their true intention.
Then tigers and rhinos, swords and soldiers, can no longer harm you,
The burning house of impermanence cannot constrain you any more.
Then precious talismans descend, and you join the court in heaven,
Softly riding up in a phoenix chariot.

Chapter Twelve

Ethics

The rules that go along with the two types of training bear the differences out in great clarity. Confucian rules, as clearly exemplified in the regulations of Zhu Xi's academy, are socially oriented and emphasize proper relationships, order, politeness, and honesty toward others.

Daoist rules similarly never deny or denigrate the social context. They, too, emphasize that one should not kill, steal, cheat, or in any way harm living beings. Yet they always place the rules in a cosmic context, threatening punishments in hell for any violation, and providing specific instructions against cosmic infringements, such as the prohibition to expose one's naked body to the sky or plot against the Three Treasures: Dao, scriptures, and masters of the religion.

The Cosmic Connection

From *Chisongzi zhongjie jing* 赤松子中戒經 (Essential Precepts of Master Redpine, DZ 185; 4th c.). Earlier translation in Kohn 2004a.

[1a] Xianyuan, the Yellow Emperor, knocked his head to the ground and asked Master Redpine: I have seen the myriad people receive life, but why is it not equal? There are those rich and noble, there are those poor and humble. There are those with a long life, there are those with a short life. Some are met by obstruction and troubles and undergo punishment in the cangue [punishment board]; others again suffer from extended illness and have their bodies all tied up. Some die suddenly without apparent disease, others live a long life with good emoluments. Like this, people are not equal. I pray you, sir, to explain the situation to me.

Master Redpine said:

People coming to life are all in isolation, each depending on one particular star. There are big stars and small, each governing a specific person's longevity and shortness [of life], decline and prosperity, poverty and wealth, death and life. As for those who do good, good *qi* will cover them, good fortune and virtue will follow them, all nasty evils will leave them, the spirits and numinous forces will guard them, other people will have respect for them, and all misfortunes will stay far away from them. As for those who do evil, bad *qi* will cover them, disasters and misfortunes will follow them, all lucky and auspicious signs will avoid them, baleful stars will shine on them, other people will detest them, and all sorts of unpleasant and disastrous affairs will crowd around them.

[1b] Day or night, whatever people do in their actions and minds, all the good and evil they commit, whether they secretly violate the prohibitions and taboos of Heaven and Earth, or give rise to personal blame and the accumulation of sins, is not the same at all. Day or night, whenever people do evil, the body gods and the Director of Fates [Siming] will submit a report to the stars and constellations above. They in turn will effect a subtraction from the sinners' lives, so that the [light] *qi* of Heaven will leave them and the [heavy] *qi* of Earth will cluster around them. This is why they go into decline.

The Yellow Emperor asked: Altogether, how long should a human life expectancy be?

Master Redpine replied:

When people first come to earth, Heaven endows them with a life expectancy of 43,800 days, that is 120 years of life, each of which corresponds to one calendar year. So people originally receive a total life expectancy of 120 years. But if they violate the prohibitions and taboos of Heaven and Earth, certain amounts of time are subtracted from it and it will come to an end.

The Yellow Emperor asked further: On occasion there are those dying while still in the womb or those who only live to see a few years. They have not yet done anything in the world, so what prohibition or taboo could they have violated?

Master Redpine explained:

Things like these happen because the sins of the ancestors and forebears bequeath calamities upon their descendants. Ever since antiquity, heroes and wise men have established a corresponding teaching, which has remained in the books of the immortals. [2a] They all admonish people to do good and to know the very incipience of evil, so that even in ten thousand ages they give nothing but good fortune to their numerous generations of descendants.

Now, human beings live between Heaven and Earth and are endowed with the two *qi* of yin and yang. Sovereign Heaven, although high, yet has its correspondence down below. Mother Earth, although low, yet has its correspondence far above. Heaven does not speak, yet the four seasons move in order. Earth does not speak, yet the myriad beings come to life. People reside right between the two. All their licentious intentions and passionate desires, whatever they do or do not do, Heaven and Earth know all about it. For this reason we say that Heaven has four-sided [all-round] knowledge.

Normally, people never say anything to recompense the grace Heaven and Earth have shown to them; on the contrary, they utter frequent complaints against them. Still, Heaven brings forth people and endows them with the trigrams *Qian* and Kun manifest in their father and mother, with the sun and the moon manifest in their two eyes, with the stars and constellations manifest in their nine orifices, and with the movement of wind and the power of fire manifest in their warm [body] *qi*. Then, when life ends, all these return to the soil.

In addition, Heaven houses the [constellations of the] Three Terraces and the North Culmen as well as the offices of the Director of Fates and the Director of Emoluments. They commonly take the perfected talisman of the Great One and place it on people's heads to examine if they are full of sins. In accordance with their finding, they make a subtraction from the life expectancy.

If the celestials subtract one year, the star [essence] above the person's head loses its luster and he or she runs into lots of difficulties. [2b] If they take off ten years, the star gradually fades and the person encounters disasters, decline, and various diseases. If they subtract twenty years, the star's radiance is reduced significantly and the person runs into legal trouble and is imprisoned. If they take off thirty years, the star dissolves and the person dies. If at this time, the subtractions are not complete and Heaven needs to ruin further years, they will be taken from the person's descendants, sons and grandsons. Should that not be sufficient either, they extend destruction to his married relations and retainers. The latter, of course, have no idea where they went wrong or what they violated; they can only say that they have a reduced life expectancy.

In this way Heaven never cheats on living beings but shows them its inclinations, like a shadow following its object, through day and night, light and darkness, thunder and lightning, rain and snow, intertwining rainbows, eclipses of the sun and the moon, and floating characters of wisdom. All these are signs given by Heaven. Similarly Earth never cheats on living beings but shows them its inclinations, like an echo follows the sound, by making rivers and streams dry up and bringing forth landslides and earthquakes, hurricanes and tornadoes, sandstorms and moving stones, floods and locust plagues, famines and droughts, epidemics and other disasters. All these are signs given by Earth.

[3a] The demons and spirits cheat on living beings either. They show them their inclinations through good and bad fortune, strange omens and auspicious signs. These are the signs given by demons and spirits. Nor does the ruler cheat on living beings. Rather, shows them his good inclinations by making sure that Heaven and Earth are in harmony, the stars and constellations follow their course, disasters and calamities end, all in the four directions take refuge, and the myriad people are at peace. These are the signs of a good ruler among men.

Typically people's actions, speech, and intentions do not make any reference to these activities of Heaven and Earth. For this reason the sages often say: Sovereign Heaven has no personal feelings, only virtue. This is just it. Thus people should be in awe of the mandate of Heaven, in awe of the great man, and in awe of the words of the sages.

Whatever good and evil people egotistically commit in their daily lives, Heaven and Earth know all about their inner feelings. Even if they secretly harm the life of another being, the spirits can clearly see it in their bodies. Also, whatever they say in body, speech, and mind, the demons always listen to their voices. Then, if they violate the prohibitions a hundred times, the demons take away their essence. If they violate them a thousand times, the Earth registers their form. It they commit nothing but evil every day, they will be imprisoned and put into the cangue. Such is the retribution enacted through yin and yang. Sovereign Heaven thus has its set of precepts and agreements, any violation of which will be punished by misfortune through either spirits and demons or Heaven and Earth.

Rules and Punishments

From *Taiji zhenren shuo ershisi menjie jing* 太極真人說二十四門戒經 (The Twenty-four Precepts of the Perfected of Great Ultimate, DZ183, 6th c.). See also Kohn 2004b.

1. I must not kill living beings or cut short other lives. Nor must I fry or boil creatures to make delicious meals or in other ways add to my personal delight. I must not myself kill, allow others engage in killing, nor even watch the act of killing for my pleasure. In no case must I eat the flesh of living beings. If I violate this precept, I shall fall into hell and be tortured in the boiling cauldron.

2. I must not steal or receive unrighteous goods. Nor must I enter other people's homes in the night or peek into their private areas during the day. I must not accept someone's goods and then develop a mind to steal them. I must not steal myself, let others engage in stealing, nor even watch the act of stealing for my pleasure. If I violate this precept, I shall fall into hell and be tortured on the mountain of knives and the tree of swords.

3. I must not harbor secret plots in my mind or wrongly accuse good people. When I am bested by another, I must not desire to harm him. When I find myself the inferior in a comparison, I must not strive to gain personal pleasure and advantage. I must not accept the good others do me while at the same time being nasty and resentful toward them. If I violate this precept, I shall fall into hell and be tortured on the stove full of coal.

4. I must not say one thing while thinking another, quarrel with my kin, chatter about the Three Treasures Dao, scriptures, masters, or slander ordained Daoists. I must not let my tongue run away, ridicule good people, nor slander the sagely teaching. I must never be doubtful or of two minds. My speech must never be uneven or encourage others to be divided. If I violate this precept, I shall fall into hell and be tortured with the iron plow that cuts the tongue.

5. I must not act in opposition to the scriptures and neglect Dao. Nor must I entice others to do so. I must not desecrate the holy altar area or trespass on the rooms of permanent residents. I must not secretly hide in the place of merit and virtue nor trample willfully about the auspicious spots of Dao. If I violate this precept, I shall fall into hell and be tortured with the steel pestles that grind down the body.

6. I must not drink wine or in other ways intoxicate and confuse my mind and spirit. I must not be uncontrolled and commit inauspicious and disturbing acts under the influence nor lose my awareness of rites and music. I must not screech in outrage against the gods or my parents, nor with my cries arouse the spirits and numinous forces. I must not startle others' minds or reduce their energy. If I violate this precept, I shall fall into hell and be tortured by poisonous snakes that eat away my heart.

7. I must not speak lies or half-truths nor use bad language or words of doubtful meaning. I must not scold and curse the gods or my parents, nor must I denigrate and shame my teachers and seniors. I must not answer good words with bad nor turn them around to be resentful and inimical. If I violate this precept, I shall fall into hell and be tortured by having poured molten copper into my mouth.

8. I must not commit debauchery or be lustful, nor lie with someone in sin or hanker after sex. I must not persist in living a sinful life that separates me from the love and kindness of others, nor avail myself of others' dotage and favors, thus destroying their homes. If I violate this precept, I shall fall into hell and be tortured by having to embrace the copper pillar.

9. I must not be stingy and greedy, never use and borrow others' goods to gain personal advantage. I must not be jealous of others or put curses on their things. I must not add to interpersonal suspicions nor deepen the resentment between me and others. If I violate this precept, I shall fall into hell and be tortured by the iron wheel.

10. I must not ruin the purification ceremonies or break the precepts by being unfilial or committing actions without benevolence. I must not secretly take food from the purification ceremonies or hide in the kitchens. I must not grab others' merit and virtue, preventing them from developing it fuller. If I violate this precept, I shall fall into hell and be tortured by having to roll stones up a mountain.

11. I must not willfully break the images of the gods nor steal flowers from their altars. I must not grab food offerings for myself or lie down and sleep in my formal vestments. If I violate this precept, I shall fall into hell and be tortured by having to sleep on a bed with iron spikes.

12. I must not allow merit and virtue to be destroyed, lodges and houses to fall into disrepair, or be restored shoddily. I must not harbor ideas of cheating and transgression in my heart. If I violate this

precept, I shall fall into hell and be tortured in the forest of swords that will cut my body and mind.

13. I must not, upon visiting someone's house and there seeing that he has certain things, willfully acquire those by barter or borrowing without returning. Even when in shabby cloth and dire straights, I must not lawlessly pressure others or take from them. If I violate this precept, I shall fall into hell and be tortured in the lake of ice.

14. I must not, upon seeing others melancholy, develop delight in my heart nor, upon seeing them vexed and troubled, be full of joy. Upon seeing someone having riches, I must not constantly think of taking them from him. Nor, upon seeing someone do good, must I develop hatred and envy in my own mind. If I violate this precept, I shall fall into hell and be tortured by iron spikes being driven into my body and by being thrown into a raging fire.

15. I must not neglect to wash my hands and rinse my mouth before entering the sacred precinct of the Dao. I must not unduly touch the scriptures and sacred images nor in other ways defile the numinous writings. In my heart I must not lack veneration and respect nor be lax and lazy about the tasks of life. If I violate this precept, I shall fall into hell and be tortured by being beaten with iron rods.

16. I must not disturb nests and destroy eggs, nor harm the unborn or abort babies. I must not act against the rules or be wanton, cutting short the road of life. If I violate this precept, I shall fall into hell and be tortured by having my body crushed by a large boulder.

17. I must not walk about naked or expose my body to Heaven and Earth, the sun and the moon, or the stars. Nor must I do so during the three periods of light and six periods of darkness. If I violate this precept, I shall fall into hell and be tortured by having my body cut with an iron drill.

18. I must not plow fields where worms make their home nor pluck the flowers and fruits off plants and so reduce the bounty of the gardens and orchards. I must not defile the monastery or homestead without feeling deeply ashamed for having desecrated an auspicious place. If I violate this precept, I shall fall into hell and be tortured by having to swallow iron pellets.

19. I must not willfully eat strong smelling, hot vegetables such as onions, garlic, chives, and leeks. They make the body rot and stink inside, so that the numinous spirits will not come to reside. I must remember to chant their scriptures and thus cultivate their presence,

never harming their sagely presence. If I violate this precept, I shall fall into hell and be tortured by having to swallow fire and eat hot coals.

20. I must not deem myself a judge of right and wrong and laugh at others in any matter of the Law. I must not wildly instigate people to discussions and then stubbornly hold on to my one-sided opinion. I must not think myself always right, without seeing what is true and proper. If I violate this precept, I shall fall into hell and be tortured by being ground in a mortar and stamped by a pestle.

21. I must not, every time people give me cause for resentment or envy, skillfully distribute poisonous drugs among them and thus reduce their life expectancy. If I violate this precept, I shall fall into hell and be tortured by having my body and mind steamed and boiled in the evil juices of one hundred poisons.

22. I must not plot against the Three Treasures or plan to separate from my six relations. I must not pursue only my own pleasures without thinking of giving to others. I must not speak and act with two different minds, disregarding the trust people have in me. If I violate this precept, I shall fall into hell and be tortured by having my tongue pulled out again and again.

23. I must not eat the food prepared for the purgation ceremonies together with strong smelling, hot vegetables, meat, or wine. I must not lack in respect for the rules of the purgation ceremonies nor in proper fear of the punishments that Heaven will bestow on humanity. If I violate this precept, I shall fall into hell and be tortured by having my body locked into an iron *kang* with no hope ever coming back to life.

24. I must not falsely assume nobility and power, cheating and beguiling the poor and humble. I must not split apart men and women in disregard of the truth of heaven. I must not give expression to two opposite opinions, disregarding the differences between me and others. I must not commit any acts outside the law, disregarding the consequences of my sin. If I violate this precept, I shall fall into hell and be tortured by having my body and mind sawed to pieces.

Attaining Purity

From *Jieye benxing jing* 誡業本行經 (Scripture of Controlling Karma and Original Conduct, DZ 345, dat. 5th c.)

[1a] The Lord of the Dao said:

Formerly I was on the Jade Terrace in the Cinnabar Hill Heaven of Pervasive Brightness. There I received the *Highest Scripture of Primordial Oneness and Golden Perfection on Controlling Karma and Original Conduct According to the Wheel of the Divine Law.* I was also at the time given the title King of the Great Divine Law of All-Highest and Most Lofty Pervasive Brightness. Since then I have been residing in the Highest Capital of Jade Clarity and activated the merit of the original karmic precepts of the wheel of the divine law for people to become flying celestials. I have allowed tens of thousands of beings, dead and alive, to reach salvation.

All the suffering and good fortune of celestials and humans originate with the cycle of karmic rebirth. Once on the Three Vehicles, people can climb up to Highest Clarity and, in the course of ten cycles, become celestial perfected. Their radiant light will illuminate the dark night, widely spreading through the ten directions, reversing the roots of the ten evils and making everyone do the ten good deeds. People then will attain life without measure and be forever protected by the perfection of the Dao. . . .

[1b] The Lord of the Dao said:

The precepts controlling karma are the basis for proper action in highest virtue, for the wide spread of golden perfection, and for the original development of eternal life.

Be good and think only right thoughts, then evil will not dare to speak up. Cut off all doubt and confusion and follow all the celestials in their worship of perfection. Never give rise to evil and, if you see it, don not follow it. Such roots of suffering are deep and make you regress within the karmic wheel. They give rise to bad fortune, and there is nothing one can do against this. You will fall into the three bad rebirths with little hope of recovery.

Blocking the Dao, you are ignorant.
Envying other people, you incur punishment for yourself.
Slandering others, you have just emerged from an animal existence.

Engaging in debauchery, you are not yet free of the karmic roots of the six domestic animals. [2a]
Being greedy and avaricious, you are harming yourself.
Coveting fancy tastes, you swallow pure poison.

All these are the foundations of cruel fates—far far removed from all the good. . . .

[3a] The Heavenly Worthy told the Lord of the Dao:

I have opened the gate to the highest ranks of the wheel of the divine law, the karmic precepts of golden perfection, the proper foundations of the ten good deeds, and the myriad forms of proper behavior. Whoever wishes to follow this path, must submit in due virtue.

Thereupon the Lord of the Dao knocked his head to the ground and paid respects. Bowing low, he received the words of the precepts. [3b]

The Ten Right Actions

1. Right vision of the manifold wondrous origins: in all cases attain the result of spirit pervasion.

2. Right hearing of the mysterious and wondrous sounds: spirit pervades to know all in the ten directions [omniscience].

3. Right knowledge of the entering of fragrance and radiance: spirit pervades numinous energy forever.

4. Right sounds to open the gate of all wonders: spirit pervades the benefits and prosperity and karmic fruits without measure.

5. Right actualization of the divine law and observance of the precepts: spirit pervades all as the perfected of Dao descend.

6. Right mindfulness of the suffering of the host of living beings: spirit pervades the karmic reward of radiance and brightness.

7. Right imagination of all without duality and doubt: spirit pervades the world of the orthodox Dao.

8. Right action in great compassion and karmic awareness: spirit pervades unsurpassed perfection.

9. Right concentration on body and shadow, remaining unmoved even in the multitude of activities: spirit pervades wondrous awakening.

10. Right holding together of body and spirit, [4a] firmly and with illumination upholding rightness: spirit pervades mystery and wonder.

The Heavenly Worthy said:

These ten highest rules of right action of the golden perfection are the first step of the myriad forms of behavior that lead to spirit pervasion by following the karmic precepts. Uphold them and you will lay the foundation of pervading the immeasurable subtlety of the ten directions.

I have activated the wheel of the divine law and spread the words of these precepts to save people through kalpic disasters and remove all obstacles [to salvation] from the living and the dead. Follow them faithfully and gradually you will ascend to eternal life. The perfection of Dao will be with you till the end of your days and never will you be confronted with any path leading to the ten evils.

The Merit of the Ten Right Actions

The Heavenly Worthy said:

There are ten kinds of merit deriving from the highest good deeds, based on the former actions according to golden perfection.

1. Cut off the karmic conditions of coveting and seeking advantage through the five colors, and with right vision never again do any wrong seeing.

2. Cut off the sounds of the five tones and six disharmonies, and be free from wrong hearing, inside and out.

3. Cut off the cause of the six arousals, and waward *qi* will not enter you.

4. Cut off all empty chatter and frivolous talk, and wrong words and fancy language will never appear before you.

5. Cut off the harm of the host of misfortunes, and the multitude of wrong patterns will not assail you.

6. Cut off all imagination of the five senses, and all wrong and evil [patterns] will no longer be active [around you]. [4b]

7. Cut off all unproductive actions, and wrong patterns and disasters will not arise [near you].

8. Cut off all doubt and confusion, and the multitude of wrong patterns will no longer violate beings near you.

9. Cut off all purposeless activity, and pathogenics and diseases will no longer arise.

10. Cut off all karma of the ten evils and always keep your heart with the wheel of the divine law and the myriad demons and pathogenic spirits will leave of their own accord and never dare come approach.

. . .

The Ten Good Abilities

The Heavenly Worthy said:

Whoever develops the following good abilities by practicing the ten right forms of vision and action according to the rules of golden perfection will soon establish the myriad good deeds.

1. See the five colors without coveting, and licentious tendencies do not arise.

2. Hear the five sounds without listening, and demonic tendencies will dissolve of themselves.

3. Smell the multitude of vapors and fragrances without joy, [5a] and the six intestines will remain unharmed, all pathogenic tendencies retreating of themselves.

4. See the five flavors without coveting their sweet taste, and the multiple turbidities will not enter your body.

5. Listen to the many kinds of music without caring, and no outer coarseness will startle you.

6. Guard the One without one-sided imaginings, and to the end of your days you will not be defiled nor will any pathogenic energy arise.

7. Venerate and cultivate the precepts regarding basic forms of behavior, and all coarseness will dissolve of itself, your body and complexion becoming pure and radiant.

8. Look upon treasures and material goods without violence and possessiveness, and a myriad forms of goodness will come easily to you, as you live in peace to the end of your days.

9. Maintain a harmonious disposition without envy or jealousy and never get aroused by whatever you see, and a myriad forms of good

fortune will come down to you, all numinous powers and demons paying their respects.

10. Be at rest with yourself and relaxed in your thoughts, compassionate and mindful of all karmic circumstances, and the ten directions will protect you, reporting on your merit to the powers on-high, and allowing you to rise to highest perfection. . . .

Basic Attitudes for the Ten Good Deeds

[8b] The Heavenly Worthy said:

1. Be compassionate and filial and go along with all, joining your mind with theirs in a myriad different activities.

2. Be loving and mindful toward the host of living beings, regarding them all as your own body.

3. Be faithful toward the scriptures and precepts, so you can see the original causes of sin and good fortune.

4. Abandon all treasures and material goods, instead giving freely to the innumerable people of the world who are destitute and in danger.

5. Widely establish merit and virtue, set up Daoist centers and create good fortune for a myriad generations.

6. To maintain goodness until you can die without shame or blame, you must not kill or steal.

7. Rescue and support all living beings in danger and emergency situations without measure, and help the host of living beings whose destiny and inner nature are disjointed without end, so they can all fulfill their original destiny. [9a]

8. Present offerings to the Three Treasures, recite the scriptures morning and evening, uphold the precepts and observe the purgations, never getting lax or lazy.

9. Always provide education for people in Heaven and on earth, think of your ruler with care and mindfulness. Wish that all may attain eternal life and live in great prosperity. Help all those who are poor, destitute, orphaned, and old. Support all the innumerable suffering people without greed or grudge.

10. Always follow these rules without advancing or retreating. Do good with all your heart.

Any celestial who can follow these ten precepts can be said to have reached the merit of the ten good deeds and thus laid the foundation for a myriad deeds of bliss. . . .

The Ten Cycles of Attainment

[21b] 1. First you receive and uphold the precepts and by doing so become an earth immortal. Cultivating and practicing the precepts of the divine law, you undergo a cycle and enter the second level.

2. Now you become a wandering immortal. Continuing to maintain a mind of rightness, you undergo a cycle and enter the third level.

3. Now you become an immortal person. Venerating and practicing the precepts in all your actions, you undergo a cycle and enter the fourth level.

4. Now you become a flying immortal. Always following the scriptural precepts, never violating them in any action, you undergo a cycle and enter the fifth level.

5. Now you become a numinous immortal. Cutting off all oral desires and never coveting fancy tastes, undergoing extended purgations, reciting the scriptures, and maintaining the precepts, you undergo a cycle and enter the sixth level.

6. Now you become a divine immortal. Free from all sensory desires, greed, and passions, equanimous in all actions, establishing merit and virtue, controlling your mind, and embracing simplicity, you undergo a cycle and enter the seventh level. [22a]

7. Now you become a perfected immortal. Developing a mind that is widely mindful of the ten directions, always saving others from danger, warning them never to commit any transgressions, and supporting all beings without favor, you undergo a cycle and enter the eighth level.

8. Now you become a flying celestial perfected. Guarding the One and never moving, doing a myriad good deeds and respecting the precepts of the divine law in mindfulness, acting always as if facing the gods, you undergo a cycle and enter the ninth level.

9. Now you become a highest perfected. Eating pure frost and drinking clear energy, cultivating Dao and reciting the scriptures, offering incense and attending audiences with the perfected, facilitating salvation for people in the ten directions and everywhere saving living

beings without measure, letting your grace seep all throughout Heaven and Earth, and never being lazy or remiss in the least, you undergo a cycle and enter the tenth and last level.

10. Finally you reach the stage of the unsurpassed perfected of Highest Clarity.

Chapter Thirteen

The Ideal Human

The realized mystic or accomplished master in both traditions is altruistic and has overcome selfish ambitions. A sage in the world, he serves as an inspiring example to others, a rallying point of social harmony, and a helper to Heaven and Earth. The Confucian master, here described in the concrete example of a real historical figure, has attained control of himself, developed a wide range of learning, and understood the principle of the universe. He writes and lectures, hoping to awaken more people to the path; he is polite and friendly, full of virtue and goodness, a just administrator of the realm.

The Daoist sage, while sharing some of these characteristics, is yet ultimately a celestial who happens to spend a brief sojourn in the world. As such, he is more obscure both within and without, not so much an obviously learned man or a government servant as a being in tune with the larger universe, one who comes and goes naturally, almost invisibly. Leaving no track or trace, certainly not in lectures or writings, he (or she) yet with his mere presence makes the world truer, the universe smoother, life more harmonious.

Heavenly Registration

From *Ge Xuan neizhuan* 葛玄内傳 (Esoteric Biography of Ge Xuan, in *Sandong zhunang* 三洞珠囊 [DZ 1139, 6th c.], 8.15a-17b),

[15a] The Lord Green Lad said:

People who have a registration of immortals' bones [in Heaven] will love immortality [on Earth]. Those who love immortality accordingly all have inherent celestial tendencies. Those with celestial tendencies, however, may be weak or strong. If they are weak, their good merit from former lives is not yet sufficient. If they are strong, their destiny found in the mysterious registers is already fixed.

As the celestial registers of the Great Capital appear in the Dark Palace [in Heaven], so the rhythm of *qi* manifests in the physical body [on Earth]. As the words of the registers shine forth in the Great Ultimate, so the spirit-mind is properly at rest in the cinnabar fields [in the body]. [15b] There are several different types:

1. People [coming to life] with a jade name in the Golden Towers have sunshine in their eyes. They show pure teeth and white blood. Benevolent and compassionate in character, they love immortality. Bright and versatile, they are of high excellence.

2. People with a jade registration in the golden books of Highest Clarity have the flowing Kui star on their backs and a slanted sternum in their chests. Generous and harmonious in character, they take care of others, their virtue reaching even to insects and worms.

3. People with a clear writ in the cinnabar ledgers of the Great Ultimate have distinct patterns in their hand lines, such as the character for "man" or "great." Withdrawn and cautious in character, they love perfection. Pure and empty, they are truly exceptional.

4. People with a purple name in the dark plain books of All Directions have four-corner eyes with a purple radiance that brightly illuminates their entire bodies. Deeply dedicated to the cultivation of the wondrous, they are pure and clear and stay away from all defilements. [16a]

5. People with an entry in the jade tomes of the Cloud Chamber have round eyes and square cheeks, dragon-like mouths and soft tongues. Of open mind, they embody perfection, examine the parts and understand the whole.

6. People with a purple name in the red-character records of the Vermilion Palace have the movements of the wonder bird and dance like phoenixes. Their navel area is radiant and glossy. Excited at being among the living, they open their minds to glittering brightness.

7. People with names enrolled in the jade ledgers of Great Clarity have voices that sound like jade and gold, square mouths and round eyes. Generous to a fault, they love all widely, treating everyone as dearly as they would their mothers.

8. People with golden names in the jasper tablets of Great Simplicity have white spots on their chests and emit purple breath from their

mouths. Compassionate in virtue and pervasive in spirit, they are deeply benevolent and help the masses. [16b]

9. People with a purple register in the cinnabar writings of the Southern Ultimate radiate the five *qi* from their heads and above reach to the multi-layered clouds. Harmonious and benevolent, they love the poor, aiding people in danger and rescuing them from hardships.

10. People with a registration record in the dark jades of the Dipper have nine nipples in their heart area and damask-like lines outside their lungs. They are also marked by a jade circle on the lower cheek, green muscles in their eyes, vertical double lines straight above the eyebrows and lines around them. Bare of hairs, their foreheads shine brightly, while their Halls of Light are even and white. Their vertical lines are the ford to perfection, while there broad foreheads are the receptacle of numinosity. Compassionate and loving toward the pure and humble, they are kind even to birds and beasts. [17a]

11. People with a red entry in the clear, golden ledgers of Highest Prime in the Dark Palace have cinnabar heart areas and purple nipples. Their bones are round and give forth a yellow florescence, while fragrant breath issues from their mouths and the jade juice behind their teeth is plentiful. They love to observe the flowing haze of the sun and the moon, delight in the radiant luminosity of the stars and planets. Their bodies pure and their bones firm, they are honest and sincere, profound and withdrawn.

12. People with golden characters in the white jade tablets of the Cinnabar Terrace in Mystery Metropolis have green livers with purple lines and gray kidneys with silky lines. Their bodies are pure and their spirits clean. Their entire being oozing fragrance and softness, their blood is clear and their energy glossy. Lying down to visualize mysterious far-off lands, they taste the fabric of shining numinosity. They love to be generous and kind to others and frequently help them in danger and hardship.

13. People with a clear inscription in the jade tablets of the Palace of the Three Primes have purple brains and damask tongues, dark spots and fringed temples. Their intestines are green, their marrow is vermilion, they have square feet and round foreheads.

The Sage

From *Daode jing* (Book of the Dao and Its Virtue).

The sage rests in affairs in nonaction
and practices the teaching of no words.
The myriad beings are active through him
and he does not turn away from them.
They live through him
and he does not take possession of them.
The sage acts in the world
but does not depend on it,
His task accomplished,
he does not dwell on it.
And because he does not dwell,
it remains. (ch. 2)

Yield and you will be whole,
bend and you will be straight!
Let go and you will be rich,
grow old and you will be new!
Have little and you will gain,
have plenty and you will lose!

Therefore:
The sage embraces the One
and guides all-under-Heaven.
Not presenting himself, he is radiant;
Not thinking himself right, he is famous.
Not pushing himself forward, he is meritorious.
Not pitying himself, he is eminent.

He never competes—
none-under-Heaven can compete with him!
The ancients said:
"Yield and you will be whole!"
Are these mere empty words?
They are not!
The sage is whole.
He follows this. (ch. 22)

Good traveling leaves not track nor trace.

Good speaking has not flaw nor bent.
Good reckoning uses not counters nor devices.
A door well shut needs no bolts, yet cannot be opened.
A knot well tied needs no extra rope, yet cannot be undone.

Therefore:
The sage is always there.
He help the people and rejects no one.
He is always there.
He helps all and rejects no creature.

Thus it is said:
He is at one with universal light.
For him, good people are teachers of the bad,
the bad are their work material.
He neither specially values the teachers
nor passionately loves the material.
Knowing that, however wise,
a person may be greatly deluded.
Such is his essential mystery. (ch. 27)

The still is easy to grasp,
the open is easy to plan.
The brittle is easy to crack,
the tiny is easy to lose.
Act before there is need,
order before there is chaos!

A huge strong tree grows from a tiny shoot.
A nine-storied tower rises from a heap of earth.
A thousand-mile journey starts with the first step.
Act with intention and you will fail,
grasp hold firmly and you will lose!

Therefore:
The sage rests in nonaction and never fails,
is without grasping and never loses,
while others try to control affairs and fail close to success.
Take care of the end as much as of the beginning,
and there will be no failure!

Therefore:

The sage wishes to be free from desires
and does not value rare goods.
He learns to be free from learning
and recovers what the multitude has passed by.
He aids the spontaneous development of the myriad beings
and never dares to act with personal intention. (ch. 64)

In the World

From *Zuowang lun* 坐忘論 (On Sitting in Oblivion, DZ 1036). Earlier translation in Kohn 1987a.

5. True Observation

[8b] True observation is the foremost mirror of the knight of wisdom, the quality examination of the people of ability. Probing misfortunes and blessings which chance to come, divining the fortune and calamities inherent in activity or rest, he succeeds in seeing ahead of life's motions and arranges his acts accordingly. Deeply praying and guarding concentration, serving the completeness of life, there will never be action in attachment from beginning to end, neither will one's principles contradict one's actions. Then one can speak of "true observation."

One bite of food or a wink of sleep usually become the source of some gain or loss, one step forward or one word spoken quite possibly lay the foundation for good and bad fortune. Though one might still cleverly restrain the results, it is much better to stolidly be on one's guard against the origins. By observing the root, the branch is known. However, one must first be free from impatient, struggling emotions. This is why we practice taming the mind and detachment from affairs; we let our outward actions diminish daily, calm the bodily structure and relax the mind. Only in such a state can one truly observe the subtle. As the *Daode jing* has it: "Let there always be no desires so that the subtle may be observed" [ch. 1].

Nevertheless, even a person cultivating Dao must be provided food and clothing, there are affairs that cannot be given up or beings one cannot leave alone. Those then have to be cared about with humility, should be attended to with clear perception. Don't take it as an obstruction to Dao and let your mind give rise to anger and impatience. [9a] As soon as you give rise to anger and impatience because of some affair, the mind will be sick with agitation. How then can it be called a mind at peace?

All human affairs, all food and clothing of people are merely a boat. If I want to cross an ocean, I need a boat. After the passage is completed, the reason for the boat is no longer there. But why should one abandon it before even having gone on the voyage? Food and clothing in themselves are empty illusion and without actual value. But as a means to free oneself from empty illusion, one must obtain provision with food and clothing. One should therefore never have any feelings of gain or loss about them. Independent of whether one has things or not, the mind should remain constantly at peace. Join others in seeking but not in coveting, in achievement but not in hoarding. Without coveting one will be free from worry, without hoarding one will never experience loss. In deeds one may be like others, but in mind one should always remain aloof. This really is the essential point of practice and it should be worked on very hard.

Despite a growing detachment from affairs there might still be some disease hard to eliminate. In that case just rely on the technique and observe it. There may be, for example, a grave case of sensual involvement. Then one must observe the fact that all defiling sensuality arises from imagination. If no rise is given to imagination, there cannot be any sensuality. Realize therefore that sensual imaginings [9b] are nothing on the outside while sensual feelings are mere foolishness within. As they are nothing but foolish feelings and empty imaginings, who would be the master of sensuality? The *Dingzhi jing* 定志經 (Scripture on Firming Up Determination) says: "Sensuality is entirely imaginative. All imagination is ultimately empty. How can there be something like sensuality?" [DZ 235, 2b].

Also, people should think that the attractiveness of seductive women is even more dangerous than that of fox fairies. When fox fairies seduce men they arouse loathing and distress. Hence men even if they have to die do not enter the evil ways. Loathing and distress keep them forever away from debauchery. Human beauties, however, beguile men, make them fall in love and get attached to them. They will then hanker after them with all their might. Because of their depraved thoughts, after death they fall into hell. Forever they will have turned away from birth in the realm of people and from the road to happiness. As the *Scripture* says: "Why is it that people of one mind and joined as a couple in this world after death do not attain the human state together again? It is because of depraved thoughts."

Then again, why—if sensual attraction ultimately comes down to beauty—do fish upon seeing such beauty enter deeper into the water, and birds fly off into the sky? Immortals recognize sensuality as defilement and impurity, wise ones compare it to knives and axes of punishment. In life on earth, not eating for seven days will cause death, but a hundred years without sensuality will avert untimely departure. Realize thus that sensuality is not essential or appropriate for [10a] the personal body or the mind, but an `enemy and thief to inner nature and life. Why must you be subject to affection and lust and yourself invite calamity and destruction?

To see another do evil and give rise to enmity and hatred in one's own mind is just like seeing someone kill himself and promptly stick out one's own neck to accept the other's blade and get killed oneself. The other person commits evil by himself, he does not ask me to do likewise. Why then should I reach out to take in another's negativity and make myself sick? If one can feel enmity upon seeing someone perform evil, then one must also react with negativity upon seeing someone do good. Why is that so? Because in both cases Dao is obstructed.

Now, if one suffers from poverty, one should observe this and ask, "who made me poor?" Heaven and Earth are equable and regular, protecting and supporting without personal aims. So if I am poor now, it is certainly not the fault of Heaven and Earth. When parents give birth to a child, they desire to see him in wealth and high esteem. So if I am poor now I cannot blame it on my parents. Other men, ghosts, and spirits don't even have the time to save themselves, how then would they have the energy to make me poor? Going back and forth, I cannot find anyone to blame for my poverty. Thus I can't help realizing that it must be my own karma, my destiny before Heaven. [10b]

I produce my own karma, whereas Heaven provides me with the destiny of this life. Karma relates to destiny like shadow and echo follow form and sound. They are not to be avoided or resented in any way. Only one who has wisdom can act benevolent and realize them fully, delighting in Heaven and acknowledging his destiny, never lamenting over any eventual suffering through poverty. Therefore the *Zhuangzi* says: "Karma enters in and cannot be prevented from becoming one's own karma" [ch. 23]. Poverty and diseases come, they cannot be kept out or eradicated completely. Thus the *Scripture* says: "Heaven and Earth cannot alter their routine, yin and yang cannot revert their tasks." Judging the matter from this angle we know that one has a true destiny , not a mere mask. How could one resent it?

The situation we find ourselves in can be compared to the encounter of a brave knight with a band of brigands. Never feeling dread or fear, he brandishes his sword and rushes to the battlefront, fighting until the robbers flee. Having thus gained merit in his service, he is gloriously rewarded for the rest of his life. If now there are poverty and diseases vexing and troubling me, then these are my robbers and brigands. With an upright mind I can be a brave knight. Examining them in wisdom and by observation I brandish my sword.

The battle is won when all vexations and bondages are eliminated. To be at peace and constantly happy—this is the glorious reward. [11a] But often, when suffering or affairs come to harass us, the mind instead of using the method of observation gives rise to worry and anxiety. This then is like an encounter with brigands when one rather than gaining merit in service casts off one's weapons and turns one's back on the battlefield. One duly has to bear the guilt of desertion and defeat. Thereby one rejects happiness and invites suffering—how could there be empathy?

If there is suffering or disease, one should first realize by observation that it originates in the fact that one has a personal body. Without a body the vexations would have no place to dwell. As the *Daode jing* states: "If I had no personal body, what vexations would I have?" [ch. 13]. Next you should turn to observe the mind and find that there is no true lord. Even though you search for him inside out, you can't find him anywhere.

All plans and thoughts arise only from a deluded mind. Thus when one "makes one's body like dried wood and one's mind like dead ashes" [*Zhuangzi* 6], all the various diseases will be duly eradicated. Someone who is horrified by death, for example, should therefore think of his body as the lodge of the spirit. Thus as the body becomes old and sick, as breath and strength decline day by day, it will just be like a house with rotting walls. Once it becomes uninhabitable, it is best to abandon it soon and look for another place to stay. The death of the personal body and the departure of the spirit are a mere change of residence.

However, when one hankers after life and loathes death, resisting the natural transformations, one's spirit consciousness will be confused and let into error. It will consequently lose its proper role. The result will be that when one is entrusted to life again [11b] and receives the constituting breath, one will not lean toward the pure and refined, but end up with much turbid and disgraceful energy. Generally all those stupid and dull, dumb and greedy come into being like this.

Only when one does not feel exhilarated when alive or frustrated when facing death, can one realize the equality of life and death and thereby produce good karma for the personal bodies to come. But by craving for a myriad different things one will only end up with love and disease alternating. If even one limb is sick, the whole bodily structure is in discomfort and unrest, how much more so when the one mind is full of a myriad diseases? Desiring eternal life in one personal body—how is it possible? All craving and aversion arise from delusion. By accumulating delusion instead of expelling it one will obscure the vision of the Dao. Thus relinquish all desires and abide in nonexistence! Be placid, pure, and well-rooted, and only then turn to observation! Whatever you loved before will not only cause weariness and disdain.

On the other hand, if you practice observation with a mind attached to projected reality, you can never be aware of negativities to the end of your days. Only with a mind utterly detached from projections can you observe the structured world and a true understanding of right and wrong will become possible. The process can be compared to a sobered people who now can see the drunkard's evil deeds the wrong of which he was totally unaware of as long as he was drunk himself. The *Shengxuan jing* (Scripture of Ascension to the Mystery) says: "I uproot and cast off worldly life and give up the world completely." [12a] The *Xisheng jing* (Scripture of Western Ascension) states: "Sight and hearing of eyes and ears retain people in imbalance. Therefore the joys of taste and smell and all the other senses must be given up" [ch. 7]. So Lord Lao gave up the world, cast off worldly life. Realizing now that smell and taste are to be given up as nothing but a steady flow of craving and desires, how could one regard the fishmonger's shop as stinking?

A Daoist Life

From *Yuandai Liexian zhuan* 元代列仙傳 (Immortals' Biographies of the Yuan Dynasty), no. 38.

Tao Hongjing, also known as Daoming, was from Maoling [near Nanjing]. His mother became pregnant after she dreamt that a green dragon was emerging from her chest. At birth, Tao had wondrous signs and magical features. When he was ten years old, he acquired a copy of Ge Hong's *Shenxian zhuan* (Biographies of Spirit Immortals) and studied it eagerly day and night. "I look up into the clear clouds," he told his friends, "and glance at the brilliant sun and never feel as if they are very far away at all."

When fully grown, he stood to a height of seven feet, seven inches. His spirit was imposing, bright and refined. His eyes were shining under well-shaped eyebrows, set wide apart. His ears each had more than seventy hairs sprouting forth for about two inches. On his right knee he had a cluster of black moles that formed the pattern of the Northern Dipper.

He read through tens of thousands of learned scrolls and was good at playing the zither. He also excelled on the chessboard. Even before he reached manhood, he was appointed as an official under Emperor Gao of the Qi dynasty and served as tutor to the imperial princes. Although he held a high position, he kept himself in strict seclusion and had no close relations with the outside world. His studies and lectures were his sole occupation.

In the tenth year of Eternal Brightness [492 C.E.], he stripped off the court robes and hung his official seals above the Warrior Gate. He petitioned to be allowed to resign from office and give up his emoluments. Imperial permission was granted.

Tao then went and settled on Mount Thatch [Maoshan] in Jurong where he built himself a Daoist temple. It was known as the Monastery of Blossoming Yang [Huayang guan]. There he lived in seclusion and traveled all over the famous mountains of the empire to search immortal medicines. Whenever he passed through a valley with a fast- flowing river, he sat down in its midst and recited an incantation. However often he did so, the waters would never submerge or drown him.

The prefect of Dongyang held his spiritual endeavor and training in high esteem and wrote to him several times, inviting him. However, Tao never left his mountain.

In character, Tao Hongjing was calm and open, yet also modest and diligent. Wherever he went, even in the darkest circumstances, his mind would shine forth like a bright mirror, deeply understanding and appreciating every being he encountered.

In the first year of Eternal Prime [499 C.E.], he had a three-storied building erected, of which he occupied the top floor. Subsequently, he cut off all relations with the world and allowed only a single servant lad to enter his secluded domain.

In his youth, Tao Hongjing had been fond of horseback riding and shooting, but later he desisted from all these activities. He just loved to listen to flute music and played the flute himself, that was all. He also very much liked the sound of the wind going though the pines and for this had his courtyard planted with them. Every time he heard their rustling sound, he would be happy and delighted. On occasion he would also wander amongst rocks and springs. To all those who saw him them, he looked quite like an immortal.

When Emperor Wu of Liang established his dynasty, Tao discovered prophesies and sacred charts in various places which duly became imperial residences. When he ordered his disciples to present his discoveries to the court, the emperor received them with grace and extended his affection to Tao.

At some point Tao had also found various divine talismans and secret oral instructions. These convinced him that he could prepare an elixir of immortality. However, it was a great distress to him that he lacked the necessary materials and ingredients. The emperor, learning of this, gave him gold, cinnabar, and many other things so that he could pursue his experiment. Tao indeed succeeded in concocting a flying elixir. It looked like frost or snow and made his body feel light when he swallowed it. The emperor also took it to good effect and his esteem for Tao increased.

The emperor frequently sent presents to Tao and invited him to come to court. But Tao never went. Instead, he merely sent a picture of two oxen, one of which was grazing contentedly in a meadow, while the other was wearing a golden harness and being led away on a rope, a man poking him forward. When the emperor saw the picture, he laughed. "So the fellow wants to be a turtle who drags his tail in the mud," he said. "How can we ever get him to come and visit us at court?"

Still, the emperor continued to consult Tao on all important matters of state. Because of this he came to be called the "minister in the mountains." He grew old doing so, and even at the high age of eighty did not suffer any changes in his appearance or vigor.

Later Emperor Jianwen traveled south to Xuzhou to grace its pure atmosphere with his presence. Withdrawing to a back chamber, he summoned Tao, who arrived with his kerchief properly tied. The two spent several days together and had extended talks. After this, Emperor Jianwen too held Tao in high esteem and marveled at his powers.

One of Tao's disciples, a man named Huan Kai, attained Dao and was about to ascend into heaven. Tao wondered at this and asked him, "I, too, have cultivated Dao and practiced its teachings with extreme diligence. Why do I not ascend? Could it be that there is something wrong with me, that something keeps me tied to this world?"

Thus he commissioned Kai to make some inquiries in the otherworld on his behalf. Kai in due course returned from his heavenly journey and gave Tao the news.

"Oh, master," he said. "Your hidden merit has been abundantly manifested. Only in your compilation of pharmacological methods and recipes you have made extensive use of gadflies, leeches, and the like. Although you have plenty of merit in relation to humans, you have caused harm to the lives of other creatures. It is because of this that you must wait another twelve years before you can shed your mortal coil. Only then can you brush away the dust of this world and take up your rightful post as supervisor of in the Department of Water in the capital city of the Penglai islands."

Tao Hongjing duly proceeded to make up for his error by substituting vegetable substances for all those of animals in the three scrolls of his *Bencao jing* 本草經 (Materia Medica).

One day he became ill and knew that his departure was imminent. Looking back over the days of his life, he composed a poem on departure and one on the great identity of all. Then he expired.

At that time he was eighty-five years old, but his appearance had remained unaltered and his limbs were as supple as ever. After he left his spirit remained, spreading a fragrant perfume over the mountain.

Chapter Fourteen

Mystical Union

Mystical realization is the attainment of oneness with the ultimate at the root of existence. In Confucianism, this is the Great Ultimate, the principle underlying all, and so the Confucian mystic in his final state becomes one with the greater universe, making Heaven and Earth and the myriad beings into one body, joining the world with his mind and whole being, and merging his consciousness with that of his fellow men.

In Daoism, the ultimate is found in the heavens of the immortals, and mystical realization accordingly takes the adept beyond the world and into the glittering celestial realms. In an ecstatic journey that sees him riding through the stars in a cloudy dragon carriage, he (or she) joins the host of the perfected, feasts with them and whirls with them in purity to eventually merge with the Great Silence at the beginning of all, the hub of Dao beyond all body and all mind.

Perfection through Precepts

From *Guanshen dajie* 觀身大戒 (The Great Precepts of Self-Observation, DZ 1364). Earlier translation in Kohn 2004b, 222-24.

[17b] The Heavenly King of Primordial Beginning said:

When the lofty wisdom scriptures of Perfection Cavern had not been proclaimed in the world, students who received them in transmission often became perfected. Thus the text is hard to encounter and hard to use fully—only rarely does it appear on earth. Its precepts are venerable and serious and cannot be properly expressed in words. Through them one can observe all the various gods in the body, the numinous perfected of the three hundred joints and passes, and prevent them from leaving wantonly and creating demonic trials. Never violate them! If you receive and chant these precepts, make sure not to go against them! Nor without their proper study issue them!

[18a] Due to this, one day a turquoise chariot of clouds and mists spontaneously arrives to receive you. You ascend to heaven in broad daylight and bodily float about the waves of emptiness. You bring forth a round radiance from the top of your head that shines into the ten directions and brightly illuminates even Great Nonbeing. None among the host of celestial sages will dare not to show you respect and honor. The great demon kings of the Six Heavens at this time will elevate all practitioners who venerate the precepts to be registered in the Palace of Eastern Florescence. This office will then pass their names on to the Heavenly Palace of Great Brahma, which in turn will transfer them to the Golden Towers of Jade Capital, where they are inscribed into the ranks of the highest immortals.

The Heavenly King of Primordial Beginning said:

The *Dadong zhenjing* 大洞真經 (Perfect Scripture of Great Profundity), if recited ten thousand times, makes a cloudy carriage descend to receive you. The scriptures of Numinous Treasure in Mystery Cavern are texts that survive the kalpas. Some people cultivate them and yet do not attain immortality or successfully concoct the numinous fluid of golden cinnabar. Why is this? It is because they do not venerate the precepts of self-observation in wisdom. These precepts are the most wondrous of all the wonders—all the nine hundred majestic deities, ultimate worthies, and immortals of golden florescence stand up and offer incense to them. They contain the perfect and arcane Dao which cannot be transmitted in words. You have to chant and practice them—and that is all.

[18b] Anyone studying Dao who does not receive these precepts can ever attain immortality. Instead, they create karmic conditions and are enticed by sound and sights; start out diligently but soon lapse into laziness; enter mountain hermitages and encounter trials by the host of demons; give rise to strange thoughts and begin to doubt and misread the perfected scriptures; revert to following ordinary goals and lose their mind for the Dao; despise their teachers and friends or defame and shame their fellow students; develop signs of madness and let their temper and energy fall into wrong patterns; covet wealth, love, and sex, and go against the Three Treasures; are hindered by family involvement and develop resentment against all kinds of or-

ganizations; have bad dreams and confused imaginings—all this from not having the great precepts to sustain their mind and spirit. They thus allow the three worms, poisonous and fickle, to cunningly deceive the five organs. Be sure to realize this affliction!

Also, this way you prevent the demon kings from erasing your name from the [ledgers of] the underworld springs of the dead. Instead, you will remain in the Three Worlds and never cross over to the ranks of the immortals.

The Heavenly King of Primordial Beginning said:

[19a] These precepts first appeared through the numinous immortals. Now all the immortals of the various heavens, earthly realms, and famous mountains venerate and practice them. Every new moon and full moon, on the days of the eight nodes and of original destiny as well as the constellations of the Primes—on all the purgation days of the various heavens—all students, teachers, and friends [of the Dao] enter the chamber to recite the precepts once in their entirety. They first pay obeisance to the ten directions, bowing once in each direction to the various heavens. As they present the precepts to the hearing of the gods, again they perform a bow for each.

If a disciple wishes to venerate the precepts, he or she must first give five pounds of gold as a pledge to the Five Emperors and ten *zhang* [100 feet] of cinnabar brocade as a gift to the ten directions. They must also swear an oath to be entered into the ledger that they will not disclose the precepts and statutes. The master in charge of the veneration of the precepts then sets up a three-day purgation for mindful meditation and instruction in the precepts. On the eve of the event, participants first light ten lamps to present an offering of light to the ten directions. The great sages of the ten directions accordingly will come to manifest in their minds. If at the time there is violent wind and rain, thunder and lightning, transmission cannot take place. In that case, set up another purgation for the precepts and again prepare all with proper dignity. Then, as the time approaches, open your spirit and relax your intention.

After having observed the precepts for nine years, your spirit candle will be naturally bright like the sun and the moon or the florescent cinnabar, and you will have a golden complexion rising from the inside, giving you the looks of a youngster with full and firm flesh. [19b] Your spirit will pervade the four ends [of the universe], your virtue will be on par with that of the immortals, and you will be able to enter and leave the spaceless. Venerating these great statutes and precepts, you can bathe in the Pond of Flowing Calm, release your cloak on the Terrace of the Seven Treasures, wander to gaze beyond the Flowery Pool, or seclude yourself in the Fragrant Wood of Recovering Life, full of golden radiance, fresh and verdant. From kalpa to kalpa, forever you will enjoy the perfection of Dao.

Stages of Attainment

From *Cunshen lianqi ming* 存神鍊氣銘 (Inscription on Visualization of Spirit and Refinement of Energy, DZ 834). Earlier translation in Kohn 1987a.

1. The diseases inherited from former lives diminish, the body grows light and the mind luminous. The mind is now totally at rest within, the spirit is tranquil, and the energy at peace. The four elements are joined in harmony, the six emotions are deeply calmed. With the mind resting peacefully in the mysterious realm, continue to practice one-pointedness and inner concentration. Joy and exultation are daily new—this is called "realizing Dao."

2. The limits of normal life are left behind. In appearance one recovers a youthful complexion. The body in a state of joy, the mind constantly at peace, one numinously attains a vision of the deep and mysterious. At this stage, one should move to a different part of the country, choose a spot and settle down. It is better not to be a too old acquaintance with the local folk.

3. Extending one's years to a thousand—one is called an immortal. One travels extensively to all the famous mountains, flying or walking in spontaneity, with azure lads as one's guards and jade maidens for entertainment. Stepping high on mist and haze, colored clouds support the tread.

4. Refining one's body to pure energy, this energy will duly radiate throughout the entire body. This is called the stage of the realized one. Appearing and disappearing to the common world in accordance with spontaneous change, one's glittering clarity will radiate of itself, night and day in equal brightness. With immortals in attendance one traverses through grottos and palaces.

5. Refining the energy to pure spirit, one becomes a spirit man. Changing and passing on spontaneously, one is utterly boundless,

one's power can move Heaven and Earth, remove mountains and drain the sea.

6. Refining the spirit to unify with the world of form, one becomes a perfect being. As one numinously pervades all existence, one's appearance and body are no longer definite. One changes according to occasion, appears in different shapes, as one goes along with beings.

7. Going beyond all beings in one's body, one whirls out of normal relations and comes to reside next to the Jade Emperor of the Great Dao in the Numinous Realm. Here the wise and sagely gather, at the farthest shore and in perfect truth. In creative change, in numinous pervasion, all beings are reached. Only one who has attained this level of cultivation has truly reached the source of the Dao. Here the myriad paths come to an end. This is called the final ultimate.

Ecstatic Excursions

From *Buxu ci* 步虛詞 (Songs on Pacing the Void, DZ 1051), 2.30b-31b, by Wu Yun (d. 778). Translation based on Schafer 1981.

ONE
The host of immortals looks up to cosmic rule;
In dignified carriages they rise to bow to the divine ancestor.
Golden stars, they illuminate each other brilliantly;
Winding along slowly, they ascend to the great void.

The mysterious Dipper stars have flown high already.
With fiery refinement, they arise in the Red Palace of the south.

Overflowing happiness fills the heavenly lands;
Overarching harmony permeates the royal rule.
The spirits of the eight trigrams shine on floating energies.
The lords of the ten directions dance on auspicious winds.

Through them I scale to the very source of yang,
Coming, as I am, from the merit of deep yin.
Freely I wander above great morning light,
Penetrating with true sight all and everywhere!

TWO
Reins relaxed, I mount to Purple Clarity;
Striding on light, I overtake swift lightning.
Mount Kunlun's top right here, the Three Heavens there!
I look down and seem see them clearly:

A porch of jade, with bright light shining forth;
A jasper forest, like a jungle of fresh green.
Unless made with bones of jade and gold,
How could I ever fulfill my deepest wish?

The community of the perfected—what a dense crowd!
Matching my radiance to theirs, I enjoy a banquet.
What a party! I forget myself and protract my stay.
Here a thousand years shrink to the winking of an eye.

THREE
The Three Heavens shine forth with brilliant light,
So bright, indeed, as if they were the sun.
Whirling away, I drive the rising winds,
To pluck some leaves from the greenery of emptiness above.

It makes me all filled with the color of pure gold;
A radiant jasper figure in the Later Heaven.
My heart in harmony with the great void's quiet,
Serene and calm, what would I think about?

Deep in mystery, there is perfect happiness;
Tranquil, I am at rest in nonaction always.
Only with my perfected divine companions,
I ramble at pleasure, borne up by the winds.

FOUR
My inner being changes into congealed pure *qi*;
My body now refined, I become perfected, an immortal.
My heart oblivious, I match the primal ancestor of all;
Reverting to my roots, I'm one with spontaneity.

The Emperor Great One settles in my heart;
As streaming light pours from my elixir field.
The gods, like Nonradiance and Lord Peach,
Chant brightly from the chapters of long life.

My six viscera glow with luminous morning light;
My hundred joints are like a net of purple mist.
My whirlwind carriage traverses endless spaces:
Slow and steady, I rise on light itself.

Unaware how far the road of clouds,
In an instant, I wander through ten thousand heavens.

FIVE
The sun's mulberry diffuses the first glow of day,
My feathered carriage skims the morning light.
Swift and sudden I reach attain the western lands,
Where joyfully I roam the palace of the Queen Mother.

A green stream, fathomless in its uncanny depth,
Vivid and flaming, is spread with lotus flowers.
A blazing glitter, the palace of blue sapphires,
Sparkling and vibrant, is covered with jade blossoms.

True cosmic energy overflows in my heart;
All spontaneity, my thoughts are free from wrong.
Looking down, I feel sorry for the people in the world:
Their sky always stays muddy—isn't it regretful?

SIX
The jasper terrace, measurable in kalpas,
Glitters alone beyond even Grand Network.
Always there are the clouds of Three Simplicities,
Crowding their brilliance, flying all around.

Feathered luminants drift by in bright morning light,
Rising and falling—how ever light and hazy.
Phoenixes cry forth in elegant melodies,
Perching and soaring above the rosy woods.

All jade emptiness, there's neither day nor night,
The wondrous luminants, blazing ever brightly.
I take a look at the Highest Capital
And know how small really all the heavens are.

SEVEN
Gleaming bright, the forest of blue blossoms,
As wondrous winds shake their jasper stems.
Neither winter nor spring is there in the Three Primes,
Just the one energy, clear and harmonious.

I turn my head as I get closer to power cluster,
Twist to look down, so near the net of planets.
"Free Fall" talisman controls all the Six Heavens,
While "Floating Bell" awes all the hundred evils.

On and on forever, oh, happy without end—
Who says the *chun* tree is a long-lived one?

EIGHT
Intense luxury—yet neither waste nor extravagance,
I meet beings bringing forth flowery radiance.
Perfect music—yet neither flute nor song,
Pure jade tones tinkling of themselves.

I climb the Terrace of Radiant Perfection,
Feast at the Hall of Feathered Luminants.
Dark clusters weave into precious cloud-streams,
As subtle vapor spread a wondrous fragrance.
A celestial now, I am truly free in time,
My joy so great, I cannot measure it.

NINE
Ascending further from Great Tenuity,
I get to meet the Sovereign of Emptiness.
Riding an eight-luminaries carriage,
I slowly and majestically enter the Gate of Heaven.

I go up into the Jade-Dawn Gardens,
Solemnly look up to the purple throne.
I dare to ask, "How, at the end of Dragon Country kalpa,
Did Your Majesty start the new Heaven and new Earth?"

With pleasure he puts down his celestial instrument,
Speaks words to me about the invisible and subtle.
Happily I listen to the most essential rules,
See finally the deep source of creation.

TEN
The two *qi* spread the myriad forms of life,
The creative pivot never stops its turning.
Now I am grasping its beginning
And can go beyond the maker's wheel.

Through solitary vastness I ascend to Great Silence,
Meeting only the clear and the perfected.
Pure and shining I encompass primordial harmony,
Joined with pure energy in mutual relation.

Reddish trees bear cinnabar treasures,
Purple haze floats with blue-green streams.
I wish to preserve my youth and infancy,
Use it forever to go beyond the body and the spirit.

Appendix

Confucian Texts in Translation

1. The Ultimate

Taiji tushuo (Explaining the Diagram of the Great Ultimate) by Zhou Dunyi (1017-1073).Translated by Wing-tsit Chan, *A Source Book in Chinese Philosophy* (Princeton: Princeton University Press, 1963), 463-64.

Zhuzi quanzhu (Collected Works of Master Zhu), by Zhu Xi (1130-1200). Translated by Wing-tsit Chan, *A Source Book in Chinese Philosophy* (Princeton: Princeton University Press, 1963), 638-41.

2. Language

Yuanshan (Inquiry into Goodness), by Dai Zhen (1723-1777). Translated by Chung-ying Cheng, *Tai Chen's Inquiry into Goodness* (Honolulu: East-West Center Press, 1971), 105-07.

3. The Self

Kunxue ji (Recollections of the Toils of Learning) by Gao Panlong (1562-1626).Translated by Rodney L. Taylor, *The Religious Dimensions of Confucianism* (Albany: State University of New York Press, 1990), 60-62.

4. Training

Beixi daquan ji (Collected Works of Chen Chun), by Chen Chun (1159-1223).Translated by Wing-tsit Chan, *Neo-Confucian Terms Explained* (New York: Columbia University Press, 1986), 176-78 and 79-73.

Zazen to seiza (Sitting in Zazen and Quiet-Sitting), by Okada Takehiko (Tokyo, 1972). Translated by Rodney L. Taylor, *The Confucian Way of Contemplation: Okada Takehiko and the Tradition of Quiet-Sitting* (Columbia, S.C.: University of South Carolina Press, 1988), 78-80.

5. Ethics

Bailu shuyuan zhi (Rules of the White Deer Hollow Academy), by Zhu Xi (1130-1200), with commentary by Yi T'oegye (1501-1570). Translated by Michael Kalton, *To Become a Sage: The Ten Diagrams on Sage Learning by Yi T'oegye* (New York: Columbia University Press, 1988), 102-06.

6. The Ideal Human

Jinsi lu (Reflections on Things at Hand), by Zhu Xi (Chu Hsi) and Lü Zuqian.Translated by Wing-tsit Chan, *Reflections on Things at Hand:The Neo-Confucian Anthology Compiled by Chu Hsi and Lü Tsu-ch'ien* (New York: Columbia University Press, 1967), 299-302.

7. Mystical Union

Daxue wen (Inquiry on the Great Learning), by Wang Yangming (1472-1529). Translated by Wing-tsit Chan, *Instructions for Practical Living and Other Neo-Confucian Writings by Wang Yang-ming* (New York: Columbia University Press, 1963), 272-74.

Ximing (Western Inscription), by Zhang Zai (1020-1077). Translated by Wing-tsit Chan, *A Source Book in Chinese Philosophy* (Princeton: Princeton University Press, 1963), 497-98.

Bibliography

Ames, Roger T. 1992. "Taoist Ethics." In *Enclyclopedia of Ethics*, edited by L. C. Becker and C. B. Becker, 1226-31. New York: Garland.

Anderson, Eugene N., and Marja L. Anderson. 1977. "Modern China: South." In *Food in Chinese Culture*, edited by K. C. Chang, 317-82. New Haven: Yale University Press.

Andersen, Poul. 1994. "The Transformation of the Body in Taoist Ritual." In *Religious Reflections on the Human Body*, edited by Jane Marie Law, 181-202. Bloomington: Indiana University Press.

Arthur, Shawn. 2006. "Life Without Grains: *Bigu* and the Daoist Body." In *Daoist Body Cultivation*, edited by Livia Kohn, 91-122. Magdalena, NM: Three Pines Press.

Assandri, Friederike. 2009. *Beyond the Daode jing: Twofold Mystery in Tang Daoism*. Magdalena, NM.: Three Pines Press.

Baier, Kurt. 1958. *The Moral Point of View*. Ithaca: Cornell University Press.

Baldrian-Hussein, Farzeen. 1984. *Procédés secrets du joyau magique*. Paris: Les Deux Océans.

Bauer, Wolfgang. 1971. *China und die Hoffnung auf Glück*. Munich: Carl Hanser.

Bäumer, Friederike. 2004. *Die Ausführungsvarianten des Qigong*. Frankfurt: Peter Lang.

Becker, Lawrence C., and Charlotte B. Becker, eds. 1992. *Enclyclopedia of Ethics*. New York: Garland.

Belgum, David. 1967. "Patient or Penitent." In *Religion and Medicine*, edited by David Belgum, 207-15. Ames, Iowa: Iowa State University Press.

Bell, Catherine. 1992. "Printing and Religion in China: Some Evidence from the *Taishang Ganying Pian*." *Journal of Chinese Religions* 20:173-86.

Bemporad, Jack. 1987. "Suffering." In *Encyclopedia of Religion*, edited by Mircea Eliade, 14:99-104. New York: Macmillan.

Benn, Charles. 1987. "Religious Aspects of Emperor Hsüan-tsung's Taoist Ideology." In *Buddhist and Taoist Practice in Medieval Chinese Society*, 127-45. Edited by David W. Chappell. Honolulu: University of Hawai'i Press.

______. 2000. "Daoist Ordination and *Zhai* Rituals." In *Daoism Handbook*, edited by Livia Kohn, 309-38. Leiden: E. Brill.

Bidlack, Bede. 2006. "Taiji Quan: Forms, Visions, and Effects." In *Daoist Body Cultivation*, edited by Livia Kohn, 179-202. Magdalena, NM: Three Pines Press. Komjathy, Louis. 2006. "Qigong in America." In *Daoist Body Cultivation*, edited by Livia Kohn, 203-36. Magdalena, NM: Three Pines Press.

Bokenkamp, Stephen R. 1983. "Sources of the Ling-pao Scriptures." In *Tantric and Taoist Studies*, edited by Michel Strickmann, 2:434-86. Brussels: Institut Belge des Hautes Etudes Chinoises.

______. 1989. "Death and Ascent in Ling-pao Taoism." *Taoist Resources* 1.2:1-20.

______. 1994. "Time After Time: Taoist Apocalyptic History and the Founding of the T'ang Dynasty." *Asia Major* 7.1: 59-88.

______. 1997. *Early Daoist Scriptures*. With a contribution by Peter Nickerson. Berkeley: University of California Press.

Boltz, Judith M. 1987. *A Survey of Taoist Literature: Tenth to Seventeenth Centuries*. Berkeley: University of California, China Research Monograph 32.

Brokaw, Cynthia. 1990. *The Ledgers of Merit and Demerit: Social Change and Moral Order in Late Imperial China*. Princeton: Princeton University Press.

Bumbacher, Stephan Peter. 2001. "Zu den Körpergottheiten im chinesischen Taoismus." In *Noch eine Chance für die Religionsphänomenologie?*, edited by D. Peoli-Olgiati, A. Michaels, and F. Stolz, 151-72. Frankfurt: Peter Lang.

Cabezon, José Ignacio. 1994. *Buddhism and Language: A Study of Indo-Tibetan Scholasticism*. Albany: State University of New York Press.

Cahill, Suzanne. 1985. "Sex and the Supernatural in Medieval China: Cantos on the Transcendent Who Presides Over the River." *Journal of the American Oriental Society* 105:197-220.

______. 1986. "Reflections on a Metal Mother: Tu Kuang-t'ing's Biography of Hsi-wang-mu." *Journal of Chinese Religions* 13/14:127-42.

______. 1990. "Practice Makes Perfect: Paths to Transcendence for Women in Medieval China." *Taoist Resources* 2.2:23-42.

______. Cahill, Suzanne. 1993. *Transcendence and Divine Passion: The Queen Mother of the West in Medieval China*. Stanford: Stanford University Press.

______. 2006. *Divine Traces of the Daoist Sisterhood*. Magdalena, NM: Three Pines Press.

Campany, Robert F. 2002. *To Live As Long As Heaven and Earth: A Translation and Study of Ge Hong's Traditions of Divine Transcendents.* Berkeley: University of California Press.

Cedzich, Ursula-Angelika. 2001. "Corpse Deliverance, Substitute Bodies, Name Change, and Feigned Death: Aspects of Metamorphosis and Immortality in Early Medieval China." *Journal of Chinese Religions* 29:1-68.

Chan, Wing-tsit. 1964. *A Source Book in Chinese Philosophy.* Princeton: Princeton University Press

______. 1967. *Reflections on Things at Hand: The Neo-Confucian Anthology Compiled by Chu Hsi and Lü Tsu-ch'ien.* New York: Columbia University Press.

Chang, Kwang-chih. 1980. *Shang Civilization.* New Haven, Conn.: Yale University Press.

Chen, Nancy N. 2003. *Breathing Spaces: Qigong, Psychiatry, and Healing in China.* New York: Columbia University Press.

Chen Yingning. 1934. *Sun Buer nüdan shizhu.* Shanghai: Yihuo tangshan.

Chia, Mantak. 1983. *Awaken Healing Energy Through the Tao.* Huntington, NY: Healing Tao Books.

______. 1985. *Taoist Ways to Transform Stress into Vitality.* Huntington, NY: Healing Tao Books.

______, and Maneewan Chia. 1993. *Awaken Healing Light of the Tao.* Huntington, NY: Healing Tao Books

______, and Michael Winn. 1984. *Taoist Secrets of Love: Cultivating Male Sexual Energy.* Santa Fe: Aurora Press.

Ching, Julia. 1976. *To Accumulate Wisdom: The Way of Wang Yang-ming.* New York: Columbia University Press.

______. 1997. *Mysticism and Kingship in* China. Cambridge: Cambridge University Press.

Cleary, Thomas. 1989. *Immortal Sisters: Secrets of Taoist Women.* Boston: Shambhala.

______. 1992. *The Secret of the Golden Flower: The Classic Chinese Book of Life.* San Francisco: Harper.

Cohen, Kenneth S. 1997. *The Way of Qigong: The Art and Science of Chinese Energy Healing.* New York: Ballantine.

Cole, Alan. 1998. *Mothers and Sons in Chinese Buddhism.* Stanford: Stanford University Press.

Creel, Herlee. 1970. *What is Taoism?* Chicago: Chicago University Press.

Darga, Martina. 1999. *Das alchemistische Buch von innerem Wesen und Lebensenergie: Xingming guizhi.* Munich: Diederichs.

Deikman, Arthur J. 1982. *The Observing Self: Mysticism and Psychotherapy.* Boston: Beacon Press.

Despeux, Catherine. 1990. *Immortelles de la Chine ancienne: Taoïsme et alchimie feminine.* Paris: Pardès.

______. 1994. *Taoïsme et corps humain: Le Xiuzhen tu.* Paris: Guy Tredaniel.

______. 2000. "Women in Daoism." In *Daoism Handbook*, edited by Livia Kohn, 384-412. Leiden: E. Brill.

______. 2006. "The Six Healing Breaths." In *Daoist Body Cultivation*, edited by Livia Kohn, 37-67. Magdalena, NM: Three Pines Press.

______, and Livia Kohn. 2003. *Women in Daoism.* Cambridge, Mass.: Three Pines Press.

DeWoskin, Kenneth. 1982. *A Song for One or Two.* Ann Arbor: University of Michigan Press.

Dobson, W. A. C. H. 1974. *A Dictionary of Chinese Particles.* Toronto: University of Toronto Press.

Eberhard, Wolfram. 1967. *Guilt and Sin in Traditional China.* Berkeley: University of California Press.

Engelhardt, Ute. 1987. *Die klassische Tradition der Qi-Übungen. Eine Darstellung anhand des Tang-zeitlichen Textes Fuqi jingyi lun von Sima Chengzhen.* Wiesbaden: Franz Steiner.

______. 1989. "*Qi* for Life: Longevity in the Tang." In *Taoist Meditation and Longevity Techniques*, edited by Livia Kohn, 263-94. Ann Arbor: University of Michigan, Center for Chinese Studies Publications.

Erkes, Eduard. 1958. *Ho-Shang-Kung's Commentary on Lao Tse.* Ascona: Artibus Asiae.

Eskildsen, Stephen. 1998. *Asceticism in Early Taoist Religion.* Albany: State University of New York Press.

______. 2001. "Seeking Signs of Proof: Visions and Other Trance Phenomena in Early Quanzhen Taoism." *Journal of Chinese Religions* 29:139-60.

______. 2004. *The Teachings and Practices of the Early Quanzhen Taoist Masters.* Albany: State University of New York Press.

Faioli, Edoardo. 1986. *Chinese Calligraphy.* New York: Abbeville Press.

Forke, Alfred. 1907. *Lun-Heng: Wang Ch'ung's Essays.* 2 vols. New York: Paragon.

Fukunaga Mitsuji. 1946. "Sō Shu no yu ni tsuite." *Shinagaku* 12:33-73.

______. 1973. "Dōkyō ni okeru kagami to ken." *Tōhō gakuhō* 45:59-120.

Fung Yu-lan, and Derk Bodde. 1952. *A History of Chinese Philosophy*. 2 vols. Princeton: Princeton University Press.

Gert, Bernard. 1970. *The Moral Rules*. New York: Harper & Row.

Girardot, Norman. 1985. "Behaving Cosmogonically in Early Taoism." In *Cosmogony and Ethical Order: New Studies in Comparative Ethics*, edited by Robin W. Lovin and Frank E. Reynolds, 67-97. Chicago: University of Chicago Press.

Gombridge, Richard F. 1971. *Precept and Practice. Traditional Buddhism in the Rural Highlands of Ceylon*. Oxford: Clarendon.

Graham, A. C. 1960. *The Book of Lieh-tzu*. London: A. Murray

______. 1983. "Taoist Spontaneity and the Dichotomy of 'Is' and 'Ought'." In *Experimental Essays on Chuang-tzu*, edited by Victor H. Mair, 3-23. Honolulu: University of Hawai'i Press.

______. 1990. "The Origins of the Legend of Lao Tan." In *Studies in Chinese Philosophy and Philosophical Literature*, 111-24. Edited by A.C. Graham. Albany: State University of New York Press. Originally published 1981.

Green, Ronald M. 1978. *Religious Reason*. New York: Oxford University Press.

______. 1987. "Morality and Religion." In *Encyclopedia of Religion*, edited by Mircea Eliade, 10:92-106. New York: Macmillan.

Gyatso, Kelsung. 1982. *Clear Light of Bliss*. London.

Hare, R. M. 1965. *Freedom and Reason*. New York: Oxford University Press.

Hawkes, David. 1959. *Ch'u Tz'u: The Songs of the South*. Oxford: Clarendon Press.

______. 1981. "Quanzhen Plays and Quanzhen Masters." *Bulletin d'Ecole Française d'Extrême Orient* 69:153-170.

Hayashi, Ryoichi. 1975. *The Silk Road and the Shoso-in*. New York: Weatherhill.

Heise, Thomas. 1999. *Qigong in der VR China: Entwicklung, Theorie und Praxis*. Berlin: Verlag für Wissenschaft und Bildung.

Hendrischke, Barbara. 1993. "Der Taoismus in der Tang-Zeit." *Minima sinica* 1993/1:110-43.

Henricks, Robert. 1983. *Philosophy and Argumentation in Third Century China: The Essays of Hsi K'ang*. Princeton: Princeton University Press.

Hervouet, Yves, ed. 1978. *A Sung Bibliography; Bibliographie des Sung*. Hong Kong: The Chinese University Press.

Hildenbrand, Gisela. 1999. "Unterrichtsmaterialien von Jiao Guorui zum Lehrsystem Qigong Yangsheng." *Zeitschrift für Qigong Yangsheng* 1999: 5-13.

Holt, John C. 1981. *Discipline: The Canonical Buddhism of the Vinayapitaka.* New Delhi: Motilal Banarsidass.

Homann, Rolf. 1971. *Die wichtigsten Körpergottheiten im Huang-t'ing-ching.* Göppingen: Alfred Kümmerle.

Hopkins, Jeffrey, ed. 1982. *Tantric Practice in Nying-ma.* Outlined by Khetsun Sangpo Rinbochay. Ithaca, NY: Snow Lion Publications.

Hou Ching-lang. 1975. *Monnaies d'offrande et la notion de tresorerie dans la religion chinoise.* Paris: Memoires de l'Institut des Hautes Etudes Chinoises 1.

Hsia, Emil C. H., Ilza Veith, and Robert H. Geertsma, trans. 1986. *The Essentials of Medicine in Ancient China and Japan: Yasuyori Tamba's Ishimpô.* 2 vols. Leiden: E. Brill.

Idziak, Janine Marie. 1980. *Divine Command Morality.* Lewiston, NY: Edwin Mellen Press.

Jackowicz, Stephen. 2003. "The Mechanics of Spirit: An Examination of the Absorption of *Qi*." Ph. D. Diss., Boston University, Boston.

______. 2006. "Ingestion, Digestion, and Regestation: The Complexities of the Absorption of *Qi*." In *Daoist Body Cultivation*, edited by Livia Kohn, 68-90. Magdalena, NM: Three Pines Press.

Jahnke, Roger. 2002. *The Healing Promise of Qi: Creating Extraordinary Wellness Through Qigong and Tai Chi.* New York: Contemporary Books.

James, William. 1936 [1902]. *The Varieties of Religious Experience.* New York: The Modern Library.

Jiang Weiqiao. 1985. *Jingzuo fa jiyao.* Taipei: Jiyou.

Jordan, David K. 1972. *Gods, Ghosts and Ancestors.* Berkeley: University of California Press.

Kaltenmark, Max. 1953. *Le Lie-sien tchouan.* Beijing: Université de Paris Publications.

______. 1965. "La mystique taoïste." In *La mystique et le mystiques*, edited by A. Ravier, 649-69. Paris.

______. 1968. *Lao-tzu and Taoism.* Stanford: Stanford University Press.

______. 1969. "*Liexian zhuan* yu liexian." *Zhongguo xuezhi* 5:63-77.

Kant, Immanuel. 1959. *Foundations of the Metaphysics of Morals.* New York: Bobbs-Merrill.

______. 1960. *Religion within the Limits of Reason Alone.* New York: Harper & Row.

Keightley, David N. 1978a. *Sources of Shang History: The Oracle Bone Inscriptions of Bronze Age China.* Berkeley & Los Angeles: University of California Press.

______. 1978b. "The Religious Commitment: Shang Theology and the Genesis of Chinese Political Culture." *History of Religions* 17: 211-225.

Keown, Damien. 1992. *The Nature of Buddhist Ethics.* New York: St. Martin's Press.

Kirkland, J. Russell. 1986. "Taoists of the High T'ang: An Inquiry into the Perceived Significance of Eminent Taoists in Medieval Chinese Society." Ph.D. Diss., Indiana University, Bloomington.

______. 2001. "Responsible Nonaction in a Natural World: Perspectives from the *Neiye, Zhuangzi,* and *Daode jing.*" In *Daoism and Ecology: Ways Within a Cosmic Landscape,* edited by Norman Girardot, James Miller, and Liu Xiaogan, 283-304. Cambridge, Mass.: Harvard University Press, Center for the Study of World Religions.

Kjellberg, Paul, and Philip J. Ivanhoe, eds. 1996. *Essays on Skepticism, Relativism, and Ethics in the Zhuangzhi.* Albany: State University of New York Press.

Kleeman, Terry. 1991. "Taoist Ethics." In *A Bibliographic Guide to the Comparative Study of Ethics,* edited by John Carman and Mark Juergensmeyer, 162-94. Cambridge: Cambridge University Press.

______. 1998. *Great Perfection: Religion and Ethnicity in a Chinese Millenarian Kingdom.* Honolulu: University of Hawai'i Press.

Knaul, Livia. 1985a. "The Winged Life: Kuo Hsiang's Mystical Philosophy." *Journal of Chinese Studies* 2.1:17-41.

______. 1985b. "Kuo Hsiang and the *Chuang-tzu.*" *Journal of Chinese Philosophy* 12.4:429-47.

Kobayashi Masayoshi. 1992. "The Celestial Masters Under the Eastern Jin and Liu-Song Dynasties." *Taoist Resources* 3.2: 17-45.

Kohn, Livia. 1987a. *Seven Steps to the Tao: Sima Chengzhen's Zuowanglun.* St.Augustin/Nettetal: Monumenta Serica Monograph XX.

______. 1987b. "The Teaching of T'ien-yin-tzu." *Journal of Chinese Religions* 15: 1-28.

______. 1988. "Medicine and Immortality in T'ang China." *Journal of the American Oriental Society* 108.3: 465-69.

______. 1989a. "Die Emigration des Laozi. Mythologische Entwicklungen vom 2. bis 6. Jahrhundert." *Monumenta Serica* 38: 49-68.

______. 1989b. "Taoist Insight Meditation: The Tang Practice of *Neiguan*." In *Taoist Meditation and Longevity Techniques*, edited by Livia Kohn, 191-222. Ann Arbor: University of Michigan, Center for Chinese Studies Publications.

______. 1989c. "The Mother of the Tao." *Taoist Resources* 1.2: 37-113.

______. 1990. "Transcending Personality: From Ordinary to Immortal Life." *Taoist Resources* 2.2: 1-22.

______. 1991a. *Taoist Mystical Philosophy: The Scripture of Western Ascension*. Albany: State University of New York Press.

______. 1991b. "Taoist Visions of the Body." *Journal of Chinese Philosophy* 18: 227-52.

______. 1992a. *Early Chinese Mysticism: Philosophy and Soteriology in the Taoist Tradition*. Princeton: Princeton University Press.

______. 1992b. "Selfhood and Spontaneity in Ancient Chinese Thought." In *Selves, People, and Persons*, edited by Leroy Rouner, 123-38. South Bend: University of Notre Dame Press.

______. 1993a. *The Taoist Experience: An Anthology*. Albany: State University of New York Press.

______. 1993b. "Quiet Sitting with Master Yinshi: Medicine and Religion in Modern China." *Zen Buddhism Today* 10: 79-95.

______. 1994. "The Five Precepts of the Venerable Lord." *Monumenta Serica* 42: 171-215.

______. 1995a. *Laughing at the Tao: Debates among Buddhists and Taoists in Medieval China*. Princeton: Princeton University Press.

______. 1995b. "Laozi: Ancient Philosopher, Master of Longevity, and Taoist God." In *Religions in China*, edited by Donald Lopez. Princeton: Princeton University Press.

______. 1998a. *God of the Dao: Lord Lao in History and Myth*. University of Michigan, Center for Chinese Studies.

______. 1998b. "Mind and Eyes: Sensory and Spiritual Experience in Taoist Mysticism." *Monumenta Serica* 46:129-56.

______. 1998c. "Counting Good Deeds and Days of Life: The Quantification of Fate in Medieval China." *Asiatische Studien/Etudes Asiatiques* 52: 833-70.

______. 1998d. "Steal Holy Food and Come Back as a Viper: Conceptions of Karma and Rebirth in Medieval Daoism." *Early Medieval China* 4: 1-48.

______. 2001. *Daoism and Chinese Culture*. Cambridge: Three Pines Press.

______. 2003. *Monastic Life in Medieval Daoism: A Cross-Cultural Perspective*. Honolulu: University of Hawai'i Press.

______. 2004a. *Cosmos and Community: The Ethical Dimension of Daoism*. Cambridge, Mass.: Three Pines Press.

______. 2004b. *Supplement to Cosmos and Community*. Cambridge, Mass.: Three Pines Press, E-Dao Series.

______. 2004c. *The Daoist Monastic Manual: A Translation of the Fengdao kejie*. New York: Oxford University Press.

______. 2005. *Health and Long Life: The Chinese Way*. Cambridge, Mass.: Three Pines Press.

______. 2008a. *Chinese Healing Exercises: The Tradition of Daoyin*. Honolulu: University of Hawai'i Press.

______. 2008b. *Meditation Works: In the Daoist, Buddhist, and Hindu Traditions*. Magdalena, NM: Three Pines Press.

______, and Robin R. Wang. 2009. *Internal Alchemy: Self, Society, and the Quest for Immortality*. Magdalena, NM: Three Pines Press.

______, and Russell Kirkland. 2000. "Daoism in the Tang (618-907)." In *Daoism Handbook*, edited by Livia Kohn, 339-83. Leiden: E. Brill.

Komjathy, Louis. 2008. "Mapping the Daoist Body (1): The *Neijing tu* in History." *Journal of Daoist Studies* 1:67-92.

Kroll, Paul W. 1996. "Body Gods and Inner Vision: *The Scripture of the Yellow Court*. In *Religions of China in Practice*, edited by Donald S. Lopez Jr., 149-55. Princeton: Princeton University Press.

Kübler-Ross, Elizabeth. 1979. *Death: The Final Stage of Growth*. New York: Macmillan.

LaFargue, Michael, and Julian Pas. 1998. "On Translating the *Tao-te-ching*. In *Lao-tzu and the Tao-te-ching*, edited by Livia Kohn and Michael LaFargue, 277-302. Albany: State University of New York Press.

Lagerwey, John. 1981. *Wu-shang pi-yao: Somme taoiste du VIe siecle*. Paris: Publications de l'Ecole Francaise d'Extrême-Orient.

Lévi, Jean. 1983. "L'abstinence des céréals chez les taoïstes." *Etudes Chinoises* 1:3-47.

Levy, Howard S. 1956. "Yellow Turban Rebellion at the End of the Han." *Journal of the American Oriental Society* 76:214-27.

Liang, Shou-yu, and Wen-ching Wu. 1997. *Qigong Empowerment: A Guide to Medical, Taoist, Buddhist, Wushu Energy Cultivation*. East Providence: Way of the Dragon Publishing.

Lienau, Dagmar. 1999. "Psychologische Aspekte des Qigong Yangsheng in der Arbeit mit Krebspatientinnen." *Zeitschrift für Qigong Yangsheng* 1999: 97-102.

Link, Arthur E., and Timothy Lee. 1966. "Sun Cho's *Yü-tao-lun*: A Clarification of the Way." *Monumenta Serica* 25: 169-96.

Liu Zhongyu. 1990. *Zhongguo daojiao wenhua xiushi*. Shanghai: Xielin.

Liu, Ts'un-yan. 1970. "The Penetration of Taoism in the Ming Confucian Elite." *T'oung Pao* 52:31-103.

Liu, Xun. 2009. "Numinous Father and Holy Mother: Late-Ming Duo-Cultivation Practice." In *Internal Alchemy: Self, Society, and the Quest for Immortality*, edited by Livia Kohn and Robin R. Wang, 122-41. Magdalena, NM: Three Pines Press.

Lo, Vivienne. Forthcoming. *Healing Arts in Early China*. Leiden: E. Brill.

Loewe, Michael. 1979. *Ways to Paradise: The Chinese Quest for Immortality*. London: George Allan and Unwin.

______. 1982. *Chinese Ideas of Life and Death*. London: George Allan and Unwin.

Loon, Piet van der. 1984. *Taoist Books in the Libraries of the Sung Period*. London: Oxford Oriental Institute.

Lu, Kuan-yü. 1970. *Taoist Yoga —Alchemy and Immortality*. London: Rider.

Ma Daozong, ed. 1999. *Zhongguo daojiao yangsheng mijue*. Beijing: Zongjiao wenhua chubanshe.

Mabbott, J. D. 1969. *An Introduction to Ethics*. Garden City, NJ: Anchor Books.

Mahony, William K. 1987. "Karman: Hindu and Jain Concepts." In *Encyclopedia of Religion*, edited by Mircea Eliade, 8:261-66. New York: Macmillan.

Maslow, Abraham H. 1964. *Toward a Psychology of Being*. New York: Van Nostrand Reinhold.

Maspero, Henri. 1971. *Le taoïsme et les religions chinoises*. Paris: Gallimard.

______. 1981. *Taoism and Chinese Religion*. Translated by Frank Kierman. Amherst: University of Massachusetts Press.

Middendorf, Ilse. 1999. "Es ist der Atem." *Zeitschrift für Qigong Yangsheng* 1999:89-90.

Mitomo, Ryōjun. 1991. "The Ethics of Mahāyāna Buddhism in the *Bodhicaryāvatāra.*" In *Buddhist Ethics and Modern Society: An International Symposium*, edited by Charles W. H. Fu and Sandra A. Wawrytko, 15-26. New York: Greenwood Press.

Mizuno, Kogen. "Karman, Buddhist Concepts." In *Encyclopedia of Religion*, edited by Mircea Eliade, 8:266-68. New York: Macmillan.

Mochizuki Shinkō. 1936. *Bukkyō daijiten.* 7 vols. Tokyo: Sekai seiten kankō kyūkai.

Mugitani Kunio. 1987. "Yōsei enmei roku kunchu." *Report of the Study Group on Traditional Chinese Longevity Techniques*, no. 3. Tokyo: Mombushō.

Munroe, Kristen Renwick. 1996. *The Heart of Altruism: Perceptions of a Common Humanity.* Princeton: Princeton University Press.

Murakami Yoshimi. 1956. *Chūgoku no sennin.* Kyoto: Heiraku shoten.

Nagel, Thomas. 1970. *The Possibility of Altruism.* Oxford: Clarendon Press.

______. 1979. *Mortal Questions.* Cambridge: Cambridge University Press.

Nakamura Hajime. 1975. *Bukkyōgo daijiten.* Tokyo: Tokyo shoshiki.

Needham, Joseph, et al. 1983. *Science and Civilisation in China*, vol. V.5: *Spagyrical Discovery and Invention—Physiological Alchemy.* Cambridge: Cambridge University Press.

Ni, Hua-ching. 1992. *Mysticism: Empowering the Spirit Within.* Santa Monica: College of Tao and Traditional Chinese Healing.

Obeyesekere, Gananath. 1968. "Theodice, Sin and Salvation in a Sociology of Buddhism." In *Dialectic in Practical Religion*, edited by Edmund Leach, 7-40.

Ōfuchi Ninji. 1952. "Shoki no sensetsu ni tsuite." *Tōhō shūkyō* 2:23-44.

______. 1979. *Tonkō dōkei: Zurokuhen.* Tokyo: Kokubu shoten.

Outka, Gene, and John P. Reeder. 1973. *Religion and Morality.* New York: Doubleday.

Pachow, W. 1955. *A Comparative Study of the Pratimok.sa.* Santinitekan: Sino-Indian Cultural Society.

Palmer, David. 2007. *Qigong Fever: Body, Science and Utopia in China.* New York: Columbia University Press.

Panikkar, Raimundo. 1973. "Common Patterns of Eastern and Western Scholasticism." *Diogenes* 83:13-113.

Peerenboom, R. P. 1991. *Law and Morality in Ancient China: The Silk Manuscripts of Huang-Lao.* Albany: State University of New York Press.

Poo, Mu-chou. 1997. *In Search of Personal Welfare: A View of Ancient Chinese Religion*. Albany: State University of New York Press.

Porkert, Manfred. 1974. *The Theoretical Foundations of Chinese Medicine: Systems of Correspondence*. Cambridge, Mass.: MIT Press.

Raz, Gil. 2008. "The Way of the Yellow and the Red: Re-examining the Sexual Initiation Rite of Celestial Master Daoism." *Nannü: Men, Women and Gender in China* 10:86-120.

Ren Jiyu and Zhong Zhaopeng, eds. 1991. *Daozang tiyao*. Beijing: Zhongguo shehui kexue chuban she.

Richards, David. 1971. *A Theory of Reasons for Action*. Oxford: Clarendon Press.

Robinet, Isabelle. 1976. "Les randonées extatiques des taoïstes dans les astres." *Monumenta Serica* 32:159-273.

______. 1977. *Les commentaires du Tao to king jusqu'au VIIe siècle*. Paris: Mémoirs de l'Institute des Hautes Etudes Chinoises 5.

______. 1979a. "Introduction au *Kieou-tchen tchong-king*." *Journal of Chinese Religions* 7: 24-45.

______. 1979b. "Metamorphosis and Deliverance of the Corpse in Taoism." *History of Religions* 19:37-70.

______. 1983. "Kouo Siang ou le monde comme absolu." *T'oung Pao* 69:87-112.

______. 1984. *La révélation du Shangqing dans l'histoire du taoïsme*. 2 vols. Paris: Publications de l'Ecole Française d'Extrême-Orient.

______. 1986. "The Taoist Immortal: Jester of Light and Shadow, Heaven and Earth." *Journal of Chinese Religions* 13-14:87-106.

______. 1989. "Original Contributions of *Neidan* to Taoism and Chinese Thought." In *Taoist Meditation and Longevity Techniques*, edited by Livia Kohn, 295-38. Ann Arbor: University of Michigan, Center for Chinese Studies Publications.

______. 1989. "Visualization and Ecstatic Flight in Shangqing Taoism." In *Taoist Meditation and Longevity Techniques*, edited by Livia Kohn, 157-90. Ann Arbor: University of Michigan, Center for Chinese Studies Publications.

______. 1991. *Histoire du taoïsme: Dés origins au XIVe siècle*. Paris: Editions Cerf.

______. 1993. *Taoist Meditation*. Translated by Norman Girardot and Julian Pas. Albany: State University of New York Press.

______. 1995. *Introduction a l'alchimie interieure taoïste: De l'unité et de la multiplicité*. Paris: Editions Cerf.

______. 1997. *Taoism: Growth of a Religion.* Translated by Phyllis Brooks. Stanford: Stanford University Press.

______. 1999. "Neidan—Inneres Elixier." *Zeitschrift für Qigong Yangsheng* 1999:25-40.

Robinson, Richard. 1967. *Early Mādhyamika in India and China.* Madison: University of Wisconsin Press.

Saddhatissa, H. 1970. *Buddhist Ethics.* London: George Allan and Unwin.

Sakade Yoshinobu. 1986. "Chō Tan *Yōsei yōshu* itsubun to sono shisō." *Tōhō shūkyō* 68:1-24.

Sasaki, George H. 1956. "The Concept of Kamma in Buddhist Philosophy." *Oriens Extremus* 3:185-204.

Saso, Michael. 1995. *The Gold Pavilion: Taoist Ways to Peace, Healing, and Long Life.* Boston: Charles E. Tuttle.

______. 1997. "The Taoist Body and Cosmic Prayer." In *Religion and the Body,* edited by Sarah Coakley,231-47. Cambridge: Cambridge University Press.

Schafer, Edward H. 1963. *The Golden Peaches of Samarkand: A Study of T'ang Exotics.* Berkeley: University of California Press.

______. 1973. *The Divine Woman.* Berkeley: University of California Press.

______. 1979. "A T'ang Taoist Mirror." *Early China* 4:387-98.

______. 1980. *Mao-shan in T'ang Times.* Boulder, Col: Society for the Study of Chinese Religions Monograph 1.

______. 1981. "Wu Yün's 'Cantos on Pacing the Void'." *Harvard Journal of Asiatic Studies* 41:377-415.

Schipper, Kristofer M. 1978. "The Taoist Body." *History of Religions* 17:355-87.

______. 1982. *Le corps taoïste: Corps physique — corps social.* Paris: Fayard.

______. 1984. "Le monachisme taoiste." In *Incontro di religioni in Asia tra il terzo e il decimo secolo d. C.,* edited by L. Lanciotti, 199-215. Firenze: Leo S. Olschki.

______. 1994. *The Taoist Body.* Translated by Karen C. Duval. Berkeley: University of California Press.

______., and Franciscus Verellen, eds. 2004. *The Taoist Canon: A Historical Companion to the Daozang.* 3 vols. Chicago: University of Chicago Press.

Schlicht, Carlos Cobos. 1999. "Die Leiberfahrung von Geistwesen im *Neijing tu.*" *Zeitschrift für Qigong Yangsheng* 1999:53-65.

Seidel, Anna. 1969. *La divinisation de Lao-tseu dans le Taoisme des Han.* Paris: Ecole Francaise d'Extreme Orient. Reprinted 1992.

______. 1982. "Tokens of Immortality in Han Graves." *Numen* 29:79-122.

Shahar, Meir, and Robert P. Weller, eds. 1996. *Unruly Gods: Divinity and Society in China.* Honolulu: University of Hawai'i Press.

Shi, Dao. 2002. "A Meeting on the Pathless Path: An Interview with Ken Cohen and Shi Jing." *The Dragon's Mouth,* Summer 2002:2-9.

Short, Lar, and John Mann. 1988. *The Body of Light.* San Francisco: Fourth Way Books.

Siivals, Aarne. 1962. "The Meaning of an Illness." *Journal of Religion and Health* 1.2:153-64

Silber, John R. 1960. "The Ethical Significance of Kant's *Religion.*" In *Religion Within the Limits of Reason Alone,* by Immanuel Kant, edited by Theodore M. Greene and Hoyt H. Hudson, lxxix-cxxxiv. New York: Harper & Row.

Simmons, Harold E. 1956. *The Psychosomatic Aspects of Cancer.* Washington, D.C.: Peabody Press.

Sivin, Nathan. 1968. *Chinese Alchemy: Preliminary Studies.* Cambridge, Mass.: Harvard University Press.

Skar, Lowell, and Fabrizio Pregadio. 2000. "Inner Alchemy (*Neidan*)." In *Daoism Handbook,* edited by Livia Kohn, 464-97. Leiden: E. Brill.

Stein, Stephan. 1999. *Zwischen Heil und Heilung: Zur frühen Tradition des Yangsheng in China.* Uelzen: Medizinisch-Literarische Verlagsgesellschaft.

Strickmann, Michel. 1979. "On the Alchemy of T'ao Hung-ching." In *Facets of Taoism,* edited by Holmes Welch and Anna Seidel, 123-92. New Haven, Conn.: Yale University Press.

______. 1978. "The Longest Taoist Scripture." *History of Religions* 17: 331-54.

Stuart, G. A. 1976. *Chinese Materia Medica.* Taipei: Southern Materials Center.

Sunayama Minoru. 1980. "Dōkyō chūgenha hyōi." *Shūkan tōyōgaku* 43:31-44.

Suzuki, D. T., and Paul Carus. 1973 [1906]. *Treatise on Response and Retribution.* LaSalle, Ill.: Open Court Publishing.

Switkin, Walter. 1987. *Immortality: A Taoist Text of Macrobiotics.* San Francisco: H. S. Dakin Company.

Taylor, Paul. 1972. *Problems of Moral Philosphy.* Encino, Cal.: Dickenson.

Taylor, Rodney L. 1978. *The Cultivation of Selfhood as a Religious Goal in Neo-Confucianism.* Missoula, Mont.: Scholars Press.

Tonkō kōza, ed. 1983. *Tonkō to Chūgoku dōkyō.* Tokyo: Daitō.

Tsuchiya, Masaaki. 2002. "Confession of Sins and Awareness of Self in the *Taiping jing.*" In *Daoist Identity: History, Lineage, and Ritual*, edited by Livia Kohn and Harold D. Roth, 39-57. Honolulu: University of Hawai'i Press.

Tsukamoto, Senryū, and Leon Hurvitz. 1985. *A History of Early Chinese Buddhism.* 2 vols. Tokyo: Kôdansha.

Underhill, Evelyn. 1911. *Mysticism.* London: Methuen & Co.

Valussi, Elena. 2003. "Beheading the Red Dragon: A History of Female Inner Alchemy in China." Ph. D. Diss., School of Oriental and African Studies, University of London, London.

______. 2009. "Female Alchemy: An Introduction." In *Internal Alchemy: Self, Society, and the Quest for Immortality*, edited by Livia Kohn and Robin R. Wang, 142-64. Magdalena, NM: Three Pines Press.

Van Gulik, Robert H. 1940. *The Lore of the Chinese Lute.* Tokyo: Sophia University.

______. 1941. *Hsi K'ang and His Poetical Essay on the Lute.* Tokyo: Sophia University.

Vankeerberghen, Griet. 2001. *The Huainanzi and Liu An's Claim to Moral Authority.* Albany State University of New York Press.

Varma, Vishwanath P. 1963. "The Origin and Sociology of the Early Buddhist Philosophy of Moral Determinism." *Philosophy East and West* 13:25-48.

Verellen, Franciscus. 1989. *Du Guangting (850-933): Taoïste de cour a la fin de la Chine médiévale.* Paris: Collège du France, Mémoires de L'Institut des Hautes Etudes Chinoises 30.

______. 1992. "Evidential Miracles in Support of Taoism: The Inversion of a Buddhist Apologetic Tradition in Tang China." *T'oung Pao* 78:217-63.

von Brunn, Isabel. 1999. "Schmuckobjekte—Spiel polarer Kräfte." *Zeitschrift für Qigong Yangsheng* 1999:84-85.

Ware, James R. 1966. *Alchemy, Medicine and Religion in the China of AD 320.* Cambridge, Mass.: MIT Press.

Watson, Burton. 1968. *The Complete Works of Chuang-tzu.* New York: Columbia University Press.

Wen Yiduo. 1956. *Shenhua yu shi.* Beijing: Zhonghua.

Wieger, Leon. 1965. *Chinese Characters.* New York: Dover.

Wilhelm, Richard. 1962 [1929]. *The Secret of the Golden Flower.* New York: Harcourt, Brace and World.

Wile, Douglas. 1992. *Art of the Bedchamber: The Chinese Sexology Classics Including Women's Solo Meditation Texts*. Albany: State University of New York Press.

Williams, Bernard A. 1980. *Three Rival Versions of Moral Inquiry*. University of Notre Dame Press.

Winn, Michael. 2001. "Daoist Internal Alchemy: A Deep Language for Communicating with Nature's Intelligence." Paper Presented at the Conference on Daoist Cultivation, Vashon Island.

______. 2002. "The Quest for Spiritual Orgasm: Daoist and Tantric Sexual Cultivation in the West." Paper Presented at the Conference on Tantra and Daoism, Boston University, Boston.

______. 2006. "Transforming Sexual Energy with Water-and-Fire Alchemy." In *Daoist Body Cultivation*, edited by Livia Kohn, 151-78. Magdalena, NM: Three Pines Press.

______, and Mantak Chia. 1984. *Taoist Secrets of Love: Cultivating Male Sexual Energy*. Huntington, NY: Healing Tao Books

Wright, Arthur F. 1978. *The Sui Dynasty*. New York: Knopf.

Wu Shouju. 1981. *Sima Chengzhen ji jijiao*. Beijing.

Yamada, Toshiaki. 2000. "The Lingbao School." In *Daoism Handbook*, edited by Livia Kohn, 225-55. Leiden: E. Brill.

Yan Lingfeng. 1983. *Jingzi congzhu*. Taipei: Xuesheng.

Yetts, Percifal. 1916. "The Eight Immortals." *Journal of the Royal Asiatic Society* 1916, 773-807.

Yoshikawa Tadao. 1987. "Seishitsu kō." *Tōhō gakuhō* 59:125-62.

______. 1990. "Ō Genshi kō." *Tōhō gakuhō* 62:69-98.

Yoshioka Yoshitoyo. 1959. *Dōkyō to bukkyō*. Vol. 1. Tokyo: Kokusho kankōkai.

______. 1960. "*Shisōji chūkaikyō* to kōka shisō." *Fukui hakase soshu kinen Tōyō shisō ronshū*, 722-37. Tokyo: Waseda daigaku shuppansha.

______. 1961. "Bukkyō jūkai shisō no Chūgoku shūyō." *Shūkyō kenkyū* 35.1: 51-72.

______. 1970. *Dōkyō to bukkyō*. Vol. 2. Tokyo: Kokusho kankôkai.

Yü, Ying-shih. 1965. "Life and Immortality in the Mind of Han-China." *Harvard Journal of Asiatic Studies* 25: 80-122.

______. 1987. "O Soul, Come Back: A Study of the Changing Conceptions of the Soul and Afterlife in Pre-Buddhist China." *Harvard Journal of Asiatic Studies* 47: 363-95.

Zhou Shaoxian. 1974. *Daojia yu shenxian*. Taipei: Zhonghua.

Index